# Structural reform of British local government

MANCHESTER
UNIVERSITY PRESS

# Structural reform of British local government

## *Rhetoric and reality*

MICHAEL CHISHOLM

Manchester University Press

Manchester and New York

*distributed exclusively in the USA by St. Martin's Press*

*Published by* Manchester University Press
Oxford Road, Manchester M13 9NR, UK
*and* Room 400, 175 Fifth Avenue, New York, NY 10010, USA
http://www.man.ac.uk/mup

*Distributed exclusively in the USA by*
St. Martin's Press, Inc., 175 Fifth Avenue, New York,
NY 10010, USA

*Distributed exclusively in Canada by*
UBC Press, University of British Columbia, 2029 West Mall,
Vancouver, BC, Canada V6T 1Z2

*British Library Cataloguing-in-Publication Data*
A catalogue record for this book is available from the British Library

*Library of Congress Cataloging-in-Publication Data applied for*

ISBN 0 7190 5771 X *hardback*

First published 2000

07 06 05 04 03 02 01 00     10 9 8 7 6 5 4 3 2 1

*JS*
*3111*
*.C49*
*2000*

Typeset in Times
by Northern Phototypesetting Co. Ltd, Bolton
Printed in Great Britain
by Bookcraft (Bath) Ltd, Midsomer Norton

For

those who serve in

and are served by

local government

# Contents

# List of tables

# Preface

July 1995: three very strenuous years as a member of the Local Government Commission for England (LGCE) had just ended and the last thing that I thought I wanted to do was to write a history of the structural reforms to local government in which I had played a part.

However, early in 1996, Derek Thomas, sometime Chief Executive of Surrey County Council, suggested that a book really ought to be written while the whole process was fresh in people's minds, and why not myself as author? Enquiries revealed that nobody else was planning a text covering the whole of Great Britain. The nearest to a full analysis that was identified was the preparation for special issues of *Local Government Studies* and *Public Administration*, both of which subsequently appeared in 1997. Additionally, a study of the Commission itself by Stewart *et al.* was in hand which was also published in the same year. It was clear that, even taken together, these would not provide a coherent analytical account of the whole episode for England, let alone Scotland and Wales.

So I decided to take up Derek's challenge but other projects meant that, although preliminary work could be done, it was not until 1998 that sustained attention could be given to the task. This delay was probably fortunate, for two separate reasons. First, it allowed some distance between myself and the events analysed, a distance which was personally necessary and which has served to improve the sense of proportion. Second, with the passage of even a few years, we are in a better position to know what the actual costs and benefits of change have been. Had the work been completed earlier, it would have been necessary to place greater reliance on the *ex ante* assessments made as part of the review process leading up to reorganisation.

Yet, some may opine, given the antagonisms that erupted between counties and districts during the reform process, would it not now be better to let sleeping dogs lie? After all, the Association of County Councils (ACC) and the Association of District Councils (ADC) have joined forces with the Association of Metropolitan Authorities to create, with effect from 1996, the new Local Government Association in England, with the important purpose of trying to heal the long-standing divisions between the various kinds of authority, so that energies may be directed to the major issues, such as funding, which affect all councils. To be reminded of the recent conflicts over structural change might be regarded as unhelpful.

However, the book is not just about an episode in the history of local government, for it also examines some important lessons regarding the governance of the United Kingdom. Why was the task of recommending change or no change given to an independent commission in England, whereas in both Scotland and Wales the Westminster Parliament chose to legislate the precise details of a new structure, and what lessons may be derived from the differing experiences? The efforts made by the Government to control the LGCE in its work on England raise some basic issues regarding the relationship between Parliament and Government on the one hand, and between the Government and a supposedly independent body on the other, matters that go to the heart of national governance. Arching over these issues, relevant to the whole of Britain, was the dangerous gulf that existed between political rhetoric and the requirements of sound evidence as the basis for policy.

There is another reason why it is appropriate to see what lessons there may be from recent history. Many observers consider that the limited structural change which has occurred in shire England leaves an unstable situation. Indeed, some twenty shire districts have formed a Local Governance Review Group to press for the granting of unitary status to authorities, such as Norwich, which were not included with bigger cities such as Nottingham and Stoke-on-Trent in the changes implemented in England. Thwarted ambitions may well extend beyond the twenty members of this group. In addition, despite the formation of the Local Government Association, there are still groupings, within that body, of authorities in terms of their standing and powers, so that the new Association has not put an end to the old rivalries, though it seems to have them in check for the present. Thus there is the potential for instability for these reasons; but there are other and more general potential pressures for further structural change which affect *all* local authorities in Great Britain (Davis 1997). With the advent of a Labour administration in 1997, a form of two-tier elected local government is being reinvented for London; Scotland now has its own Parliament and Wales an Assembly, in both cases with possible implications for local government which may take some time to work through. In England, the Labour Government might wish to proceed with some form of elected regional assemblies and if it does there may well be questions raised regarding the appropriate structure for local government.

If, or when, further change to the structure of local government is contemplated in any or all of the countries which comprise Great Britain, some lessons from the 1990s are unequivocal. First, it is essential to clarify the purpose or purposes which it is intended should be achieved by structural change. Second, and of equal significance, consideration must be given to the options that may be available to achieve the given ends, options which may take the form of changes in the powers and responsibilities of local authorities, of changes in funding, of changes in their internal organisation and functioning, or of changes in the manner in which councils are regulated by the Audit Commission and in other ways. Only if it is clear that structural change is a *necessary* condition for achieving the stated goals should an administration be minded to proceed. Assuming that the decision is taken at some future date to proceed with major structural change, on no account should anyone be deluded that such change on its own is likely to be a *sufficient* condition for achieving the stated ends. The 1990s have repeated a lesson which has been ignored too often in the past. For it to be sensible to consider the structure of local authorities, account must be taken of the purpose for which the institution of local government is needed, what the relationship between central and local government should be, and how the powers, financing and internal management of councils should be organised. To deal with just one element, *structure*, in isolation from all the others makes for downright bad governance of the national polity.

The present book focuses on the issues which are relevant for determining the structure of local government and for this reason omits a very considerable amount of detail which, however important in its own right, would obscure the narrative and impede analysis. Therefore, the volume cannot claim to be a complete history in the sense of an exhaustive chronicle. For example, virtually nothing is said about the staff commissions which were established to facilitate the staff appointment and allocation procedures where structural change occurred. There is an important story to be told about this work but it is not central to decisions about whether structural change should occur and the nature of such change. Another subject which is not discussed is the impact of local government structure on the number of councillors and hence their representative role in relation to the electorate. Conversely, more attention is paid to the estimation of the financial costs and benefits of reorganisation than has been common in the published literature, partly because this literature has not fully recognised the role that these costings actually played and partly because the evidence reveals some very serious issues for national governance.

In writing this book, I owe a very large debt to many people, too many to name individually. My greatest debt is to two individuals. Derek Thomas has already been mentioned; not only did he sow the seed for this book but he stayed around to nurture the seedling with constant help and advice. To Colin Wilby my debt is quite different. For almost three years at the Local Government Commission as the officer with whom I worked, his unflagging care and cheerfulness, his professional dedication in the best tradition of public service, made possible a task that might otherwise have been too daunting. He also provided invaluable help during the writing of this book.

At this point, it becomes difficult to do full justice to the numerous debts which I owe, for the following reason. I have interviewed a large number of people. For the conduct of these interviews, I proposed that the conversation should be under Chatham House rules; that is, non-attributable. If the interviews had been 'on the record', and particularly if they had been recorded on tape, most, if not all, of the individuals with whom I spoke would have felt much more constrained in what they said. The interviews provided invaluable material, not least in helping with the interpretation of events, and evidence culled from these discussions is distributed throughout the text. To list the individuals interviewed would allow the diligent and knowledgeable reader to make some strong inferences regarding the identity of those who supplied certain pieces of information, which might cause them embarrassment and would breach the understanding which formed the basis for their cooperation. Therefore, I do not list them but wish them to know that I owe them all a very great debt indeed.

I have also received valuable help from many other individuals and also from a number of institutions. The staff of the University Library in Cambridge were exceedingly helpful in tracking down disparate material, some of which is a cataloguer's nightmare: Bill Noblett in the Official Publications room and Neil Hudson in Periodicals came to my aid on numerous occasions. Invaluable help was also provided by the Local Government Commission. Through the good offices of Roger Latham and Alan Sumby, I had the benefit of access to the files of the Society of County Treasurers, a privilege that yielded a great deal of information which I would not otherwise have found.

Draft text has been seen and criticised by a number of people; their comments and suggestions have been of great help but they are, of course, not responsible for the use which I have made of their contributions. The list comprises: Alan Barnish, Tina Day, George Freeman, Malcolm Grant, George Jones, Barbara Kahan, Roger Latham, Steve Leach, Arthur Midwinter, Alan Sumby, Derek Thomas, Robin Wendt, Colin Wilby and Julian Wolfson. Derek Thomas was rash enough to volunteer to read the entire text at the time of completion, having seen most of it at earlier stages of drafting.

My wife has also been a pillar of strength. During the three years I was a member of the Commission she cosseted me; she has read and commented on the text; and she was very patient as the book neared completion and became an absorbing mistress of my time.

Michael Chisholm
Cambridge

# 1

# Introduction

Fashion, though Folly's child, and guide of fools, Rules e'en the wisest, and in learning rules. (George Crabbe, *The Library*)

Late in 1990, the Government embarked on the structural reorganisation of local government throughout much of Great Britain, leading to the complete re-shaping of councils in Scotland and Wales, and to a partial reform in shire England: Northern Ireland was not affected. By April 1998, all the new councils which were created had come into existence and were operational. This episode in the history of local government provides the subject-matter for this book. The purpose is to bring together the histories for England, Scotland and Wales into one volume, this being something which has not hitherto been done. In an important sense, therefore, this is a historical record of some years in which local government was re-shaped in a radical manner. But the intention runs beyond the provision of a chronicle, to consider in a critical fashion what happened, why and with what results, providing, for want of a better term, an analytical history. An important aspect of that analytical approach is the treatment of events in the three countries of Great Britain, since this allows comparisons and linkages which have not previously been made, yielding new insights. Although the subject-matter is the reform of local government, the study throws light on the working of central government and it will be remembered that the Conservatives had come to power in 1979 and retained office until May 1997, so this is essentially a history of events under Conservative administrations.

At the time reform was initiated, the whole of Scotland, Wales and shire England possessed a two-tier structure of local government – counties (or regions in Scotland) and districts. Legislation was enacted to convert this two-tier structure of principal authorities into a single-tier, or unitary, system throughout both Scotland and Wales. Change in England was effected in a different way. The Local Government Act 1992 provided for the establishment of the Local Government Commission for England, charged to review the structure of local government outside London and the Metropolitan areas, in that region known as shire England, to recommend to the Government whether or not the two-tier arrangements should be replaced by unitary authorities. In the event, forty-six such councils have come into existence; the remainder of shire England retains the two-tier structure of counties and districts. Table 1.1 summarises the position in Great Britain before and after structural reorganisation in the 1990s.

**Table 1.1**  *Summary of the effects of structural reorganisation in Great Britain*

| Area, with total population (000) | Number of authorities and average population (000) Two-tier structures | | Unitary structures |
|---|---|---|---|
| | Counties/regions | Districts | |
| **Shire England** | | | |
| Pre-reform | 39 | 296 | |
| (30,711) | (787) | (104) | |
| Post-reform | | | |
| Two tier | 34 | 238 | |
| (22,506) | (662) | (95) | |
| Unitary councils | | | 46 |
| (8205) | | | (178) |
| **Scotland** | | | |
| Pre-reform | | | |
| Mainland | 9 | 53 | |
| (5065) | (563) | (96) | |
| Islands | | | 3 |
| (72) | | | (24) |
| Post-reform | | | |
| Mainland | | | 29 |
| (5065) | | | (175) |
| Islands | | | 3 |
| (72) | | | (24) |
| **Wales** | | | |
| Pre-reform | 8 | 37 | |
| (2917) | (365) | (79) | |
| Post-reform | | | 22 |
| (2917) | | | (133) |

*Sources*: *Municipal Yearbook* and *Regional Trends*.
*Note*: The population figures are mostly for 1995 except that those for the unitary authorities in shire England are more recent.

The first question considered is why reorganisation occurred in the 1990s, this being addressed in Chapter 2, which explores a number of long-term pressures that had been building up, as well as the contingent political circumstances which led to the announcement that reform would be put in hand. These considerations were, to a large extent, general to the whole of Great Britain, though there were nuances which distinguished the three constituent countries. Chapter 3 describes the process of change in England, with a summary of the outcome, and necessarily focuses on the role of the LGCE; the complementary account of the changes in Scotland and Wales, conducted by the Government itself, is contained in Chapter 6. Chapters 4 and 5 concentrate on the issues which were relevant to the review process; namely, the costs and benefits of change, and the significance of service delivery, communities and public opinion. The first of this pair of chapters deals with the costing of change in England only, the equivalent data for Scotland and Wales being contained in Chapter 6. In contrast, although Chapter 5 concentrates on the evidence for England, some relevant material from elsewhere is also included. Then, the *ex ante* estimates for the one-off costs of change having been considered in earlier chapters, Chapter 7 examines the evidence for the actual, or *ex post*, costs of reorganisation, to see how closely the prior estimates have matched the actual costs. This chapter is followed by an enquiry into how well the new arrangements are working throughout Great Britain and the extent to which the benefits which had been expected as a consequence of reorganisation have been realised in practice. Given the multiplicity of changes affecting local government and the need for new councils to settle down to their tasks, Chapter 8 can offer only a preliminary assessment of the changes which have been effected, an assessment which will undoubtedly be up-dated with the passage of time. Finally, Chapter 9 draws a number of conclusions from the evidence which has been reviewed, conclusions which are relevant for local government and also for the general governance of Britain.

Taken together, these chapters map a journey which started with certain concepts and political imperatives, which provided the rhetoric in favour of change. The confrontation of that rhetoric with the realities of the real world, and the negotiation of a way through the conflicting pressures to achieve certain goals, led to outcomes which may or may not be durable for the foreseeable future.

Since so much rhetoric was used, it is well to pause a moment to reflect on one's understanding of this word. *The Shorter Oxford English Dictionary* gives two meanings which are relevant in the present context. The first of these is 'the art of using language so as to persuade or influence others', an art which is integral to the concept of language and to the communication of information and ideas. Used in this sense, rhetoric has a long and honourable ancestry traceable to Ancient Greece. But it also has a baser meaning, as 'language characterised by artificial or ostentatious expression', designed to persuade whether or not the message conveyed is actually correct. This meaning of rhetoric is part of the daily political combat and the reporting thereof in newspapers and on television screens. As the tale unfolds, the reader will find that an uncomfortable amount of the rhetoric which was important for local government reorganisation is better described by the baser version than by the first and more honourable one.

This confident assertion presupposes that the statements which have been made, designed to persuade the public and key decision makers, can be tested for their veracity against some generally accepted version of what is true. Therein lies a serious methodological problem, for when it comes to estimating the costs and benefits of structural change (whether these be *ex ante* or *ex post* estimates), to identifying the sense of community, and so on, we do not have an objective reality on which everyone is agreed. The best that we can do is to establish realities which have a high probability of being true, such that most observers, when presented with the evidence, will agree that the reality portrayed is likely to be correct. Therefore, the dictionary definition of reality as 'being real or having actual existence' must be interpreted in terms that are essentially those used by Popper (1959): that which we 'know' is the knowledge which we accept subject to the possibility that additional evidence may show it to be wrong. In essence, that which we accept as true is something for which the probabilities of falsification are perceived to be low. Consequently, in the pages which follow considerable efforts have been made to ensure that what is portrayed as 'reality' can be shown to be based on high-quality evidence with which most people will agree.

As the story unfolds, it will be seen that there was considerable divergence between much of the rhetoric employed and the realities about which that rhetoric was used. That divergence occurred at several levels in the public discourse, including the local level and the national. The latter throws light upon the working of central government and the manner of national governance. Consequently, although the subject-matter of this book is about local government, it will be found that an inter-weaving theme is about the quality of central government and that, in many respects, this is the most important aspect of the history which is revealed.

There are some other terminological niceties which need to be clarified. Recurring through the text is the term 'two tier', used for a structure of local government in which powers are divided between the counties (or regions in Scotland) and the districts within these larger units. Conceptually, this structure is based on the belief that certain functions are best carried out locally, at the district level, whereas other functions require a larger area and population; housing and park maintenance are examples of the former, while the latter includes education and social services. This terminology applies to the two principal tiers but ignores the existence of parish, town and community councils. These latter were not directly involved in the re-structuring which is the subject of this book; however, a literally correct description of the structures which existed in 1990 would be 'three tier', not 'two tier'. However, the term 'two tier' is part of common usage, but it should be employed with the qualification in mind that there are in addition the parish, town and community councils. By the same token, the term 'unitary' is also misleading, for it too ignores the existence of this lowest tier of local government. In any case, these are tiers of *elected* local government, so that the terminology omits any reference to the existence of unelected bodies, commonly called quangos (Cole and Boyne 1996). It would be tedious to repeat these qualifications at every turn and the reader is enjoined to keep them in mind in reading what follows.

The term 'unitary' must be qualified in another way. In formal usage, the term applies to the authorities in England, Scotland and Wales which were formed in the 1990s to combine most of the former powers of the counties (or regions) and districts. For the purpose of the present book, the responsibilities of these new authorities may be regarded as sufficiently similar that there is no serious confusion in using the term in all three countries. The more serious complication is that in London and the Metropolitan areas of England, the upper or county layer of local government was removed in 1986, creating a form of unitary local government. However, there are contrasts between these two groups of authorities in their powers, and between them and the new unitary authorities. On occasion, it is convenient to describe all these councils as unitary authorities but the reader should be aware that this is a rather loose usage.

Until the creation in 1999 of a Parliament for Scotland and an Assembly for Wales, the principal local authorities were the main bodies below the national government legitimised by direct elections. As such, they have responsibility for a wide range of services, including education, social services, council housing and the provision of public open spaces. They also have an important role in regulating public health, weights and measures, and land use, the latter under the town and country planning laws. And, finally, they play an important part in championing the interests of their areas, reflecting the desires and aspirations of their citizens. In one way or another, local government touches the lives of everyone. For anyone who wants a reasonably complete review of the functions of local authorities in England, a useful publication has been issued by the Department of the Environment (DoE 1992a); a brief account for the three countries of Great Britain is contained in the annual *Municipal Yearbook*.

Local Government plc accounts for a large segment of the national economy. Taking net revenue expenditure, which is only one among several definitions of local authority spending and a conservative one at that, the value of the annual expenditure of councils in Great Britain is equivalent to about 7 per cent of the Gross Domestic Product at market prices. On the basis of employment, the 2.1 million full-time equivalent staff in 1990 accounted for somewhat over 8 per cent of all workers; by 1998, the absolute number had fallen to 1.7 million, or about 7 per cent of total employment. These approximate figures show that the local government sector is substantial. This implies that any proposal for radical reorganisation should only be brought forward in the confident knowledge that the change will be beneficial, since there clearly is the potential for any adverse consequences of change to be considerable in magnitude and with potentially serious effects for many citizens.

An important feature of the local government system is the high degree of central control exercised by the Government, especially from 1979 onwards. Councils operate within a tight web of controls and limitations, with most of their money coming from the Exchequer: in the early 1990s, approximately 80 per cent of local authority revenue came in the form of revenue support grants and the reallocation of the uniform business rates; the proportion thus derived has now fallen to about 75 per cent. In addition, at the time structural reorganisation was imple-

mented the total expenditure of individual authorities was capped, thereby deny-
ing them the possibility of raising additional funds by increasing the Council Tax.
In very large measure, therefore, local authorities had little financial accountability to their electorates; accountability lay in the upwards direction, to Westminster
and Whitehall (see, for example, Chisholm *et al.* 1997; Lord Hunt 1996).

Given that the Government did decide to reform the structure of local government, the following questions may be posed at this stage of the enquiry. Was there
clear evidence that replacement of the two-tier arrangements by unitary structures
was a necessary, even if not a sufficient, condition for meeting specified objectives? What were the objectives which the Government set for itself in undertaking reorganisation? How strong was the evidence that these objectives would be
attained, and that this would be done more effectively by structural change than
by other means? Was there a clear idea of what unitary structures would be appropriate? And were proper methods used to achieve change? This bundle of questions shapes the enquiry which follows, throughout which a recurring issue is the
extent to which the rhetoric employed was or was not congruent with the relevant
available evidence. As the reader will discover, there was in fact a considerable
disjuncture between rhetoric and reality, from which flow some important consequences. The subject-matter for the chapters which follow is an episode in the history of local government, and in this sense the book is focused on that sector of
the economy. However, as the history unfolds, it becomes increasingly clear that
in fact we are studying some aspects of the wider national governance, with implications which run far beyond the seemingly narrow confines of local government.

# 2

# Why structural reform in the 1990s?

Yes, Minister. It may work in practice. But it won't work in theory. (Lilley 1999)

With most major reform processes, it is possible to identify two sets of reasons for implementation of change at a particular time: long-term pressures and developments, and short-term contingent circumstances. This form of analysis seems to be entirely appropriate for examining the question as to why structural reform of local government was implemented in the 1990s. Therefore, we will begin with a brief résumé of earlier attempts at reform and the structural changes which were effected in the 1970s, and then move on to consider more recent events.

## A brief historical overview to 1975

The modern system of local government in Great Britain finally took shape with a series of Acts which went onto the statute book between 1888 and 1899 (Wilson and Game 1994, pp. 42–6). The 1888 Local Government Act established elected county councils in England and Wales; similar provision was made for Scotland one year later. The completion of the process came in 1899, with elected second-tier authorities being established in Scotland to match those which had already been put in place elsewhere in Great Britain. The larger cities were designated as all-purpose authorities, known as county boroughs in England and Wales and as counties of city in Scotland. At the time the Bill was introduced which became the 1888 Act, provision was made for only ten cities to be excluded from the jurisdiction of the counties but by the time the legislation was completed the number had risen to sixty-one (Keith-Lucas and Richards 1978, p. 13). Scotland entered the twentieth century with four counties of city.

Thereafter, as Keith-Lucas and Richards recount, there were continuing problems on a number of fronts. Rapid urbanisation meant that the county boroughs and smaller towns sought to expand their boundaries to encompass the expanding built-up area, requests that quickly became a matter of concern and then opposition on the part of other authorities. In addition, the local government structure was a complex pattern of relatively small authorities above the parish level, with a variety of powers and duties. In the 1920s, a Commission was established to review the problems and to make recommendations, the major outcome of which was legislative provision to slow down the creation and extension of county boroughs. In fact, not one was created in England between 1929 and 1964 (Richards 1973, p. 37). Another attempt was made with the Local Government Act 1929, which laid on county councils a duty to review the structure of county districts (but not county boroughs), and to do so once every ten years. By 1938, there had been some modest rationalisation under this Act but then everything was put on hold with the outbreak of the Second World War in 1939.

After the war, there was widespread agreement that the complicated system of local government should be modernised but there was lack of agreement concerning the desirable structure. That lack of agreement was manifest in the divergent positions taken by the various local authority associations. In addition, though, it was clear that the terms of reference for the Local Government Boundary Commission, the body charged with making recommendations for England and Wales, were inappropriate. In its 1947 report, the Commission said:

> We have definitely reached the conclusion that, in many areas – and these cover the great bulk of the population – our present powers and instructions do not permit the formation of local government units as effective and convenient as in our opinion they should be ... Our experience also confirms the statement made recently in Parliament by the Minister of Health (Aneurin Bevan): 'Everyone who knows about local government feels it is nonsense to talk about functions and boundaries separately. They have to be taken together'. We have no jurisdiction over functions. (Quoted in Keith-Lucas and Richards 1978, p. 205)

After a year's delay, the Commission was sacked for its temerity.

A decade later, the Local Government Act 1958 established separate Local Government Commissions for England and Wales. The former was circumscribed by labyrinthine procedures and little progress was made. The Welsh Commission issued a report in 1963 which made serious proposals for change but in a manner which suggested it had little real confidence in the results of its deliberations:

> Boundaries cannot reasonably be divorced from functions or from finance. We have tried faithfully to carry out the task assigned to us. We venture to believe that, within the limits imposed upon us, our recommendations are deserving of serious consideration. But we cannot help wondering whether, had we been allowed to consider at least the redistribution of functions, we might not have done a better job ... That we were not permitted to consider the redistribution of functions was, we believe, for reasons we have already stated, a serious mistake, and was, in fact, a disservice to Wales. (Local Government Commission for Wales, quoted in Keith-Lucas and Richards 1978, p. 216)

The unsatisfactory situation continued to fester until the newly elected Labour administration in 1966 established the Redcliffe-Maud Royal Commission to undertake a thorough review of local government in England. A parallel Royal Commission, chaired by Lord Wheatley, was at the same time set up for Scotland. No provision was made for an equivalent review in Wales. The establishment of these two Commissions in the mid-1960s marked a radical break from the ineffectual attempts to reform the local government system that had characterised the twentieth century to date outside London. The capital had seen the creation of the Greater London Council (GLC) and the Inner London Education Authority (ILEA) in 1965, following the report of the Royal Commission which had been established in 1957 under the chairmanship of Sir Edwin Herbert. The GLC covered an area and population substantially larger than had been encompassed by the previous London County Council; the administrative county of Middlesex was abolished and the number of lower-tier authorities within the enlarged jurisdiction was reduced to thirty-two boroughs plus the City of London.

The Commissions chaired by Lord Redcliffe-Maud and Sir Andrew Wheatley reported in 1969. The former proposed a radical re-structuring of English local government outside London, a structure of fifty-eight unitary authorities based on the concept of functional city-regions, except that in the case of three conurbations (Birmingham, Liverpool and Manchester) it recommended a two-tier structure. Though the Government had successfully fostered the belief that radical reform was inevitable and imminent, and though it broadly accepted the Redcliffe-Maud proposals, the backlash was immediate and powerful (Keith-Lucas and Richards 1978; Wood 1976). Opponents of the Commission's proposals for England fastened on the fact that a revised two-tier system had only just been put in place for London, that the majority report itself proposed a two-tier structure for three conurbations and that Derek Senior had written a dissenting report advocating a form of two-tier administration (the upper tier being regional governments). In addition, and compounding the problems, the Wheatley Commission recommended a form of two-tier structure for Scotland. Enthusiasm for the unitary concept embodied in the Redcliffe-Maud proposals evaporated. Finally, a general election intervened.

The advent of a Conservative administration in 1970 changed the political dynamics. The Conservatives' election manifesto had promised change based on the two-tier principle, change that would be much less radical in England than had seemed probable under the previous Labour administration. The opinion was widespread that a two-tier structure would recognisably be a continuation of established patterns, would allow for a larger number of councillors than would be the case in a unitary structure and would be more accessible to citizens. No doubt there was also the political calculation that a two-tier arrangement in which the county boroughs became districts within counties would allow the Conservatives a greater measure of political control of the local authority system than would be the case with the Redcliffe-Maud proposals, which were more likely to tilt the balance towards the Labour Party.

The incoming Conservative administration could have put off local government reform pending the report of the Commission on the Constitution, set up in

1969 to consider the relations between central government and the countries, nations and regions of the United Kingdom. Instead, proclaiming that local government reform need not wait on the resolution of these wider constitutional matters, the Government chose to proceed. The outcome was two Acts, one for England and Wales (1972), the other for Scotland (1973). In England and Wales, the legislation retained the two-tier principle which had been rejected by the Redcliffe-Maud Commission, modified the county structure and resulted in a sharp reduction in the number of second-tier authorities. Former county boroughs in shire England lost their all-purpose status to become districts on a par with the districts formed from the antecedent urban and rural districts; and big cities such as Birmingham found that a Metropolitan county council had significant authority in respect of conurbation-wide matters. In Scotland, a modified version of the Wheatley recommendations was adopted; that is, a two-tier structure of regions and districts on the mainland and three most-purpose authorities for the islands. As in England and Wales, the big cities lost status and power.

Keith-Lucas and Richards point out that the passage of the 1972 legislation was much less contentious than one might have expected:

> A general agreement emerged that the Bill should pass. The endless arguments over local government reform petered out in an anti-climax. Why did this occur? There was a consensus that some change was long overdue; that many authorities were too small; that the isolation of county boroughs must end; that the conurbations needed a measure of separate treatment. Granted this degree of harmony, the disagreements move towards details. Certainly, a degree of weariness surrounded the whole question. (Keith- Lucas and Richards 1978, pp. 228-9)

The major complaints came from the county boroughs, which in future would become districts like any other district within their respective counties. However, the county boroughs were much more likely to be Labour controlled than Tory and so the Government felt able to ignore their arguments against the loss of powers.

The net effect of the Act was to reduce very sharply the number of principal authorities below the level of the counties outside London. While 58 counties in England and Wales were reduced to 53, the number of non-county councils was slashed from 1,332 to 369 (Chisholm 1975, p. 306). The reduction in number and consequential increase in size was even more apparent in Scotland; a total of 431 authorities was transformed into just 65 (Wilson and Game 1994, p. 53). This nation-wide reduction in the number of local authorities was surprisingly uncontentious. The perception was widespread in the early 1970s that there were too many councils that were too small for the efficient delivery of services and for the coordination of wider initiatives. There was also the generally held view that the local government system is subject to economies of scale and that therefore to achieve greater efficiency substantial consolidation was essential.

The new authorities came into existence in England and Wales in 1974 and in Scotland a year later, bringing the whole of mainland Great Britain into line with the two-tier principle embodied in the Greater London Council in 1965. With the exception of the Inner London Education Authority and the three island councils of Scotland, a roughly uniform two-tier system was in place everywhere, though the functions and relative importance of the two tiers were not the same throughout Great Britain.

Northern Ireland was and remained quite distinct. A 1972 Act provided for twenty-six single-tier authorities, elected by proportional representation (compared with the first-past-the-post electoral system otherwise used throughout the British political system at that time). However, health and education responsibilities were given to nine appointed area boards.

One feature of the reforms in Great Britain in the 1970s is worth noting. The relevant Acts specify the powers and duties of the local authorities in England, Scotland and Wales. In other words, this particular reform gave simultaneous consideration to both structure and powers, a major step forward in comparison with earlier attempts at reform. Whether the particular combination of structures and powers was really appropriate is another matter but credit should be accorded for the fact that two of the key ingredients were recognised to be inseparably linked. On the other hand, the legislation avoided questions of finance.

The explanatory and financial memorandum published with the Local Government Bill 1971 for England and Wales expressed the view that, over-all, the proposed changes would have little impact on the income and expenditure of local authorities (a similar assessment was made for Scotland). Yet, despite the establishment of a Local Government Staff Commission to oversee the staffing implications of change, the number of employees rose by nearly 5 per cent, an increase only some of which was attributable to changes in the duties of authorities. In addition, there was a substantial upwards drift in wage levels. All in all, 'there was a substantial increase in administrative costs' (Keith-Lucas and Richards 1978, p. 235); these extra costs contributed to the financial crisis which affected local government in the mid-1970s, a crisis which led to the Layfield enquiry into the funding of local authorities (Layfield 1976, pp. 28–9).

An issue that was not resolved with the reforms of the 1970s was the over-all purpose of local government. Many of those who advocated reform did so in the belief that this was essential if local authorities were to make a more general and positive contribution to society. If local authorities were to raise their sights, however, this would almost certainly imply higher expenditure and the possibility of becoming ever more dependent upon central government grants. On the other hand, the Conservative Government under Edward Heath clearly took the view that the purpose of reform was to achieve more economical service delivery and a better quality of management, though recognising the desirability of decisions being taken locally where practicable (Keith-Lucas and Richards 1978, pp. 239–42). Additional points to note are:

1 The Government was aware of the need for counties and districts to work together and made certain provisions which were intended to facilitate this,

such as ensuring that authorities could hire services from each other and engage in joint purchasing and agency arrangements.
2  Nevertheless, the 1972 Act gave counties and districts some functions which obviously and directly overlapped, as with planning.
3  The former county boroughs and counties of cities were deeply disenchanted with the demotion into which they had been forced.
4  In England, three entirely new counties were created – Avon, Cleveland and Humberside – cutting across traditional loyalties in the name of functional integrity around an estuary or river. This was somewhat ironic given the rejection of the functional city-region concept of Redcliffe-Maud and the fact that the Scottish regions were based on this idea.
5  Many of the counties were perceived to be remote from their electorates, despite the efforts that were made to close the credibility gap.

All of these issues were to achieve prominence within two decades, by which time the context in which local government was viewed had changed dramatically.

## The changing scene, 1975–90

In the mid-1970s, it was generally thought that there would be a long period before further major changes in the structure of local government were contemplated and that incremental change would be the order of the day (e.g. Chisholm 1975; Lord Redcliffe-Maud and Wood 1974). In the event, within a decade the county level of government had been abolished in London and in the six Metropolitan areas outside the capital identified in the 1974 reforms. Although, as we shall see, these changes were prompted by considerations that had little to do with fostering local government and much to do with the wish of central government to impose its political will, the 1986 elimination of these urban county councils provided some encouragement for the protagonists of unitary, or 'all purpose', local authorities elsewhere in Britain. That hope was reinforced by some much wider and more fundamental intellectual and practical developments, at least some of which can be identified with the New Right movement which came to prominence. It is with these more general ideas that we shall begin this section.

### Public choice theory and the post-welfare society

The advent of Margaret Thatcher as leader of the Conservative Party in Opposition and then as Prime Minister from 1979 coincided with some powerful New Right thinking. The post-war consensus regarding the collective provision of goods and services, and the role of the state in relation to individual responsibilities, was challenged at its foundations. Inspired by thinkers such as Hayek, the New Right emphasised the responsibility which individuals have to provide for their own welfare, emphasised the superiority of markets over collective provision and proclaimed the need to roll back the frontiers of state provision, including provision by local authorities. These ideas, and the policy conclusions to which they led, were not unique to Britain. Ronald Reagan became President of the United States in 1980, espousing concepts very similar to those of Thatcher, and Bennett (1990) has shown that equivalent developments were occurring quite generally throughout Europe.

An important component of this thinking was based in public choice theory, a body of thought with quite long antecedents (Arrow 1951; Dowding 1996; Dowding *et al.* 1994; Gray 1994; D. N. King 1984; D. S. King 1987, 1989; Oates 1972). One premiss of this thinking is that bureaucracies are inherently inefficient for the allocation of resources in comparison with market mechanisms. Another is the proposition that bureaucracies have an in-built tendency to grow and also to supply excessive quantities of the goods and services for which they are responsible. From this starting point, it is easy to conclude that society would be better off if bureaucracies could be tamed and if markets could be encouraged to extend their share of the totality of socio-economic transactions.

The proposition that bureaucracies are fundamentally inefficient can be justified in the following manner. It is asserted that they produce a limited range of standardised goods and services, an assertion which is consistent with the interpretation of the early post-war decades as a period dominated by 'Fordist' mass production – standardised products from rather inflexible production systems in which scale economies are important. This view of the world is captured in the old joke that one could have any colour of Model T Ford so long as it was black. Stoker (1989) certainly seemed to think that this characterisation fitted local government in Britain and other authors have used the same framework (Goodwin and Painter 1996; Painter 1991). More generally, though, it is asserted that the limited range of goods and services produced by bureaucracies reflects the need to cater for some concept of the average person. In the context of local government, this would be an assessment of the needs of the majority of citizens, with the possibility that needs which are diverse might be overlooked or downplayed. To the extent that a bureaucracy does indeed direct its attention to the average, serious inefficiencies will occur in the allocation of resources because of the mismatch that will exist between the range of services on offer and the range that citizens actually need or desire. The electoral system is held to be an inherently inefficient means for people to express complex bundles of need and aspiration. The allocative inefficiency of a bureaucracy will be compounded by the inefficiencies that arise from the lack of competitive stimulus, given that in many or most cases the bureaucracy will have a virtual monopoly in the provision of particular services.

This train of thought leads to two policy strategies. The first is to remove responsibilities from the bureaucracy and transfer them into the market sector of the economy – in effect to privatise the provision. Where privatisation is deemed to be inappropriate for whatever reasons, the second strategy is to introduce some form of quasi-market, as with the separation of customer and contractor in the

National Health Service (NHS) and the publication of school examination league tables so that parents may be better informed in making choices for their children.

Applied to local authorities, these ideas resulted in three sets of policy conclusions. The first was the need to improve the efficiency of local authorities in the discharge of their duties, notably through the introduction from 1980 of Compulsory Competitive Tendering and a general shift towards a business ethos (Ascher 1987). In fact, this was part of a more basic change, to view citizens as customers and local authorities as, in effect, the contractors engaged to provide services, something that was helpfully codified by the Audit Commission with its 1988 publication, *The Competitive Council*. This concept of the role of local authorities was put with particular clarity by the Department of the Environment in its evidence to the Select Committee of the House of Lords on relations between central and local government (Lord Hunt 1996, vol. 2, p. 1).

The second strategy of Government was to remove some functions from local government altogether, either into the private sector or into the hands of unelected quangos (Kellner 1997; Stoker 1991, 1997a). While he was a Minister in the last Conservative administration, William Waldegrave sought to justify this shift in the following terms: 'The key point in this argument is not whether those who run our public services are elected, but whether they are producer-responsive or consumer-responsive' (Waldegrave 1993, p. 13). This statement followed an earlier passage in which he asserted that local authorities have *unfettered* control over the services they provide, for which they raise only a small part of the necessary funds; the first part of this assertion, of unfettered control, is one that most observers would find hard to accept. It was also curious that Waldegrave should imply that the proportion of funds derived from central government was fixed and immutable. Nevertheless, his comments are worth reporting because they illustrate as clearly as any other text the direction of thinking in Government circles in the late 1980s/early 1990s.

The third policy conclusion to note is one that has particular relevance in the present context. Given that local authorities would in practice continue to exist, albeit with modified powers and discretion, public choice theory leads to the argument that efficiency will be increased if local authorities are individually small. The reasoning for small authorities runs as follows. If it is accepted that there are allocative inefficiencies in the delivery of local authority services because their provision is aimed at the common denominator and fails to reflect the diverse pattern of needs and desires among the 'customers', it follows that efficiency would be improved if the residents of individual local authorities were homogeneous in their socio-economic characteristics; that is, if there were only a small dispersion about the local norm. If there were small differences among the residents in each local authority, the standardised package of services provided by each council would closely reflect the local circumstances and allocative inefficiencies would be minimised. The simple way to achieve greater homogeneity in the populations of local authorities is for them to be small and based on identifiable communities.

Furthermore, following Tiebout (1956), these small authorities would then be faced with the direct stimulus of competition, since residents in one area who were dissatisfied with the bundle of services on offer at the particular level of local tax, and who felt that the electoral system precluded the recognition of their wishes, would have the option of moving to a nearby authority where the combination of services and tax level more nearly matched their circumstances. This spatial redistribution of population would, on the premises chosen, serve to increase the allocative efficiency of the system as provision and need would be brought more into line. In other words, if citizens felt that 'voice' would avail nothing, they would have the option of the 'exit' strategy. As John (1997) points out, this reasoning was offered as a justification for introducing the Poll Tax, which first became payable in 1988. Curiously, though public choice thinking clearly influenced attitudes to the structure of local government, the links were apparently never articulated formally.

This interpretation of public choice theory concentrates on the *horizontal* implications of the Tiebout propositions, ignoring the fact that a *vertical* dimension can also be inferred which would yield two or more tiers of local administration (Boyne 1996). This vertical dimension was almost completely ignored in Britain, so that public choice theory seemed clearly to point to the abolition of the counties in England and Wales, and of the Scottish regions, because they encompassed very diverse populations. Those who might have wished to defend these larger authorities on the ground that there are in fact real economies of scale in the provision of services were met with the following argument. With the progressive privatisation of services, local authorities would cease to be service providers and would concentrate on ensuring that the necessary contracts with the independent sector were in place and being implemented. The local authority would be responsible for ensuring that services were provided to a defined standard but would not actually supply these services directly. This concept of local authorities as enablers rather than providers was articulated by Ridley in 1988 and a year later by the Adam Smith Institute (1989a, 1989b). Very quickly, guidance began to appear on how these enabling authorities should be managed (e.g. Brooke 1989), and one commentator even went so far as to opine that: 'It is quite possible to envisage the local authority of the future as a set of contracts, and a network of internal and external trading' (Walsh 1989, p. 30). According to this scenario, any benefits that there may be from scale economies would be reaped by the firms operating in the private sector and would be reflected in the contract prices paid by the local authorities. Consequently, so it was argued, the size of the local authorities themselves would be immaterial so far as scale economies were concerned, opening the way for small authorities which would have homogeneous populations for whom services would be delivered economically. However, given that there are observable economies of scale in contracts, larger authorities with larger contracts to offer should be able to operate more economically than smaller ones, but this possibility was effectively ignored.

The idea that scale economies need no longer be taken very seriously in determining the size of local authorities seemed to be supported by the observable fact that small and medium-sized firms had taken on a new lease of life. In the 1950s and 1960s, it had seemed inevitable that the smaller firms would progressively lose out to bigger and more efficient competitors. Come the 1980s, the evidence was accumulating that small firms were not an endangered species and indeed that they were rapidly increasing in significance (see, for example, Keeble 1987, 1990; Mason 1987; Storey 1994). This change of fortunes was easily interpreted as a feature of the 'post-Fordist' mode of production, in which large and inflexible mass-production systems were giving way to more flexible arrangements involving the careful linkage of small (and often specialised) firms. Modern electronic/computer technology allowed for the quick and flexible adaptation of production systems, the 'customisation' of durable articles such as cars, and a revolution in the whole chain of supply/stock and control/orders. A large literature interprets the changing industrial and commercial scene in these terms (e.g. Lipietz 1987; Piore and Sabel 1984). Thus it is no surprise that, writing in 1989, Stoker explicitly linked changes in local government to the transition to a 'post-Fordist' society, just as the same ideas were linked to the Conservative political agenda a decade later (Willetts 1997).

Though one may share the doubts expressed by Cochrane (1993) concerning the utility of this paradigm for the analysis of local government, the key fact is the following. The re-structuring of economies, and particularly of manufacturing, that undoubtedly was going on in the 1980s, appeared to diminish the significance of scale economies in all sorts of ways. This contributed to an important change in the presumptions brought to the examination of local government. Although in the past it had been difficult to identify scale economies in local government (Dearlove 1979), it was assumed that they must exist and the onus of proof was on those who thought otherwise. By the end of the 1980s, the view was widespread that the obligation had shifted; it could be assumed that scale was not important and it was up to those who believed size did matter to come forward with evidence.

This position was articulated by the Adam Smith Institute with two publications in 1989. It was argued that local authorities had already lost certain powers and, furthermore, that it would be a good thing if the process were taken much further: 'One result of such a radical reduction in the role of local government would be completely to remove the case for a two-tier system of local councils' (Adam Smith Institute 1989a p. 46). The argument then proceeded as follows: 'If some theoretical optimum size can be disregarded as a factor in determining how big authorities must be, then it becomes possible to move towards a new pattern of local councils related to the kind of natural communities that people themselves identify with' (Adam Smith Institute 1989a, p. 49).

The population suggested for these 'natural communities' was in the range 40,000 to 60,000, with the interesting proviso that they could be smaller. However, the Institute did not explore the implication that many large cities would be split up if authorities of this size were to be created, cities such as Glasgow, Hull and

Plymouth, the populations of which run well above the upper threshold suggested. Nor was discussion vouchsafed for the areas of England which by that time had already had the upper tier of local government removed, as discussed in the next section; the London boroughs and Metropolitan districts had populations which were several multiples of the upper limit suggested. Nevertheless, for our purpose the cardinal fact is that the thinking embodied in the Adam Smith Institute's documents is entirely congruent with the ideas of public choice theory, even though no explicit reference is made to this body of thought. The documents also demonstrate very clearly the logical conclusions to be reached for local government if the premisses from which the theoretical thinking starts are accepted.

All of these ideas intersected with another strand of public choice theory, that bureaucracies tend to expand and to aggrandise. Viewed from this perspective, one could interpret the often uneasy relations between counties and districts in two-tier structures as evidence of attempts by both parties to extend their sphere of operations; the solution seems simple; remove one tier. However, if one looks beyond the establishment of the successor unitary authorities, one has to ask why it should be assumed that they would not fall prey to the same malaise, in the form of competition horizontally one with another. In any case, in so far as there were tensions between tiers, an alternative interpretation would be that these reflected genuine differences of interest between areas and differing judgements about priorities, something which would remain whatever structure of administrative areas might exist. Nevertheless, there was a propensity to interpret conflicts as a fault of structure and the habits of bureaucracies rather than as reflecting a basic spatial differentiation of society and hence interests that could not always be congruent.

In outlining the above structure of thinking, several caveats and qualifications have been entered on the way. In addition to these, there are some more general problems which we should note. According to the rhetoric of public choice theory, it would be desirable to have numerous small local authorities, each tailoring its pattern of service delivery to the needs of the relatively homogeneous population it served. This implies that there would be considerable diversity in the provision of services, both in the relative importance attached to services such as education, housing and social services, and in the quality and diversity of these services. Such a pattern would conflict with an alternative viewpoint, which notes the small size of Great Britain and the widespread desire to have roughly similar services available everywhere – health and education being two in particular (King 1989). An increase in local diversity would run counter to the strong tendency, which accelerated after 1979, for powers and decisions to be transferred from local councils to Westminster and Whitehall (Kellner 1997). Consequently, attempts to implement the rhetoric of local diversity and consumer choice faced an uphill battle in face of the fact that local authorities had little real discretion in their work, and diminishing discretion at that. As is well known, the proportion of local government finance under the direct control of local authorities declined very sharply with the introduction of the Poll Tax. The dilemma was not confined to those on the political right. For those on the left, there has long been the belief that the state should foster equality for all citizens; a public choice case for diversity would therefore be anathema. Diversity might be good for democracy but it could not be good for equality among citizens.

A key feature of the changes introduced into the governance of localities during the 1980s was the fragmentation of service delivery. In so far as this was privatisation which gave consumers a choice of service providers, residents could exercise genuine options within their financial means. In practice, though, much privatisation gave individuals no greater choice than existed before. A privatised refuse collection service does not allow the householders to choose which firm will collect their rubbish but it does extend the lines of communication for putting things right if they go wrong. Similarly, in so far as services were removed from the jurisdiction of local authorities and put into the hands of agencies, whether quangos or bodies such as school governors that are hard to distinguish from quangos, it is not clear that *de facto* the choice available to an individual citizen was actually increased. What is not in doubt is that a much more diverse pattern of provision has been created, which amounts to the fragmentation of the system (Stoker 1989). It may be that the net effect has been to increase over-all efficiency. Two things do seem to be quite clear. From the viewpoint of the citizen, the greater complexity of service delivery has been accompanied by greater obscurity regarding lines of accountability. And from the vantage of the service providers, effective provision implies a more intricate web of negotiations and cooperation between agencies than was the case in the past, solely by virtue of the larger number of players involved (Painter *et al.* 1997; Peters 1998). As a consequence, any local authority, whether in a two-tier system or a unitary system, has to work with an increased number of agencies. That being the case, the removal of one tier of local government might have rather less impact in improving accountability and reducing overlap in service provision than the advocates of change suggested.

There were, and continue to be, other serious doubts about the applicability of public choice theory in the local government domain. Could all, or virtually all, the services for which local authorities remained responsible really be put out to contract? Would there actually be the markets in which these services could be bought? Is it also the case that there are no economies of scale in the management of contracts? – the officers who are responsible for drawing up and monitoring contracts need to have considerable skill, skill which may be a function of the number and complexity of the contracts with which they are familiar. Finally, the whole of the public choice approach to local jurisdictions assumes that there are no spillover, or externality, effects between jurisdictions. A classic example of such externality effects is the usage of libraries and museums, which are usually located in towns and cities but which may serve a population living in neighbouring or even distant places. Should such facilities be free for the inhabitants of the authority in which they are located but for others only on payment? Not surprisingly, therefore, voices were indeed raised questioning the validity of some of the claims that were made for the benefits to be expected from the changes to which local government was subjected in the post-1979 period (e.g. Smith 1985; Stoker 1991).

It is quite clear, though, that between 1975 and about 1990 a major change had occurred in the intellectual and political climate so far as it affected local government. It is that change which provided the context within which other events had their impact on attitudes to the structure of the local authority map, and also provided the context for a sustained campaign to change the settlement of the 1970s.

### 1986–90: abolition of the Greater London Council, the Metropolitan county councils and the Inner London Education Authority

Within a decade of setting up a much modified two-tier system throughout mainland Great Britain, moves were afoot by the Conservatives to unpick part of the structure which they had created. The administration elected in 1979 under Margaret Thatcher energetically set about controlling public expenditure, including the expenditure of local authorities. Some councils sought every means available to resist the pressure to reduce spending (Boddy and Fudge 1984), leading some ministers to conclude that powers would have to be taken to place enforceable limits on the budgets of authorities. Michael Heseltine, then Secretary of State at the Department of the Environment, opposed this proposition, arguing that the significant over-spenders were limited in number, mainly the Greater London Council and the Metropolitan counties. His solution, suggested in 1981, was simple: these authorities should be abolished (Crick 1997, p. 215). Heseltine's hostility to the Metropolitan counties was shared by Thatcher, who also detested the GLC and its leader, Ken Livingstone. It was at her behest that the 1983 Conservative election manifesto included the commitment to abolish these county councils, the commitment being made in haste and despite general advice from ministers and civil servants that the structures should be left intact (Forrester *et al.* 1985, pp. 64–6). By 1 April 1986, they had ceased to exist. Four years later, in 1990, the ILEA was also abolished and the Inner London boroughs took over responsibility for education.

In the case of the Metropolitan counties, the 1974 reforms had created a real problem, in that large cities with a proud tradition of civic governance had been stripped of many powers and disliked their status, seemingly subordinate to the counties. There was certainly an arguable case for reviewing the roles of the counties and the other authorities in London and in the conurbations but the Government chose outright abolition of the upper tier. In doing so, it identified a narrow set of reasons, namely the alleged wastefulness of having two layers of local administration. The evidence to back this claim was limited and questionable, and in any case ignored advice from Coopers & Lybrand that extra costs would outweigh savings (Forrester *et al.* 1985, pp. 124–30). Subsequently, on the basis of reductions in staffing, which were attributed entirely to the structural change, the Government claimed that abolition of these county councils had resulted in an annual saving of £100 million (*Hansard*, written answers 26 July 1990, col. 381).

It was this figure which surfaced during the 1992–95 structural review of shire England, which is the subject of the next chapter.

In fact, the abolition of the county tier did not eliminate a tier of administration but transformed its character. Many county-wide functions continued to be discharged in the form of joint arrangements, administration by central government, and so on (Leach *et al.* 1991; Wilson and Game 1994). For example, in London, with its thirty-two boroughs and the City of London, almost one hundred separate bodies came into existence, elected or selected in four different ways and with twenty-one different means of raising revenue. In their study of the former Metropolitan counties, Leach *et al.* (1991) concluded that between 1984/5 and 1987/8, being years before and after the change, total net expenditure in real terms had risen by 9 per cent. For those services which had been transferred to the Metropolitan districts, the rise was 4 per cent. At November 1986 prices, the extra costs over-all were in excess of £600 million p.a., and for the transferred services the additional annual expense was £50 million (Leach *et al.* 1991, pp. 250–1). It is clear that the abolition of the GLC had similar consequences (Hebbert and Travers 1988, p. 3), while the claim that the Inner London Education Authority was wasteful and inefficient does not stand close scrutiny (Smith and Watson 1988). Consequently, the claim that abolition of the GLC and Metropolitan counties had yielded an annual saving of £100 million does not appear to be plausible.

In any case, the assessments cited above ignore numerous costs that are hard to quantify, as may be illustrated by reference to child care services. For a significant period, London local authorities agreed to provide very specialised residential child care facilities, such as Community Homes with Education and Assessment Centres, on the basis that total usage costs were shared with whoever provided the facility. The use made of such facilities by any one London local authority would rarely have justified provision solely for an individual authority, even though they were an essential part of the spectrum of services required. The organisation and management of the scheme was carried out by the London Children's Regional Planning Authority on behalf of all the London councils, all of which served on the responsible committee, which agreed rates and other matters of mutual interest. These specialised facilities were expensive and commitment to the scheme weakened gradually until, with the abolition of the GLC in 1986, it finally collapsed, leaving the individual boroughs to manage as best they could. This in turn led to the closure of a number of facilities which the providers could no longer afford to maintain in the absence of certainty regarding the regular use thereof. The reduced range of facilities tended adversely to affect the choice available, and hence suitability for meeting the needs of young people, including proximity to their own homes. Experience and skills formerly concentrated on a particularly needy segment of the population were, inevitably, dispersed (Kahan 1999a). The consequences have been two-fold. First, to relieve pressure on the limited number of residential places available, councils have been forced to place as many children as they can for fostering or adoption, irrespective of whether this is truly in the best interests of the individuals. Second, residential placements are scattered quite widely. An example is provided by Ealing. In March 1999, the borough had 163 youngsters placed in residential homes; 77 were within Ealing and 35 else-where in London, with a further 51 placed outside the capital. Of this last group, the largest concentrations, in descending order, were in Surrey, Essex, Kent and Hampshire, but individuals were as far afield as Leeds and Somerset (Tutt 1999). Distant placements are in fact contrary to provisions in the Children Act 1989 and inevitably imply the rupture of such family and friendship ties as may exist. Any placement outside the responsible authority, even if nearby, involves a change of education authority and therefore interruption to schooling. In addition, the local authority itself has an increased load of administration in dealing with numerous education and health authorities for the children in its care. Thus, although out-wardly the system works, it does so with increased costs, including the human costs imposed on unfortunate young people.

In addition to claims about administrative savings, advocates of the change also asserted that elimination of the county tier would improve the democratic respon-siveness of the local government system, a view that was not supported by the actual evidence: 'We are thus left with the inescapable conclusion that on any cri-teria of accountability, based on any conception of democracy, there has, since abolition, been a marked reduction in accountability' (Leach *et al.* 1991, p. 169). The basic reason for this conclusion lies in the nature of the arrangements put in place across the former county areas, involving non-elected bodies of one kind or another.

In the present context, the main significance of the abolition of the GLC, the Metropolitan counties and then the ILEA was the impact which this had on per-ceptions regarding the durability of the two-tier structures elsewhere (Leach *et al.* 1991). No longer was it perceived that the re-structuring of local government was an episodic affair with long intervals of stability, as had seemed to be the case pre-viously. The fact that the rhetoric of cost saving bore rather little relationship to the essentially political reasons for the abolition of powerful counties was not par-ticularly relevant. Major foundations of the two-tier structure had been up-rooted, destabilising the entire structure. It is doubtful that this was the intention of the Government; there is little doubt that it was the effect.

But the impact was not immediate. The opinion was widespread that the 1986 changes were occasioned by political considerations of a relatively short-term nature, focused on specific authorities. It was clear that for all the rhetoric about improving efficiency, the real reason for the change was the dislike that the Gov-ernment had for powerful authorities which held different ideological views and were resistant to the wishes of ministers. As a consequence, it was equally clear that the demise of the GLC and Metropolitan counties did not mark the start of a considered programme of local government reform. Nevertheless, there is little doubt that those who wanted to see an end to the counties elsewhere were encour-aged, most notably the Association of District Councils, though it took a few more years and the Poll Tax fiasco to trigger major change.

## The major cities

With the 1974 structural changes in England and Wales, the former county boroughs lost status and powers; they became equal to the other districts within their respective counties. Many of these cities had a long and proud history of self-government, derived from ancient royal charters, recognised in the 1888 legislation and symbolised in many cases by the grand council house in the city centre. The new structure had been imposed by Parliament against their will and for reasons which appeared to be at least in part a matter of rather short-term political calculation than a considered change designed for the long-term welfare of local government as an institution. The big cities were not happy. Representatives of eleven of these cities, nine from shire England and two from Wales, met in 1975 in Derby, forming the group which came to be known as the Major Cities; along with Bristol, Derby and Hull there were six other English cities of comparable importance. The purpose of the group was to campaign for a modification of the 1974 two-tier structure so that the big cities could take over the powers of the counties and in this sense return to the pre-1974 position of county boroughs. However, from the outset the task confronting the cities was considerable, partly because in the mid-1970s there was a general sense that the then existing system was likely to endure for some time, and partly because several of the big cities were very important components in their counties – Bristol in Avon and Hull in Humberside, for example – so that a change in their status would raise serious questions about the county structure.

Nevertheless, it soon appeared that the Major Cities would achieve their goal when the Labour Government issued proposals that would return some powers to the larger cities in England, doing so in a cautious and essentially evolutionary manner (DoE 1979). Though ministers noted that there was pressure for more radical transfers of powers to all districts, they decided not to proceed down that road. However, these proposals were swept off the political agenda when the Conservatives won the 1979 general election. The new Government had no interest in modifying the structure that the Heath administration had put in place, particularly since the *Organic Change* proposals would give greater power to authorities which were generally more likely to be controlled by the Opposition parties. The campaign by the Major Cities became a low-key affair, and remained so even during and immediately after the abolition of the GLC and Metropolitan counties; the cities did not perceive this change as providing them with an opening. It was not until late 1990 that a serious push was made, a delegation going to see Heseltine, the newly appointed Secretary of State at the Department of the Environment. The context was the replacement of Margaret Thatcher by John Major as Prime Minister, the determination to find an alternative to the Poll Tax (DoE 1991a) and the announcement by Heseltine that the structure of local government would be reviewed, matters which are discussed below.

In response to the consultation document on the structure of local authorities issued by the DoE (1991b), the Major Cities submitted a document which is interesting for what it tells us about the cities themselves and about their links with the Association of District Councils (Major Cities 1991). The document was in fact a joint submission with the ADC, signifying the close cooperation between the Association and this sub-set of its members and the support being given to the big cities' case. Conversely, the cities would not stand in the way of the claims being made on behalf of all the districts that they should assume the powers of the counties to become unitary authorities, though at least some of those representing the big cities had doubts about the strength of the case for a general move to a district-based unitary structure. The cities which signed up to the June 1991 submission were: Bristol, Cardiff, Derby, Hull, Leicester, Nottingham, Plymouth, Portsmouth, Southampton, Stoke-on-Trent and Swansea. The burden of the case put to the Government was that county powers should be transferred to these cities immediately, ahead of any other changes that might be put in train. To support this case, they claimed that following the 1974 reforms the relevant counties had set up agency arrangements for the delivery of services in the cities. Consequently, the cities asserted, the transfer of the county functions could be achieved at minimal cost and 'with no disruption to existing county services'. The text continues: 'The restructuring of local government should take account of the fact that, in effect, the Major Cities have never stopped performing certain functions and can simply resume immediate responsibility for their future management' (Major Cities 1991). To put it mildly, this claim was an exaggeration. But the text illustrates as graphically as anything the continuing pride of the big cities and the anger with which they viewed what had happened in 1974.

### Association of County Councils and Association of District Councils

The Association of District Councils began to formulate the case for a district-based system of most-purpose, or unitary, authorities as early as 1983. Two years later, shortly before the GLC and Metropolitan counties ceased to exist, the annual conference of the Association voted in favour of a motion which called on the Government to abolish the county councils and transfer their functions to the existing district councils. For reasons already mentioned, this proposal cut little ice with the Government, which at that time was not contemplating additional structural change, but the ADC continued to work on its ideas and, having commissioned some research which supported its case, in 1987 published a position paper, *Closer to the People*, of which a second version was published in 1990.

The various arguments advanced by the ADC in favour of unitary district councils boil down to the following propositions. The two-tier structure involves inefficiency in the delivery of services and obscures the lines of accountability. In any case, with the erosion of the powers and duties of local government which had been going on for some time, the case for having two layers of local administration had become weak. As local authorities were becoming enablers rather than providers, the concept of the self-sufficient (county) provision of services was no longer relevant (i.e. the scale economy argument no longer held). In addition, a structure of local government based on communities would make for a more responsive and democratic system. The final step in the argument was implied rather than stated, namely that the existing districts coincided with the geography of communities tolerably well and were therefore the appropriate community-based units to form unitary authorities.

These arguments are clearly very closely related to the public choice thinking which has already been discussed but, curiously, the ADC seems to have been unaware of the case that can be derived from that thinking in favour of small units of local administration. Nevertheless, the 'closer to the people' slogan chimed pretty exactly with important strands of New Right thinking, a fact which must have given their campaign some impetus in important quarters. In any case, there is no doubt that under the guidance of Roy Thomason the ADC pursued a dedicated and effective campaign, such that when it was announced in December 1990 that there was to be a review of the structure of local government the Association was well prepared.

In contrast, the Association of County Councils had not bothered unduly about the possibility of structural change, despite the abolition of the GLC and Metropolitan counties in 1986 and other developments, including the ADC campaign: 'During the 1980s, though by no means neglecting the issue, the ACC had kept a relatively low profile on the subject of local government structure' (Wendt 1997, p. 1). This policy had appeared to be vindicated when Chris Patten, Secretary of State at the Department of the Environment, opined in November 1989 that local government had as much need of structural reorganisation as a 'hole in the head'. However, only twelve months later, the Association of County Chief Executives, meeting in Cheltenham and with the ACC represented, decided to commission a paper on the value of county government; by that time, it realised that there was a strong possibility that structural change would come back onto the political agenda. In fact, an announcement was made in Parliament on 5 December that there would be a structural review. The day before that, the ADC re-launched its document *Closer to the People*, somewhat revised; the ACC pre-empted both by launching its own *Strengths of the Counties* (ACC 1990) on 3 December; this document had been written following the Cheltenham conference (Wendt 1997, p. 2).

It would be wrong to suggest that the counties had done nothing until their November 1990 meeting. Individual counties, Essex and Nottinghamshire being notable cases, had been busy considering the possibility of change and the case that they could make in favour of their respective authorities; and the ACC had hired consultants and had issued a number of briefing papers. Nevertheless, there had not been a sustained pro-county campaign to counter the ADC's attack and the fact that it was only in November 1990 that the counties seriously began to get their act together meant that they had an uphill task in face of the groundwork which the ADC had undertaken. Perhaps of greater importance, though, was the fact that a strong case could indeed be made for a limited number of big cities to assume the powers vested in the counties. Therefore, the ACC would have had difficulty in sustaining the case that there should be no change whatsoever and was faced with the intellectual and political need to consider more than one possibility. Consequently, the document which the ACC submitted to the Government in February (ACC 1991a) envisaged three scenarios:

1  Retention of the existing two-tier structure.
2  Reorganisation into unitary authorities based on counties.
3  A mixed or hybrid system of unitary councils and two-tier arrangements.

The second of these scenarios was the direct counter to the ADC case for unitary districts but it was one for which prior spadework was largely lacking. While the ACC was absolutely right to acknowledge the possibility of more than one outcome, the problem was that in the cut and thrust of the political roughhouse this intellectually sound position was in danger of being overwhelmed by the single-minded advocates of a district-based unitary structure. Indeed, by September 1991, the ADC felt sufficiently confident about the way events were apparently unfolding that it was shifting its energies to assisting individual districts in preparing the cases they would submit to the Local Government Commission which the Government intended to establish (ADC 1991a, pp. 3–4).

## The main political parties

Although the Opposition parties in Scotland and Wales had already adopted the unitary concept, local government reform was not seriously on the political agenda at the time of the 1987 general election. Of the main parties, only Labour mentioned it in its manifesto, with the promise to 'examine' the situation. By the time of the next election in 1992, legislation had been passed by the Conservatives, providing for a structural review in shire England, and consultations were in progress for radical re-structuring in both Scotland and Wales. The Conservatives' 1992 election manifesto reflected this position, and Labour promised a unitary structure for shire England based, in general, on the existing districts. The Liberal Democrats made a similar promise, except that the unitary authorities would be based on 'natural communities'. There was general support for unitary structures in Scotland and Wales, though the Opposition parties explicitly linked such a change to the creation of elected bodies for the two countries, in parallel with their view that there should be devolved regional government in England as part of the reform package (Jones 1993; *The Times* 1992).

Consequently, when the Conservatives won the 1992 general election, it could be thought that a fairly high degree of consensus existed and that there was momentum in the reform process. However, the parties had not spelled out the reasons for embarking on reform, the Opposition parties had linked reform to regional devolution and nobody had offered the electorate a map showing actual proposals. Even so, the ADC could justifiably feel that its campaign was making good progress. However, it did not take long to discover that the devil lies in the detail.

## The rush to reform

The downfall of Thatcher in November 1990 opened the floodgates to change in local government. All three contenders in the second ballot for party leadership – Heseltine, Hurd and Major – pledged to do something about the Poll Tax, which was widely seen to be an albatross around the neck of the Government (Butler *et al.* 1994). Heseltine had always opposed the Poll Tax and made its abolition the centrepiece of his leadership campaign. In addition, though, he argued for the introduction of elected mayors and for the reorganisation of local government (Leach 1992a, p. 1).

Major took over the reins of government on 27 November and made Heseltine Secretary of State at the Department of the Environment. There was a strong political imperative to get the Poll Tax issue sorted out quickly, since a general election was due no later than 1992. The speed with which Heseltine acted was consistent with his track record (Crick 1997). On 5 December, in a debate on the Poll Tax, he announced not just a national review of this particular tax but also a wide-ranging consideration of the organisation and structure of local government in England. At the time, most observers regarded these additional reviews as a means of deflecting criticism about the policy U-turn over the Poll Tax, as a cover for the political retreat. That was the view of Nigel Lawson, who described the general review as a 'somewhat oversized cloak' (Lawson 1993, p. 1004; see also Young 1994, p. 83), a view emphatically confirmed to the author by one of the ministers who was involved in the English structural review. Nevertheless, and in apparent contradiction of this cynical assessment, the initial consultation put in hand by the Department of the Environment appeared to presage a thorough examination of structure, finance and powers. However, very quickly it was clear that a considered review of anything other than the Poll Tax was not on the cards. In so far as the 5 December announcement dealt with matters other than the Poll Tax, it related solely to England and it was only subsequently made clear that Scotland and Wales would be included. That in itself suggests policy making on the hoof. More important, though, was the humiliating Ribble Valley by-election defeat suffered by the Government in February 1991. This seems to have accelerated the already fast consultation and legislative process to get rid of the Poll Tax and at the same time to have resulted in the abandonment of any attempt at a considered and comprehensive review of local government and instead the implementation of ideas some of which 'stem[med] from one man's vision – not from the mainstream of recent Conservative ideology' (Leach 1992a, p. 1).

Subsequent to the 5 December announcement, it was made clear that the structure of local government in Scotland and Wales would also be examined. On 21 March 1991, Heseltine announced his interim conclusions with respect to the Poll Tax (to be replaced nationally by the Council Tax) and also with respect to the structure of local government in England. He proposed to consult on the idea of establishing a local government commission charged to examine the shire counties on an area-by-area basis, to recommend whether the two-tier structure should be retained or replaced by unitary authorities. Although no blueprint was in mind, he indicated that 'it seems likely that we shall move to a larger number of unitary authorities' (*Hansard*, 21 March 1991, col. 402). These proposals contained a dash of populism, in that local people were to have a say in the structure appropriate for their area. On the same day, Ian Lang announced that: 'I believe that we should now prepare to move to single-tier local authorities throughout Scotland' (*Hansard*, 21 March 1991, col. 462); he promised a consultation paper on options for a unitary structure. No reasons were given for the different approaches in England and Scotland. As for Wales, David Hunt was much more circumspect: 'I have made no proposals for unitary authorities … I have received some representations that we should move towards such a system, but I do not intend to make any decisions until I have had the benefit of further discussions with the Welsh local authority associations' (*Hansard*, 27 March 1991, written answer, col. 414).

Outwardly at least, the drive for structural change was coming from England and in particular from Heseltine. Yet Lang, then Secretary of State for Scotland, considers that, irrespective of any decision about England, sufficient preparatory work had already been done before the great flurry of activity that he would have proceeded with the introduction of unitary local government north of the Border (Lord Lang 1999). His counterpart in Wales believes that the consultation which he was conducting would also have resulted in unitary proposals quite independently of policy in England (Lord Hunt 1999). However, at least one Cabinet colleague of the time doubts whether ministers would have agreed to structural change in Scotland and Wales without parallel proposals being made for England.

In April 1991, proposals were issued for structural change in England (DoE 1991b), with other documents for Scotland and Wales appearing in quick succession (Scottish Office 1991; Welsh Office 1991). Later in the year, the Department of the Environment (1991c) issued a further consultation paper, this time on the internal management of local authorities and the possibility of introducing elected mayors. Several features of these documents stand out. First, they were issued as separate and essentially unconnected papers; a proper review of local government would have attempted to tease out the inter-connections between the three aspects of the local government system, and would have considered financial matters running well beyond the Poll Tax/Council Tax issues to include the proportion of revenue for local authorities raised locally. In any case, no attempt was made to examine why local government is needed and hence what changes might be desirable so that the objectives could better be met. Finally, although for Scotland and Wales it was clearly proposed that the existing two-tier structure should be replaced with unitary councils, and although it was clear that the Government favoured unitary authorities in England as well, the procedures proposed for England differed sharply from those envisaged for the other two countries. Whereas a commission would make recommendations regarding change in England, Parliament would legislate for a unitary structure in both Scotland and Wales.

On 23 July 1991, Heseltine announced the conclusion of his consultations on the Poll Tax replacement and, almost as an aside, added that: 'The response to the consultation paper, "The Structure of Local Government in England", has been very positive. Nearly 1,900 individuals and organisations have written in with their views, overwhelmingly in support of our proposals. There have been some useful suggestions for minor improvements' (*Hansard*, 23 July 1991, col. 1049). His comment about 'some useful suggestions for minor improvements' ignored serious contributions by important organisations, including calls for the review to be conducted as part of a wider consideration of structure, powers and finance – in other words, the purpose of local government. The two local government associations were united on at least one thing, pointing to the limitations and risks inherent in a rolling review programe (ACC 1991b; ADC 1991b). These representations were ignored and a Bill was introduced in the autumn which became the Local Government Act 1992, just before the dissolution of Parliament preceding the general election that year. Legislation for Scotland and Wales did not reach the statute book until 1994.

If Heseltine had not been put in charge of the Department of the Environment, it seems probable that nothing would have happened in 1990–91 with regard to structural reorganisation (Leach 1992a, p. 1). Indeed, it appears that initially other ministers did seriously consider the possibility of abolishing local government altogether. It was well known that Thatcher as Prime Minister had detested the institution and in her memoirs she makes no bones about her attitude (Thatcher 1993). There is little doubt that these attitudes were shared by members of Major's administration: 'With so much of its revenue now under Treasury control, some ministers felt that the time had come for a shift of functions (as well as powers) to Whitehall. Observers felt that local government in the early months of 1991 came nearer to total abolition in Britain than at any time under Thatcher' (Jenkins 1995, p. 60). Under these circumstances, a thorough consideration of all the inter-locking issues could hardly be expected.

Ministers seem to have thought that the electorate was disenchanted with the existing two-tier structure of local government and would welcome the thorough shake-up of the system implied by the removal of one tier (Boyne *et al.* 1995). After all, the Association of District Councils, representing the districts in shire England, was at that time controlled by the Conservatives and was pressing for change. On the assumption that voters would welcome a change in local government structure, there were clear political advantages in prospect through starting with England. The Government's electoral prospects depended on English voters rather than those in Scotland and Wales, since the core of its political support lay there rather than further north and west. It was Heseltine who 'secured approval for a fundamental examination of the management and structure of local government' (Crick 1997, p. 363) and did so from his base at the Department of the Environment, whose remit runs only in England. The main impetus for the structural review seems to have come from England, though some preparatory work had been done in both Scotland and Wales.

The lack of commitment to the institution of local government, compounded by the short-term political pressures on the Government, was reflected in the haste

with which the consultation process was pressed and in the form of the consultation itself. Though ministers could and did claim that finance, internal management and structure were being dealt with simultaneously, this conveniently
overlooked a number of crucial matters which deserve to be emphasised:

1  There was no consultation on what the purpose of local government should be
   and what relationship there should be between central and local administrations.
2  Finance was treated in a very limited way – just the replacement of the Poll
   Tax.
3  The three consultations were undertaken in isolation the one from the other, so
   that no account could be taken of the inter-relations of the various aspects of
   structure, powers, finance and internal management.

The ostensible reasons for changing the structure of local government were
given by the Department of the Environment in the following terms. The abolition
of one tier of local administration:

> should reduce bureaucracy and improve the coordination of services, increasing
> quality and reducing costs. This argument holds even if both the county council and
> the district councils in a county are efficient and if the two tiers cooperate closely
> with each other; there can still be benefits in a clearer and more streamlined struc-
> ture. Such a structure is also important for proper financial accountability on the part
> of local authorities to local taxpayers: people must know who is responsible for set-
> ting a budget and achieving value for money in services in their area, and how the
> size of their local tax bills relates to what is spent on local public services. (DoE
> 1991b, p. 6)

The financial accountability argument referred to the fact that the local tax,
whether the Poll Tax or Council Tax, was collected by the districts on behalf of the
counties, which were responsible for the greater part of expenditure.

In advocating the merits of unitary local councils, the Government also made
the following claims:

1  That local authorities were in the process of becoming enablers rather than
   providers, with maximal use of the private and voluntary sectors.
2  That some of the authorities which had come into existence in the 1970s were
   'still not wholly accepted by all the local communities which they serve' – an
   ill-disguised code for the new counties of Avon, Cleveland and Humberside.
3  That citizens were often confused as to which tier of local government was
   responsible for what.
4  That it is desirable for there to be close coordination of certain services, responsibility for which was divided between tiers; social services and housing were
   identified as one pair, the other being litter clearance and road cleaning.
5  That in some matters where the two tiers need to work together there was at
   times 'conflict and tension', planning being the case cited.
6  That the introduction of unitary authorities where they did not then exist would

'offer the opportunity of relating the structure of local government more closely to the communities with which people identify'.
7 Finally, that with the changing role of local government, there was no longer any presumption 'that there is an ideal size of authority for the most efficient delivery of services'. By implication, the Government seemed to be saying that it could see no reason for either an *upper* or *lower* limit to the size of authorities, though reference to communities suggested smaller rather than larger councils.

With the Opposition parties committed to the principle of unitary authorities, there was relatively little parliamentary dissent during the passage of the Local Government Bill, which began in November 1991. The structural provisions contained in this Bill related only to England. The main point of real contention arose over amendments designed to ensure that the Local Government Commission would have to recommend all-unitary solutions. The Government, furiously lobbied by the Association of County Councils, resisted this change, on the grounds that there was no national blueprint for England and that the proposed Commission should examine the circumstances in each area. It was of course known that Bills would subsequently be tabled for Scotland and Wales which would determine the structure of unitary authorities throughout both countries. At least at the level of national party politics, the Government was right in its judgement that the legislation for England would be uncontentious.

Thus, in a period of rather less than eighteen months, the apparent stability of the two-tier system had been overtaken by a general move towards unitary structures throughout much, if not all, of Great Britain where they did not already exist. The rhetoric adopted by Government clearly had its roots in the belief that markets are the superior way in which to allocate resources, that the country had moved into a post-welfare phase and that public choice theory provided a suitable framework for analysing local government. The fact of pending reform generally, if not universally, on the basis of unitary authorities represented a major victory for the Association of District Councils, which had lobbied hard for just such a change. However, it had not achieved a commitment to transfer county functions to the existing district councils.

In these few months, the Government had signalled a remarkable change of policy. As recently as 1986, a Green Paper had been issued setting out proposals for the abolition of domestic rates and their replacement by the Poll Tax. That document considered the possibility of structural change and dismissed it in robust terms:

It is true that there could in theory be some gain in accountability if there were to be all-purpose local authorities throughout the country. Ratepayers would then know that the spending decisions of one authority lay behind their bills. But this gain would be achieved at the cost of enormous disruption which a further large-scale local government reorganisation would cause. And, in the course of that reorganisation, it would be necessary, yet again, to face up to the fact that different local government services can best be provided by authorities of different sizes. (Secretary of State for the Environment *et al.* 1986, para. 1.46)

The DoE, the Scottish Office and the Welsh Office were, at that time, united in opposing structural reform.

For all the rhetoric about structural reform improving accountability, the replacement of the Poll Tax did nothing to change the proportion of local government finance raised locally – 15 per cent in England, 11 per cent in Scotland and only 8 per cent in Wales (Burns *et al.* 1994, p. 259). Nor was there any change to the capping regime which limited total expenditure. Compared with these and other constraints on local authorities, the possible improvements in accountability arising from the removal of one tier of local administration must be regarded as small. Furthermore, the Government offered no criteria by which to determine the size of the proposed unitary authorities or the extent to which they might reflect the identities of local communities. Indeed, some commentators felt that the whole re-structuring project, and in particular the rhetoric used to justify it, was so removed from reality that a hidden agenda was in play, especially in England:

> The approach has provoked an almighty battle between the counties and districts as each camp fights for survival. Cynics argue that the government's strategy has been to ignite a series of squabbles between counties and districts so that many of those involved in local government will be distracted from much more strategic issues – such as the increasing centralisation of power in Whitehall and the new opportunities opening up for local government in the emerging Europe of regions. (Burns *et al.* 1994, p. 260)

Note also that the Government's rhetoric in support of unitary authorities emphasised the cost savings which *should* occur as a result of the change. This neatly side-stepped the perfectly reasonable question of whether the abolition of the GLC and Metropolitan counties had in fact achieved the savings which had been claimed (Leach *et al.* 1991; Leach 1992b).

## Conclusion

The 1990s structural reform of local government had been a long time a-building. Numerous strands of argument and interest converged: the general appreciation that rapid change was occurring in the economic and social dimensions of society; the theorisation of some aspects of these changes in the form of public choice theory; and the influence of specific interest groups, notably the district councils, including the Major Cities. However, these pressures for a re-think of local government structure had little impact on the Government until the Poll Tax disaster provided a catalyst. Then, a whole new set of considerations entered the picture, including the role of particular politicians, most notably Heseltine, and the electoral imperatives facing a Government which was forced to acknowledge its unpopularity and needed to redeem its electoral fortunes. There is little doubt that the structural changes were initiated for the wrong reasons and in such haste that little real thought can have been given to the complex implications. Equally, had change not been initiated for England it is doubtful whether Scotland and Wales would have been reformed separately.

It is also clear that in launching the reform process the Government's rhetoric was at odds with many realities. In particular, the argument that removing one tier would improve accountability sat ill with the high degree of financial and other control over local authorities exercised by central government on the one hand, and the increased complexity of service provision that had come about in the years leading up to 1990 on the other. If improved accountability and greater efficiency were the primary objectives, there were many things that could have been done which would have yielded much greater benefit than structural change. If community identity was the primary concern, then an alternative approach would have been to examine the internal workings of councils to see whether major improvements could be achieved. And if the problem was conflict between the upper and lower tiers of local government, one has to ask why there would not be conflict horizontally between neighbouring unitary authorities and what mechanisms should be in place in either case to help minimise the difficulties. All of these considerations add up to a picture of Cabinet government that is far from flattering but fully consistent with the harsh judgement which has been forcefully articulated by Foster and Plowden (1996) and Foster (1999).

If it was an inauspicious start to the process of structural change, might it be the case that events confounded the critics and cynics? Thus the focus of the chapters which follow is two-fold: to tell the main elements of the story that unfolded; and to see how far the rhetoric used matched the realities. In the light of the evidence thus presented, it will be possible to draw some conclusions which are relevant for the time when the structural reform of local government may again be back on the political agenda. These conclusions will run wider than just the local government field; they apply much more generally to the way in which central government is conducted.

# 3

# The roving review of shire England

> The Government does not wish to impose a national blueprint for reform. (DoE 1992b, para. 3)

Following passage of the Local Government Act 1992, the Local Government Commission for England was established to conduct area-by-area reviews of the structure of local government throughout shire England. Very quickly, that review became the subject of heated public debate, the process being regarded by many as a shambles (*Financial Times*, 25 August 1993; Johnston *et al.* 1997; S. Leach 1994, 1995; Stoker 1993; and special issues of *Local Government Studies* (vol. 23:3 1997) and *Public Administration* (vol. 75:1 1997)). That the review was highly contentious is not in doubt, nor that it pursued a somewhat zig-zag course. For some observers, a major reason for the difficulties lay with the Commission itself: 'The accusations are … that the Commission has not simply wasted the opportunity to build structures which would strengthen the institution of local government but has debased the coinage of debate about it' (Stewart *et al.* 1997, p. 1). Though Stewart and his co-authors hasten to say that some at least of these accusations cannot be sustained, the impression became widespread that in important ways the Commission was author of its own difficulties. However, as Leach and Stoker (1997) point out, the drama involved several additional actors: they explicitly note the Government, the Association of County Councils, the Association of District Councils, professional associations and the public. Some care is necessary to weigh the respective roles of all these participants and others beside.

Though a considerable amount has been written about the English review, there are significant elements of the story which have either been exaggerated or downplayed, or even overlooked. The purpose of this chapter is to give a brief history of events and the outcome of the review process, paving the way for the two chapters which follow, the over-all intention being to present a balanced account of events and an interpretation of what was going on through four turbulent years in England. Chapter 4 is devoted to one important aspect of the review, the problem of estimating the costs and benefits of reorganisation, while the succeeding chapter discusses the issues which surrounded matters of service delivery, community identity and public opinion.

## The evolution of the main review: 1992–95

Power to direct the Commission to carry out structural reviews in specified areas is given by the 1992 Act to the Secretary of State, to whom the Commission must report with recommendations for change or no change. Where changes are recommended, the Secretary of State may accept them (with or without modifications) or reject them; no power is given to substitute a completely different set of proposals for change. Any change is then to be effected by the laying of an affirmative Order in both Houses of Parliament. For the purpose of the Act, structural change is defined as the 'replacement, in any non-metropolitan area, of the two principal tiers of local government with a single tier'. Such an authority quickly came to be known as a unitary authority, wielding the powers formerly enjoyed by the district(s) and county it replaced. In reviewing an area and deciding whether or not to recommend change, the Act requires the Commission to consider the 'identities and interests of local communities' and 'effective and convenient local government' and to strike a balance between these community and efficiency arguments. The Act also specifies that the Commission may be directed 'to have regard to any guidance given by the Secretary of State as respects matters to be taken into account'. Quite clearly, such guidance must be taken seriously but is subsidiary to the provisions of the legislation itself.

Sir John Banham was appointed as the prospective Chairman of the Commission in November 1991, at a time when the Local Government Bill was still being considered by Parliament. Appointments of other Commissioners only took effect on 1 July 1992, this month marking the real start of work with the publication of the final versions of the *Policy Guidance* and *Procedure Guidance* by the Department of the Environment (DoE 1992b, 1992c). Both documents are very similar to drafts which had been circulating for comment, so there had been a pretty clear idea of the nature of the task from the very beginning. Then, on 20 July the Commission received its directions for the review timetable, which consisted of five groups of counties, or tranches, to be examined in sequence over a period lasting about five years; that is, one year for each tranche. The first tranche of ten counties was to get under way on 3 August with the Isle of Wight, the other counties starting in September, with final recommendations to be completed by 23 January 1994 (see Appendix 1). Initially, the Commission was staffed by civil servants on secondment from the DoE and it was not until October that permanent staff began to take up their assignments. These staffing uncertainties in the early months compounded the general pressure under which the Commission worked and made it very difficult indeed to look beyond immediate concerns to examine the strategic issues for the whole review.

Although the *Policy Guidance* asserted that no blueprint was in mind for England, the tenor of the document unmistakably pointed towards unitary outcomes, though it left important qualifications and loopholes. This angling of the *Guidance* was at variance with the neutrality of the central provision of the Act. At the time work began, it was known that the Government was planning to bring forward legislation for both Scotland and Wales to create unitary structures, and that this would happen without the review process of an independent commission (see Chapter 6). Consequently, there appeared to be a general presumption on the part of Government that the task of the Commission was to find and recommend unitary structures. But, and here was an important elephant trap for the Commission, neither the Act nor the *Policy Guidance* gave any lead as to the size of authority that could appropriately take on the powers of both districts and counties. Indeed, the *Guidance* (para. 10) says: 'There need be no maximum or minimum size for the area or population covered by a unitary authority.'

Another major difficulty with the structure of the review related to the degrees of freedom for the Commission to re-draw the administrative map of shire England. The Secretary of State directed the Commission to review specified areas. The implication of this was that the outer boundary of the county or group of contiguous counties was sacrosanct, unless the Secretary of State issued a specific direction; therefore, there was little possibility of seeking a structure which would mean straddling these boundaries, and in fact no direction was issued. Second, by virtue of the very tight timetable imposed for the work, it was predictable that the Commission could only very rarely consider solutions other than those which involved whole districts. The time and effort that would have been required to look at numerous solutions which required drawing new boundaries across existing districts, as around some large cities, for example, would have been beyond the bounds of reasonable possibility. In both ways, the fundamental structure of the review constrained the Commission very severely in the range of options it could realistically consider. In any case, had the Commission proposed solutions which meant crossing county boundaries, there is little doubt that in many cases public opinion would have been very hostile; for example, there was a major outcry at the suggestion to transfer some parishes from northern Hampshire into a proposed Newbury unitary authority in Berkshire. Any crossing of county boundaries which involved the division of existing districts, as in the Hampshire case, would have increased the costs of reorganisation. A further complication would have arisen with pension arrangements for fire and police personnel transferred between authorities on account of the unfunded nature of pension provisions for both services, though this was not realised until the review was well advanced. All things considered, in the generality of cases, the Commission was constrained to work within existing county boundaries.

The *Policy Guidance* strongly emphasised that the structure of local government should be based on natural communities, whether these be large or small, but that any change 'should be worthwhile and cost-effective over time'. If the Commission had been able to find and recommend unitary structures which simultaneously fitted these criteria, the progress of the roving review would have been much less contentious than it turned out to be. The fundamental problem was recognised in the *Guidance*, namely that there was likely to be a trade-off between the two sets of considerations noted above and therefore scope for plenty of disagreement about the suitability of the available options.

Even before the Commission began its work, the battle lines had been drawn. As early as March 1991, the Association of County Councils had issued a briefing paper to counter the ADC's (1990) evidence on the costs and benefits of change gleaned from previous structural reforms. The Welsh Consultative Council for Local Government met on 24 February 1992 with papers tabled by the counties on the one hand and the districts on the other, costing a range of unitary options for Wales ranging from eight to twenty-seven authorities (Assembly of Welsh Counties 1992a; Council of Welsh Districts 1992). While both analyses agreed that eight unitary authorities would be cheaper than the two-tier status quo, the counties thought that twenty-seven would be more costly than the present arrangements while the district figures suggested there would be savings (see Chapter 6). Then, in May 1992, Nottinghamshire County Council published its assessment that were the two-tier structure in the county to be replaced by eight district-based unitary authorities, local citizens would have to foot a £40 million bill. To this the districts in the county responded furiously with the claim that there would in fact be savings of £13 million. If any warning were needed, it was clear that costing change was going to be a major battle ground. Thus, even before the English review had begun, it was fully apparent that Heseltine's exhortation to local authorities to make their submissions to the LGCE on the basis of consensus was unlikely to be heeded (Whitehead 1994, p. 13).

Commissioners were allocated in pairs to have particular responsibility for individual review areas and found themselves pitchforked into the battle arena. By early summer 1993, draft recommendations had been published for all ten of the first tranche counties, and the battle of competing interests intensified. Of the counties being reviewed, the Isle of Wight was the most straightforward case, since there was widespread agreement in the island itself and more generally that having a county council and two districts for a total population of the order of 130,000 was nonsensical; the draft recommendation for a unitary authority for the whole island was relatively uncontentious. In the case of the three 'artificial' counties of Avon, Cleveland and Humberside, draft proposals for unitary authorities that were fundamentally district based were contested by the counties and by some interests, but were quite widely seen as being appropriate for densely populated, urbanised areas – though parts of Humberside were essentially rural in character. However, draft recommendations for a single unitary authority in Somerset, and for three in both Gloucestershire and North Yorkshire, aroused a considerable outcry – that such authorities would be too remote. An even greater reaction was evident to the draft proposals for Derbyshire and Co. Durham, in both cases for a unitary city and a single unitary authority for the rest of the county. These concerns were, if anything, exacerbated by the fact that in Lincolnshire the Commission recommended the retention of the two-tier structure. The general pattern at this stage was clear: if there were going to be unitary authorities, they were going to be big; they might not be a whole county, but in general they were going to be much bigger than the ADC had been campaigning for. The basic reason for this lay in the costing evidence, which is discussed in Chapter 4.

At the draft recommendation stage, the districts had manifestly failed to impress the Commission with the general case for them to become unitary authorities; but the counties had not gained all they had wished for. Concern about large unitary authorities ran much wider than the district council corridors, as was evident during the summer as consultation proceeded, leading to the final recommendations for the first tranche counties published in the autumn and early January 1994. For Avon, Cleveland, Humberside, the Isle of Wight and North Yorkshire, the Commission confirmed its draft proposals for unitary authorities, either unchanged or with small alterations. Lincolnshire was also confirmed for the retention of the two-tier structure. In the case of Somerset, a single unitary authority now became three. The most radical changes were in Derbyshire, Co. Durham and Gloucestershire. In Derbyshire, two unitary authorities were recommended, one for Derby City (as before) and another for a greater Chesterfield, with the two-tier structure remaining elsewhere. A similar change of recommendation occurred for Co. Durham; Darlington was confirmed for unitary status but instead of a unitary authority for the rest of the county it was now proposed that the status quo should prevail. Finally, for Gloucestershire, it was now recommended that there should be no change in the structure of local government.

Faced with this evolving situation, aware of the clamour that attended the review process and the unhappiness of many Conservative councillors and MPs, it was widely rumoured during the summer of 1993 that the Government was on the verge of cancelling the whole exercise (Filkin and Moor 1997). In the event, with the strong intervention of the Prime Minister (Young 1994, p. 92), the Cabinet decided to proceed with reform in England but to accelerate the work of the Commission. The primary consideration was that the Commission had already made recommendations for unitary structures in some county areas which the Government was minded to accept and that the need was to achieve greater coherence in the pattern of future recommendations from the Commission (Gummer 1999). A subsidiary reason was the momentum which had been generated for radical reform in both Scotland and Wales, which would have created a difficult situation if the English review had been stopped or curtailed (Stewart *et al.* 1997, p. 10). In addition, it must be remembered that the Government was beleaguered over Europe, struggling to get the Maastricht Treaty ratified by Parliament, and coping with the trauma of the country's ejection from the European Exchange Rate Mechanism in September 1992 and with the impact of Norman Lamont's valedictory speech in the House of Commons following his dismissal as Chancellor of the Exchequer – 'the impression of being in office but not in power' (Young 1998, p. 443). Politically, it would have been very difficult for the Government to abandon the English review and hence the decision to proceed. With the aim of obtaining a more coherent outcome from the review and minimising the political damage, the *Policy Guidance* was amended, the Commission was directed to have another look at Derbyshire, Co. Durham and Gloucestershire under the revised *Guidance*, and the remaining counties were to be reviewed as a single tranche with completion scheduled for the end of 1994. The ADC was delighted, glad that the review was to continue and equally pleased with the change to the *Guidance* which strengthened the push for unitary solutions. In the counties, on the other hand, there was widespread concern.

However, for the ADC it proved to be something of a Pyrrhic victory. Derbyshire and Lancashire County Councils both applied to the High Court, alleging that the change to the *Guidance* which strengthened the advice to find unitary solutions was unlawfully limiting the Commission's discretion, and in a landmark judgment delivered on 28 January 1994 the Court agreed with the plaintiffs (*R v. Secretary of State for the Environment, ex p. Lancashire CC* [1994] 4 All ER 165). In the original *Policy Guidance*, the relevant text read: 'In some areas the Commission may wish to recommend a continuation of the existing two-tier structure. But the government expects to see a substantial increase in the number of unitary authorities as a result of the Commission's reviews' (DoE 1992b, para. 3). The equivalent passage in the *Guidance* as amended read: 'In some areas the Commission may wish to recommend a continuation of the existing two-tier structure. *But the government expects that to be the exception, and that the result will be a substantial increase in the number of unitary authorities in both urban and rural areas*' (DoE 1993, para. 3, italics added). It was the sentence in italics which was the subject of the court case. The High Court ruled that the entire sentence must be struck out. This did more than return the *Guidance* to its original state; it actually watered down the advice to the Commission to find unitary solutions.

Although dismissed by the Government as being inconsequential, that judgment was widely seen as a turning point in the review process, a view shared by the Commission itself (Chisholm 1997, pp. 102–3; LGCE 1995a, para. 54). While this assessment is undoubtedly true, there was also the less tangible, but nevertheless potent, effect of the county council elections held in May 1993. The Conservatives suffered the humiliation of losing control of sixteen counties, being reduced to just Buckinghamshire. Also, parliamentary by-elections in May and July of that year produced stunning victories for the Liberal Democrats at the expense of the Conservatives in Newbury and Christchurch respectively (Crewe 1994). Emboldened by these electoral reverses for the governing party, opponents of wholesale change became more confident and assertive long before the court case came to judgment. There was the sense that, despite the 1992 general election victory, the Government was vulnerable, a view which was reinforced by the even more disastrous local authority elections of 1994. With the changes in political control which occurred, some councils altered their submissions to the Commission and argued for different outcomes from those previously advocated, thus providing an interesting commentary on the nature of the evidence submitted.

In summary terms, the expedited review in 1994 resulted in final recommendations for a number of unitary authorities (generally, but not exclusively, important cities) and for the maintenance of the two-tier structure throughout the greater part of shire England. Of the limited number of cases in which the Commission proposed an all-unitary solution for a whole county, the Secretary of State ultimately accepted only one, Berkshire, but with the modification of converting five unitary authorities into six. Thus by March 1995 it had become clear that less change would occur than had been expected in some quarters, with the Major Cities and a number of other authorities becoming unitary councils. For some observers, the pattern looked rather incoherent. The review process itself was widely seen to have been flawed and a good deal of opprobrium was being heaped on the Commission and on the Government. Ministers needed an exit strategy to minimise the political damage and to wrap up the review. The device selected was to make the Commission's Chairman, Sir John Banham, the scapegoat; when the Secretary of State announced to the House of Commons that Sir John had 'resigned' there was unconcealed and quite disgraceful merriment. New Commissioners would be appointed from July, when the existing appointments expired, and this re-constituted Commission under the chairmanship of Sir David Cooksey would be asked to re-examine a limited number of districts to see whether they should be accorded unitary status.

The *Guidance* which was issued to the Commission by the DoE in June 1995 for this further review stressed the need for consistency across England, noting in particular that whereas some cities and large towns had been recommended for unitary status others had not: 'Many of these councils used to be county boroughs and so have a tradition of unitary local government. They are often areas where there is a significant need for economic and social regeneration' (DoE 1995, para. 2).

The preceding historical sketch provides the framework within which a more thorough examination of certain features of the English review can now be undertaken; some of these features have not received the attention they deserve in the extant literature. Hence, the task to which we now turn is to put some flesh on the historical bones.

## The Commission, 1992–95

The opinion very quickly became widespread that the Commission lacked 'a clear sense of direction' (S. Leach 1994, p. 539). Part of the blame for that lies with the Commission itself but by no means all. As Chisholm (1995, pp. 98–9) and Thomas (quoted in Crick 1997, pp. 372–3) note, no time was allowed for the Commission to assess the nature of the problem and the extant evidence that was relevant; nor did it insist on being given this time. At the very beginning, Commissioners asked for the establishment of a library stocked with the appropriate material to allow individuals to read themselves into the task; despite several promises that such a facility would be created, the request got nowhere.

Even if the time and resources had been available for a cool assessment of the task in hand, it is an open question whether Commissioners would have found sufficient common ground in the early months of the review to avoid the appearance of inconsistency. Before the review had even begun, the Chairman had made it publicly known that he thought: 'If it ain't broke, don't fix it.' Yet, in writing a book which was published in 1994, he seems quite clearly to espouse the idea of large, county-sized unitary authorities in which there should be highly devolved internal management to give 'truly local local government' (Banham 1994, pp. 74–9). Since the Commission had no jurisdiction over the internal management of authorities, these publicly expressed opinions could be read to span the range from endorsing the status quo to unitary solutions based on small ('local') authorities to big ones. That ambivalence was manifest in the way that he ran the Commission; and it was clearly visible to other participants in the review process (Delafons 1994; Stewart *et al.* 1997, p. 17).

The other members of the Commission also held divergent views. Some were committed to the idea of small unitary authorities, while others strongly believed in large ones. Yet others were less convinced of the need for wholesale change. It is probable that in the early months there would have been agreement that the larger cities had a strong *prima facie* case, but it is unlikely that there would have been a consensus regarding an appropriate minimum or maximum size of authority for unitary structures to be compared with the status quo. The weekend seminar that was held in February 1993 did not result in a clear set of concepts and criteria for application in the review, and indeed it hardly could. The documentation that the grossly over-worked staff could prepare was limited and by that time work was far advanced on the first tranche reviews, with the first report on draft recommendations for mainland England due to be published on 22 March. This divergence of viewpoint was an entirely proper reflection of opinions held outside the Commission. Had the Commission been directed to consider the whole of shire England in a single report submitted at the end of the review, there would undoubtedly have been a convergence of views as the evidence piled up and there would have been far less scope for accusations of inconsistency. In practice, given the sequential nature of the review, these differing predilections of Commissioners had a marked impact on the review process, and especially on the ten counties of the first tranche. As the review progressed, the accumulating evidence caused most Commissioners to adjust their ideas, but the initial months had cast an aura of muddle over the review.

A fundamental problem was that when the Commission began work there was only a very hazy idea of what the independent advice on costings might show – transition costs on the one hand and ongoing costs/savings on the other (see Chapter 4). Consequently, when lead Commissioners were dispatched to their respective counties, they had perforce to say that nothing was ruled either in or out with respect to the size of possible unitary authorities. This meant that everybody believed that virtually all unitary options were open, however big or small. In addition, it quickly became apparent that Commissioners had divergent attitudes to their role. Some took the view that the task was to find and 'sell' a unitary structure for their area; some Commissioners engaged in attempts to broker deals for unitary solutions, either because that was what they believed was right or to ensure that in the event of a unitary solution being decided upon it would at least be a reasonable one. Others took a more judicial approach, regarding their role as being that of eliciting information and opinions as the basis on which to form a judgement on whether the two-tier arrangements could be bettered and if so with what structure. These differences were apparent within the Commission and were clearly visible to outsiders (Davis 1997; Game 1997; S. Leach 1994; Stewart *et al.* 1997; Stoker 1997b).

Linked to these differences were divergent attitudes to the relative importance of the Act and of the *Policy Guidance* in giving shape to the work of the Commission and hence the process of the review; the Act, in the crucial section, is neutral regarding the outcome, whereas the *Guidance* has a distinct but contradictory slant towards unitary outcomes. It seemed fairly clear that initially the majority of Commissioners were inclined to place greater reliance on the unitary interpretation of the *Guidance*.

To cap it all, from quite early on, and certainly from March 1993, there was a continuous leak of information about decisions regarding draft and final recommendations; the source or sources of these leaks was never known. The fact of the leaks reflected the 'political minefield' into which the Commission had entered (Banham 1994, p. 75), and quite possibly also the lack of coherence of the Commission as a body. Whatever the source(s), life felt pretty uncomfortable.

Possibly the worst outcome from this over-all situation was the fact that many decisions had to be put to the vote rather than being arrived at by consensus and that a number of important issues were decided by just one or two votes. One such matter was the status of the two-tier option in the consultation process, this option being either absolutely no structural change or alternatively the creation of a unitary authority for a city and no change elsewhere. In putting forward one or more unitary structures for public consideration, should not the option of the status quo be included automatically, since all the analyses relevant for unitary structures were predicated on comparisons with the present arrangements? The proposal that indeed this should automatically be included in the consultation phase was defeated by one vote. Thus, of the ten counties in the first tranche, the status quo was offered as an option for consultation in only one case, that of Lincolnshire, where it was in fact the preferred structure at that stage in the process. When the review was accelerated in 1994, to cover all the remaining counties plus the three that had been sent back for further review, the status quo, or a variant thereof, was offered as an option for consultation in twenty-seven out of the total number of thirty-two counties considered. The illogicality of declining to offer the two-tier structure as an option, especially in the first tranche reviews, caused endless trouble, calling in question the genuineness of the whole process and in particular of the consultation exercise. At public meetings and elsewhere, it was impossible to give a coherent justification for apparently ruling out the continuation of the existing arrangements.

At the start of the first tranche reviews, the possibility of district-based unitary authorities as the norm had to be regarded as a possibility, since the Commission had very little data on which initially to rely. When, in the event, it was only in three counties – Avon, Cleveland and Humberside – that something closely approximating this solution was proposed, the hopes of many individuals were rudely dashed. Indeed, the Commission had obviously moved to the view that if there were to be change larger rather than smaller unitary authorities were needed, implying either the amalgamation of districts or even whole county unitary authorities, and the anguish in some quarters was considerable. Equally important, though, was the following unspoken reality. The Commission was supposed to treat each area 'on its merits' and to find a locally acceptable solution that was also cost effective – no blueprint. Yet, from the fact of a rolling programme, it was obvious to everyone that early decisions would probably set patterns which would be reflected in later recommendations. Consequently, the nature of the draft and then final recommendations for the ten first tranche counties was seen as crucial for the remainder of the review. The probability is that whatever the pattern of those early recommendations had been, there would have been a hue and cry as the respective interests sought to swing events in the direction they championed. In a very real sense, therefore, the considerable outcry and the extent of the political upheaval that occurred in 1993 were at least as much the result of the review's structure as they were of the particular recommendations made by the Commission.

By December 1993, hard experience had convinced the Commission that for the forthcoming accelerated reviews some indication should be given to local authorities of the upper and lower population limits that in the normal course of events would be acceptable for authorities in a unitary structure. The following wording was agreed: 'The Commission expects that the areas for which it will recommend unitary authorities will in most cases have populations in the range of 150,000 to 250,000' (LGCE 1993, para. 41). The logic which led to the selection of these indicative population limits was as follows. The modelling of costs had progressed sufficiently by the spring of 1993 for the Commission to be reasonably confident that below 150,000 unitary authorities would not be cost effective. In addition, there were doubts about the ability of smaller authorities to manage the delivery of services. At the upper end of the scale, the Commission had been impressed by the widespread and general hostility shown towards very large unitary authorities – the reduction in number of councillors and hence reduced representation, and the fear that such authorities would be remote and insensitive to local needs and aspirations. It was judged that outside the big cities, a population above 250,000 would imply authorities that seemed too large to command allegiance. The choice of these two figures was a matter of judgement applied to the available evidence, a judgement on which Commissioners were divided.

Indicative limits having been agreed for the accelerated review, the Commission considered each county in the light of its special geography and suggested an upper and lower limit for the number of unitary authorities it was worth considering for comparison with the existing two-tier arrangements. The Commission believed that this range was likely to contain the unitary option which would be the best alternative to the status quo, and so the purpose was to try to focus the debate and to avoid the devotion of time and resources arguing for other structures which, *prima facie*, would be less desirable. As a matter of procedure, therefore, the Commission sought the best unitary option for comparison with the status quo. There were still differences between Commissioners' views of their role, in that some sought to promote unitary solutions whereas others maintained a more judicial approach.

The Act enjoins the Commission to consult those who may have an interest in the structure of local government in an area, obviously including residents, and the *Policy Guidance* reinforces this by stressing the importance of public opinion and the possible use by the Commission of polling to ascertain the views of citizens. In this respect, the framework for the review was consistent with the rhetoric of basing local government on communities and that local government exists for people, not for the employees and councillors. An unprecedented consultation process was put in hand by the Commission for the first tranche counties and, in some respects, an even bigger one for the counties in the expedited review. Nobody could claim that the consultation processes were perfect but, equally, most observers would agree that consultation did elicit a great deal of information and that the Commission did use that material. But this very consultation process produced a Catch 22 situation. Particularly in the first tranche counties in 1993, the public and others were apt to believe that the consultation process was a charade, the Commission having made up its mind what its final recommendations were going to be and that therefore nothing that was said or done during the consultation period would make an iota of difference. This was certainly the author's experience in Derbyshire and then in Hampshire and Surrey. It was an uphill task to persuade people that consultation was a genuine attempt to elicit information and that this information might cause the Commission to change its mind. The task was made all the greater by the fact that the impression was widespread that, even if the Commission did alter its judgement, this would signify nothing because at the end of the day the Government would impose the solution it wanted. This view of the over-all process was, quite extraordinarily, shared by the Environment Committee of the House of Commons (1994; see also Chisholm 1995). Time after time, it was necessary to explain that the Secretary of State had no power to substitute a structure which was radically different from the Commission's final recommendation. That recommendation could be accepted, modified or rejected but not replaced by a totally different scheme of the Minister's devising. The other half of the Catch 22 situation was the fact that the Commission did indeed listen to the evidence generated by the consultation and did alter several of its draft proposals when it came to formulating final recommendations. This fact was then interpreted by many observers as evidence that the Commission lacked a sense of direction, having failed to identify the right solution first time round (S. Leach 1994, p. 539).

In addition to the above aspects of the review, the Commission was exposed to a number of other pressures, so it is now appropriate to consider the other main actors in the drama of the review besides the Commission itself. But we must do so with the following context in mind. The Act itself devotes seventy-three lines to setting out the Commission's procedure in conducting structural reviews. The *Procedure Guidance* goes into minute detail about the way in which the Commission should conduct reviews. Furthermore, the initial directions given by the Secretary of State regarding review areas also gave specific dates for the completion of each stage in each area (Appendix 1). In a litigious age, the Commission had to be scrupulously careful to adhere to the procedural constraints lest an interested party sought a judicial review. As a result, the Commission's officers had to spend an inordinate amount of time ensuring that *procedures* were proof against challenge. In the event, no court challenge against the Commission succeeded. However, the eagerness of both Parliament and Government to prescribe the procedural details created a situation that was not conducive to the pursuit of proper *outcomes*, an important and little-recognised handicap under which Commissioners and staff alike laboured.

## The role of central government

The Government set up the Commission and gave it certain directions and guidance but did not then leave the Commission to get on with its task. Seen from the outside, it was obvious that the Government tried to control the review process to secure a general pattern of unitary authorities: 'Having set up an independent, roving commission the government appears to have sought to impose a national solution rather than follow the original logic of local solutions based on local views' (Stoker 1997b, p. 45). Seen from the inside of the review process, there is no doubt that Stoker's assessment is right. The basis for this assertion goes way beyond the nature of the *Policy Guidance*, which has already been discussed, and some of the main evidence has previously been described (Chisholm 1997; Stewart *et al.* 1997).

To begin at the beginning, consider the choice of counties in the first tranche review areas; there can be no doubt that these were chosen in the belief that the Commission would arrive at unitary solutions which would then set the pattern for the remaining areas. By any standards, the Isle of Wight was a special case, with a population of the order of 130,000, a county council and two district councils. There was widespread prior agreement, on the island and generally, that a single authority would make much better sense. The three 'artificial' counties formed in 1974 – Avon, Cleveland and Humberside – were perceived by the Government to be unpopular and, furthermore, that with the dense urban populations in two of them and an important part of the third (Humberside) the Government thought that they lent themselves to division into most-purpose authorities. These four counties, therefore, formed a clear core of cases where the Government could reasonably expect unitary outcomes, to which we must add Derbyshire as the fifth. Derbyshire County Council figured in the Conservative Party's pantheon of demons, partly because of some bruising experiences with the former leader, David Bookbinder, and some of the policies pursued by the Council (Mobbs 1997). The following question asked in the House of Commons by Philip Oppenheim, one of Derbyshire's Conservative MPs, illustrates the attitudes: 'Does my right hon. Friend agree that, whatever changes to local government finance are made by whichever government, they are still likely to have to face the fundamental problem of profligate, wasteful county councils, such as Derbyshire?' (*Hansard* oral answers, 12 December 1990, cols 949–50). Two other Conservative MPs in Derbyshire, Edwina Currie and Patrick McLoughlin, made public statements early in the review process that the county would be abolished. At that time, the Conservative MPs in the county were clearly determined that the County Council should cease to exist, a fact which gave considerable encouragement to the district authorities.

There were no other counties where the issues seemed so clear-cut. In order to make up numbers so that the whole review could be completed in five years, other counties were added to the group identified above, all being contiguous with the three 'artificial' counties. By putting all five of the assumed-to-be-clear-cut cases into the first tranche, the inference has to be that the Government wished to ensure a momentum towards unitary solutions.

That inference is confirmed by the details of the original timetable. Work was to start on the Isle of Wight ahead of the other counties, with draft recommendations due in December 1992. The next set of draft recommendations was to be published on 22 March 1993, for Derbyshire, with Cleveland and Co. Durham to follow a month later (Appendix 1). This sequence of publications should have the effect of creating a pattern of unitary expectations. Throughout the whole review process, the Commission kept to the timetable set for the publication of draft and final recommendations, with but one exception. That was Derbyshire, and that episode is revealing.

The Commission had agreed its draft recommendations for Derbyshire and the report was drafted in the phrenetic way that was general given the incredibly tight timetable. At the point when the text was ready for sending to the printer, just meeting the deadline, the Chairman decided to postpone publication. The draft recommendation was for a unitary Derby City and a single unitary authority for the remainder of the county: options for two or four unitary authorities outside the City were also canvassed but were not favoured, though the option for two was considered viable whereas the case for four seemed to the Commission to be weak. The explanation offered for the postponement by the Chairman at the next meeting of the Commission was wholly unsatisfactory, being that the text still needed revision; in fact it was subsequently published unchanged. It was clear to the author as one of the lead commissioners that the Chairman was under pressure to modify the draft recommendations to give greater prominence to the case for five unitary authorities in the county. The only body that could have applied such pressure was the DoE on behalf of the Government, since at that time they were the only people who would have known what the Commission had in mind; from the beginning, the Department, very properly, was kept informed about the progress of the Commission's work, on a 'no surprises' basis. Indeed, it was notable that the DoE raised no objection to the postponement of the Derbyshire report despite the fact that this meant missing the deadline which had been set in the directions given to the Commission.

The effect of two months' delay in publication, to May, should have been to lessen the impact of proposals for just two authorities in the county. Draft recommendations for Cleveland were due in April, with the other 'artificial' counties following in June, packaged with adjacent counties. However, the nature of the Commission's draft recommendations for Derbyshire leaked and on 10 March the ADC communicated with all the districts in the county with the details, saying also that 'the ADC has raised strong and serious protests' about the Commission's lack of enthusiasm for any number of unitary authorities in Derbyshire greater than three. The source of the leak is not known.

The draft recommendations for Derbyshire were the subject of consultation during the summer of 1993, leading to the formulation of revised proposals, which were published on 8 November at the same time as the final recommendations for Co. Durham. For both of these counties, the Commission's initial preference for just two unitary authorities had been sharply modified in the light of the evidence and opinions garnered during the summer months. The Commission now recommended a unitary Derby City (as before) but instead of a unitary council for the rest of the county proposed a unitary authority focused on Chesterfield and no change elsewhere. The Co. Durham recommendation was for a unitary Darlington but otherwise no structural change. The very same day that these final recommendations were published, the Chairman wrote to the DoE offering to review the two counties again in the light of the revised *Policy Guidance*, which, it will be remembered, placed much stronger emphasis on unitary solutions than did the original version. The DoE responded to the Chairman on 8 November and made the correspondence publicly available that day. A few days later, Banham publicly declined to speculate why ministers had wanted him to write to the DoE (Chisholm 1997, p. 103). In the event, both Derbyshire and Co. Durham were sent back to the Commission, along with Gloucestershire, where draft recommendations for a unitary solution had been transformed into a no-change final recommendation. Lincolnshire had been proposed by the Commission for no change all along and the Government did not send this county back, clearly deeming it to be a true 'exception'. This episode provides the clearest possible proof that ministers were actively seeking to obtain a particular outcome from the review and sought to manipulate the way in which the Commission worked.

In addition to changing the guidelines and sending back three counties, ministers offered the Chairman the opportunity to change the membership of the Commission to ensure that it 'was more committed to the unitary principle' (Stewart *et al.* 1997, p. 10). This offer was reported to the Commission by the Chairman; he had refused it, not once but thrice. Had this attempt to change the composition of the Commission become public knowledge at the time, the uproar might have been considerable. Yet Geoffrey Filkin, Secretary of the Association of District Councils at the time, believes, with the benefit of hindsight, that this is what should have happened (Filkin and Moor 1997, p. 134). In the event, the Government used another strategy, namely the filling of some vacancies which had been left when the Commission was set up in 1992 with people believed to favour the unitary principle; but, as one well-placed informant observed to the author, the impact was less than had been expected.

In January 1994, the High Court overturned the inclusion of the sentence in the revised *Policy Guidance* which stated that continuation of the two-tier structure should be the 'exception'. Nevertheless, ministers continued publicly to press for unitary solutions. For example, David Curry made it clear at a meeting of the ADC in February 1994 that this was the Government's aim (Chisholm 1995, p. 566; see also Stewart *et al.* 1997, p. 12); soon after, he publicly attacked one county for its use of costings data in a leaflet it had published, thereby explicitly joining the fray on one side (*Local Government Chronicle*, 5 April 1994, p. 1). There is no doubt that over an extended period of time ministers sought to use the Act to achieve something very close to a 'blueprint' of unitary authorities at the sub-county level. The means employed amounted to the attempted manipulation of the Commission, which makes the rhetoric employed in Parliament, that the Commission was independent, sound somewhat hollow. However, as R. Leach (1994, p. 356) observed, the second-round final recommendations for Derbyshire, Co. Durham and Gloucestershire 'required some courage in the face of government pressure', confirming that the independence was maintained despite the pressure exerted.

### The two local authority associations

As previously indicated, the Association of County Councils had a politically difficult defensive path to tread. Initially, the ACC was less prominent than the ADC, which was assiduous in cultivating links with the DoE and very public in its campaign. However, the ACC had considerable strengths in its links to influential public figures and there is little doubt that much hard work was undertaken behind the scenes, tapping the reservoir of doubt about unitary solutions which was manifest when an amendment to the Local Government Bill to make unitary recommendations mandatory on the Commission was rejected. Somewhat behind the scenes, the Society of County Treasurers, led in particular by Nottinghamshire and West Sussex, provided powerful support for the ACC on the one hand and for individual counties in their dealings with the Commission and Ernst & Young over costing issues on the other (see Chapter 4).

In the early days of the review, the ACC argued that if there were to be change then there should be unitary counties or unitary structures which would involve no more than two or three authorities for a county area. The claim was that such a structure would save money and that the large unitary authorities could and would introduce internal management systems which would ensure that local communities' interests would be properly safeguarded. As the review progressed, and it became clear that such large unitary authorities would not command the necessary support, and particularly following the High Court ruling in 1994, the ACC shifted its emphasis to the case for no change, or for no greater change than the granting of unitary status to a limited number of big cities (see, for example, ACC 1994). The Association also became more aggressive in its public posture, reflecting confidence that the review was now going its way.

The ADC was energetic and vociferous in pursuit of its goal, unitary structures across shire England. Initially, the campaign was for districts to assume the powers of the counties, creating a system of relatively small most-purpose authorities. However, as early as the spring of 1993, the ADC was beginning to realise that this might not be achievable. The circular to Derbyshire districts of 10 March, containing the leaked information about the Commission's intended draft recommendations for the county, urged them to campaign for the inclusion in the consultation process of an option for five unitary authorities, since: 'For many the prospect of getting unitary status on current boundaries has gone.'

To its credit, through 1993 and into 1994, the ADC remained true to its belief in unitary authorities at the sub-county level, even if this could only be achieved by the amalgamation of districts to give authorities of sufficient size to be cost effective. Thus, when the expedited review started in late 1993: 'The ADC advised districts on the new principles of the process, and made clear that unless they had populations over the 150,000 mark, or very strong community identities, they would have to accept mergers with their neighbours. This advice was accepted by most districts' (Filkin and Moor 1997, p. 135). However, the ADC revealed its doubts with a publication on the scope for improving the two-tier structure (ADC 1994).

The difficulty for the ADC was that acceptance by the districts in the expedited review of the need for mergers in order to achieve unitary authorities of a viable size represented the *formal* position. The reality was rather different, and had become apparent as early as 1 April 1993. A meeting of treasurers from the eighteen counties involved in first and (planned) second tranche reviews heard reports that in every single county: 'The districts in their area were universally in disarray following the leaking of the Derbyshire proposal [for two unitary authorities] and the comments of the Commission about unitary district options in their area' (Latham 1993). Latham went on to say that subsequent to the 1 April meeting he had learned that the Major Cities were to see John Redwood, Minister for Local Government, and that they were privately saying that the ADC policy of a national pattern of district-based unitary authorities was not sustainable. They appeared to be cutting loose from that lowest common denominator approach. In any case, notwithstanding the ADC's advice, the Derbyshire districts were never able to agree a convincing case for a unitary structure based on amalgamations, any more than the districts were able to in Co. Durham and Gloucestershire.

Once the accelerated review got under way, it was very common for the county association of district councils to put forward a structure of unitary authorities which, by amalgamations, reduced the number of authorities to about half the existing number (districts plus county), and in this sense the advice of the ADC was indeed followed. But the lack of conviction in these proposals was transparently obvious when, as was commonly the case, individual districts put forward their first preference schemes in which their own authority would gain unitary status, or a preference was expressed for no change to the two-tier arrangements. Many districts, realising that unitary status on present boundaries was unlikely to be achieved, became more interested in fighting to maintain their own identity (Mobbs 1997; Stewart *et al.* 1997). In other words, the ADC's membership was a good deal less biddable than the ADC would wish one to believe. In fact, the divisions between the districts served to do much of the counties' work for them, and was doing so even in the early days of the first tranche reviews and certainly within six months of the commencement of the structural review in August 1992.

The manner in which the two Associations approached the Commission deserves a brief mention. From the outset, the ADC lobbied individual Commissioners in a sustained manner, the present author included. In contrast, the ACC kept its distance and worked through the formal channels. There is little doubt that this contrast in campaigning style arose from the access which the ACC had to important professional bodies whose evidence to the Commission might be important, and its access to influential persons within Parliament and more generally (*Financial Times*, 11 January 1995).

## Twenty-one districts reconsidered in 1995

Early in 1995 it had become clear that the Government felt it needed an exit strategy from a situation which it felt was exceedingly difficult. In general terms, John Gummer (Secretary of State at the DoE) did two things. First, where the Commission had recommended all-unitary outcomes in the expedited review, he decided to accept proposals for unitary status for identifiably large towns, such as Luton and Milton Keynes, leaving the remainder of the relevant counties with their two-tier structure. In addition, and in contrast, he accepted unitary recommendations for rural Rutland and Herefordshire, and for the mixed circumstances of Berkshire (which became six unitary councils). The second part of the strategy was to re-constitute the Commission under a new Chairman and ask it to look again at twenty-one districts for which the original Commission had recommended the status quo. These councils were urban or suburban in character, some being regarded as extensions of the London conurbation.

The direction to undertake this further review was issued on 29 June 1995 and the work was completed by the end of the year. Given that the remaining parts of the relevant counties would in any case continue with the two-tier structure, this six-month reconsideration was by definition a much more limited matter than had been the case for the main review, though the time pressure was nevertheless considerable. In the event, the Commission recommended the creation of eight unitary authorities and all of these proposals were accepted. Thus the total number of new unitary authorities created by the review was forty-six.

## Concluding comments

Since this is the first of three chapters which deal with the review in England, this is not the point at which any over-all conclusions can be drawn about the process. One point, though, is abundantly clear; the review was not a straightforward matter. Equally, it is not possible to judge the performance of the Commission in the absence of a proper regard for the legislation under which it worked and proper consideration of the roles played by the other main actors, in particular the Government.

At this stage of the account, there are some features of the main review (1992–95) which need to be highlighted. In the first tranche of ten counties, the draft recommendations made by the Commission were for all-unitary outcomes in nine cases, Lincolnshire being the only exception; for this county, the proposal at this stage was for no change. By the time that the Commission formulated its final recommendations in the light of the consultations conducted on the draft proposals and the further evidence received, the number of all-unitary recommendations had fallen to six. The final recommendation for Gloucestershire was to maintain the two-tier structure intact, this county joining Lincolnshire; and in the case of Derbyshire and Co. Durham, the Commission now recommended a hybrid solution of one or two unitary urban areas and the continuation of the two tiers elsewhere. The expedited review in 1993–94 considered the three counties which the Secretary of State referred back plus the twenty-nine remaining counties, making thirty-two in total, and the Commission's recommendations followed a substantially different pattern. At the draft recommendation stage, all-unitary solutions were preferred for eighteen counties, hybrid solutions for ten and no change in the four remaining counties. Thus, instead of finding clear merit in an all-unitary outcome in 90 per cent of cases, the proportion had fallen to 56 per cent. In response to the evidence obtained during the consultation period, the number of final recommendations for the entire replacement of the two-tier structure had fallen to just four, or 12.5 per cent; hybrid structures were recommended in eleven cases, and for the remaining seventeen counties the conclusion of the review was that there should be no change. Quite clearly, as the review proceeded, the Commission became less inclined to recommend complete reorganisation. That fact suggests at least three possible interpretations. On the one hand, the Commission might have been operating in a thoroughly inconsistent manner, as alleged by the critics. Or it may be that the objective circumstances of the counties reviewed early in the process differed very considerably from those examined later. Or yet again, it may be that as the review progressed, the pattern of evidence became clearer and more persuasive that there should be no change. Of course, it could be some combination of all three reasons.

The process of resiling from unitary solutions was continued by the decisions which the Secretary of State took on the recommendations which he received. During the course of the review, he received proposals from the Commission for the complete replacement of the two-tier structure in ten counties; of these, he accepted five, opted for a hybrid solution in four cases and decided upon no change in one county. Where the Commission recommended hybrid solutions, these were generally accepted (though New Forest was exceptional in being rejected as a unitary authority), accounting for another eleven counties, with the remaining eighteen being left unchanged. Because the Secretary of State could not substitute his own entirely different solutions, he could only decide in favour of a unitary structure where he had received such proposals from the Commission, and he exercised his choice by whittling down the all-change recommendations and thus increasing the number of hybrid and status quo outcomes (Chisholm 1995). This provides the background to his decision to send back twenty-one districts for further review. By the end of the process, forty-six new unitary authorities had been accepted.

In the cases where the Secretary of State accepted, with or without modification, the Commission's recommendation for change, he then had to lay an affirmative order before both chambers of Parliament. Because Parliament had the final say in whether these orders would be passed, it was clearly necessary to be reasonably confident that the requisite majorities would be forthcoming, a matter which manifestly involved considerations of a very political nature.

The next two chapters examine the evidence which became available during the review, evidence which, if we may anticipate, certainly had an impact on both the Commission and on the Secretary of State and was a material factor in the steady move from unitary to status quo decisions. But before we turn to that material, a final comment is in order concerning the review process in England. So far as is known, nobody has provided an estimate of the costs which were incurred in the structural review. Enquiries within the Department of the Environment, Transport and the Regions (DETR) indicate that the staff costs incurred by the DoE probably did not exceed £1 million and this element of the total may be ignored. The easiest significant component to cost is the Commission itself, since from July 1992 to December 1995 virtually all its work was on the review and therefore its entire expenditure can be assigned thereto. The accounts were prepared on a cash basis but this is not an issue of great significance in the present context because the matter of interest is the aggregate sum over several years, not comparisons between years. For the purpose of estimation, we may assume that three-quarters of the 1995/6 expenditure should be assigned to the structural review, on which assumption total spending amounted to £18.2 million from July 1992 to December 1995, giving an average of £467,000 per county area. To the cost of the Commission one should add the costs incurred by the counties and districts and also by the DoE. The single most useful figure which the author has located is an over-all estimate for Derbyshire and its constituent districts, compiled immediately after the whole review process in the county was completed, an estimate which has not been disputed. Taking account of the Commission's costs and the costs of both the county and the nine districts, the sum amounted to £3 million (Hodgson 1998). This figure includes a valuation of the staff time committed to the review. A figure of £3 million is probably greater than would have been the experience in the average county, for two reasons: Derbyshire is somewhat larger in population terms than the average, having just over 900,000 residents compared with an average for the thirty-nine counties of just under 800,000; and Derbyshire had two full reviews. On the other hand, it was not involved in the further review of twenty-one districts. In any case, we can compare the Derbyshire sum with figures mentioned to the author by senior officers for the expenditure incurred by the county alone in Shropshire, of £0.25 million, and for Nottinghamshire of £0.435 million. These latter figures ignore the district and Commission costs, and take no account of the opportunity costs of staff time, which are included in the Derbyshire figure. Nevertheless, armed with this information we may employ the following simple arithmetic to obtain an estimate of the total costs incurred, other than those of central government. At the upper end of the range, the Derbyshire figure of £3 million, applied as an average cost for all thirty-nine county areas, gives a total of £117 million. If we take the more conservative figure of £2 million for each county area we would have total costs of £78 million, but that would leave only £60 million for the counties and districts once the Commission's costs had been deducted, or an average of £1.54 million per county area. This last figure seems improbably low given the figures cited for the *expenditure* of two counties, to which must be added district costs. Thus it seems probable that the costs of the review could not have been far off £100 million, a figure with which Archie Gall (1999), head of policy at the LGCE, personally would not disagree.

# 4

# Estimating the costs and benefits
# of change in England

A cynic is: 'A man who knows the price of everything and the value of nothing'.
(Oscar Wilde, *Lady Windermere's Fan*, Act III)

The 1992 Act enjoins the Commission, in making any proposal for structural change, to be satisfied that it will reflect the identities and interests of local communities and secure effective and convenient local government. The latter requirement is amplified in the *Policy Guidance* which was issued to the Commission, beginning with the assertion that: 'Unitary authorities can reduce bureaucracy and costs and improve the co-ordination and quality of services.' In the context specifically of measuring the costs and benefits of change, the *Guidance* continues: 'Change to the structure of local government should be worthwhile and cost-effective over time ... The Commission should recommend a structure which in its view best combines cost-effectiveness with a reflection of community identities and interests' (DoE 1992b, paras 7 and 8). Although a trade-off between the sets of criteria was clearly envisaged, it is also clear that the Government was expecting that proposals for change would reduce the costs of local government, an expectation (or hope) that was entirely consistent with the general policy of the Government to improve the efficiency of the British economy.

In the literature about the English review, remarkably little attention has been given to the problem of costing change and the role that the findings on costs and savings had on the thinking of the Commission. The accumulation of evidence showed that a general district-based structure of unitary authorities would cost a good deal more than the two-tier arrangements and would not be cost effective, whereas a county-based structure would yield savings. This had become apparent early in 1993 and played a significant part in the decisions taken by the Commission.

## Costing change: main review, 1992–95

Ernst & Young was initially employed as temporary assistance to help with the Derbyshire review, pending the appointment of Commission staff. The company was asked to assist in developing the Commission's general approach to the county reviews, using Derbyshire as a 'model' which could be applied elsewhere, including the costing of change, which it was hoped could be agreed with the local authorities. Very quickly it became apparent that these hopes could not be realised, and Ernst & Young's role shifted to the giving of advice on the complex problems involved in the estimation of costs and savings throughout the main review.

The main parameters for the costing of change were the following:

1  The Commission needed to be able to compare the existing two-tier structure in a given area with one or more unitary options for that area.
2  In doing so, it was to assume that the quality and quantity of services delivered would not be affected by structural change.
3  Hence the focus of the costings effort was on the overhead, or indirect, costs of administration, generally thought to amount to about 10 per cent of total expenditure.
4  Two elements of cost were to be identified: the transition costs for moving from the existing situation to a new structure; and the ongoing costs/savings that could be attributed to the new structure.

The stipulation that costings should be based on the assumption that with structural change there would be no alteration in the standard or quality of direct service provision was set out in the *Policy Guidance* and had a clear and defensible logic. In the absence of that assumption, the Commission would have been inundated with proposals from both counties and districts for the way in which services could be run in the future, proposals that would amount to worthless promissory notes because they involved issues beyond the jurisdiction of the Commission. On the other hand, the narrowing of the costing exercise to focus on about 10 per cent of the total costs highlights the limitations of considering structure without account being taken of other aspects of local government, such as its powers, financing and organisation. The ADC and the districts individually were not too pleased with the limited scope of the costing, since they were debarred from claiming radical improvements in service delivery dependent upon structural change. The ACC was equally unhappy, because it was unable to mount as strong a case as it would have wished that a pattern of small unitary authorities would increase costs. Nevertheless, the logic of the limitations had to be accepted, though a strong sense of the frustrations which were felt is conveyed by a critique written early in the review by a local government officer (West 1993).

### *Some of the problems encountered*

As outlined above, the costing exercise might look relatively straightforward but in practice it proved to be horribly complex and contentious. The five areas of particular difficulty were the following:

1 The definition of the 'indirect' staff in the existing two-tier structure.
2 The assumptions made regarding the indirect staffing needs of proposed unitary authorities, and hence the ongoing costs/savings to be expected.
3 The information technology (IT) costs for a new authority compared with the existing costs.
4 Whether the costings should be based on average circumstances or adjusted for local variations in geography, level of service delivery and level of expenditure.
5 Whether there are scale economies or diseconomies in administration and, if so, how they should be incorporated.

Working through all of these issues and many others as well took an enormous amount of effort over an extended period of time.

On 1 October 1992, the first fruits of Ernst & Young's work on costings were circulated to local authorities – a nine-page draft document giving advice on the methods to be used. During the first tranche reviews, intensive discussions were conducted with the aim of improving the guidance to local authorities and, so far as possible, to reconcile the conflicting positions taken by the counties and districts. The costing methodology, fundamentally based on staff numbers and staff grades in the category of indirect employment, was much improved as a consequence. By 26 May 1993, it was possible to circulate a revised version of the model, in a document which now ran to thirty-four pages (Ernst & Young 1993a). The covering letter from Martin Easteal, the Commission's Chief Executive, made it clear that the document embodied the methods used by the Commission in assessing costs for the unitary options considered in the first tranche review areas, and that this had been done in the absence of agreement between the counties and districts involved. In circulating the document, the Commission invited comments and suggestions for further improvements; thus, during the summer and autumn of 1993, in the run-up to the expedited review, there was a marathon series of meetings and the generation of large quantities of paper. The outcome was a revised version, which was circulated in December; by now, the document exceeded 100 pages in length (Ernst & Young 1993b).

But that was not the end of the story. Both the ACC and the ADC had pressed all along that the Ernst & Young model should be tested against 'real' situations using actual employment data: the nearest analogues suitable for testing the unitary options were the Metropolitan districts; but the model should also be tested by seeing how well it predicted actual staffing levels in two-tier county areas. The consultants and the Commission resisted this proposal. Consequently, the county treasurers undertook their own examination, to compare the model's predictions with the realities of the Metropolitan districts and of the two-tier structure in shire England. Results from this exercise were available by the end of January 1994. Taking an average two-tier county with its districts, it was found that the model

gave a very reasonable approximation to the actual staff total, with an under-estimate of 3.7 per cent. But this was on the assumption that indirect staff accounted
for 10 per cent of the total staff. If in fact the indirect staff in the existing two-tier
average county were only 9 per cent instead of 10 per cent, the model over-pre-
dicted total staff by 7 per cent; if in reality indirect staff accounted for 11 per cent
of the total, the model under-predicted by 12.5 per cent. Given that the whole exercise was to ascertain differences between the existing situation and hypothetical
unitary structures, even an error as low as 3.7 per cent could have a significant
impact on the costings; at its simplest, such an error would imply that the indirect
staff of proposed unitary authorities would be under-estimated by 3.7 per cent,
giving them a head start in the comparison with the existing actual situation.
Equally important, it is evident that the staff estimates derived from the model are
very sensitive to the assumptions made about the proportion of the total staff classified as indirect.

Even greater problems emerged when the model was run for an average Metropolitan district, on the assumption of 10 per cent indirect staff. The model gave
an under-prediction of 43 per cent compared with the actual number. Since these
authorities have strong similarities with the big cities, in terms of total population,
dense urban populations and the range of socio-economic problems loosely associated with the 'inner city', it seemed clear that the Ernst & Young model was in
danger of giving seriously erroneous estimates for the staff needs of proposed big
city unitary authorities (Sumby 1994).

That these concerns were well founded was clearly demonstrated by an analysis that was made of the material included in the submissions of eighteen county
areas whose documents had to be lodged with the Commission by 8 April 1994.
For individual county areas, the local authorities included in their papers their own
estimates of the number of indirect staff. Summing the figures for the county and
its districts in each county area, and then comparing those totals with figures for
all staff obtained from *Staffing Watch*, the average for all the eighteen counties was
12.37 per cent indirect staff, ranging from 8.94 per cent in Staffordshire to 16.71
per cent in Surrey. On the face of it, there is indeed considerable variation in the
proportion of staff categorised as indirect, with the implication that to assume a
uniform 10 per cent would introduce serious errors.

The differences identified above reflect the complex interplay of many factors.
However, the root of the problem lay with the assumption in the Ernst & Young
model that every authority spends at, or very near, its Standard Spending Assessment (SSA). This assumption introduced two separate and serious difficulties.
First, while very few councils were spending significantly below SSA, there were
some that exceeded their assessed sum, an excess that would be reflected in their
indirect staffing levels. Second, the whole of the SSA allocation system is riddled
with illogicalities and cannot realistically be taken as an aggregate measurement
of need to spend (Flowerdew *et al.* 1994; Rita Hale & Associates 1996, 1998).

The Commission did accept that re-calibration was necessary and for each
review area the model was adjusted to the datum of indirect staff in the area,

though remember that this 'actual' figure was itself somewhat problematic. However, the Ernst & Young model had been designed to assess proposals for all-unitary solutions for a whole county area. Further complications were therefore introduced in adapting it to assess costs and savings for hybrid areas – a unitary city, for example, and no change elsewhere. Consequently, during the expedited review, some adjustments were made to the costings, Derbyshire being a case in point. At the draft recommendation stage of the second review, the Commission estimated that a unitary Derby City and no change elsewhere would alter the annual ongoing costs somewhere in the range of from £2 million extra costs to £2 million savings: at the time of the final recommendations, these figures had been amended to £3 million additional expenses and £1 million reduced expenditure (LGCE 1994, 1995b).

Another bone of contention was that of scale economies. The 1992 *Policy Guidance* (para. 2.9) asked the Commission to identify the economies and diseconomies of scale in different structural options. The Ernst & Young (1993a) model for costings, used in the first tranche reviews, incorporated the concept that larger authorities reap certain cost advantages by virtue of their size. Nevertheless, Banham acknowledged publicly that the model appeared to be biased, by under-stating the costs of running a small unitary authority. During the summer of 1993, considerable further effort was put into refining the model to remove such biases as existed. Apart from the practical problems of incorporating the scale effect to obtain unbiased estimates as the basis for decision making, note also the implications for the statement made in the *Guidance* (para. 10) that: 'There need be no maximum or minimum size for the area or population covered by a unitary authority.'

This brief account of the process of costing change makes one or two things clear. At the start of the review in 1992, the Commission had only the haziest idea of what the costing data would show. By the time draft recommendations for the first tranche had to be formulated, the picture had become a good deal clearer, but throughout the remainder of the review there was still plenty of scope for the costings in each county area to be altered significantly by the nature and extent of any re-calibration that might take place. The fact of this evolution of costing methodology as the review was in progress contributed to the uncertainties that surrounded the whole operation. The whole task had been an inherently contentious exercise which 'turned out to be a considerably more difficult problem than had been expected' (LGCE 1993, para. 92).

*Evolving estimates of the costs and benefits of change*

At the beginning of the review process, the ADC and most districts believed that a district-based unitary structure would be cheaper than the existing two-tier arrangements and would therefore fully justify the transition costs (ADC 1990, pp. 23–4). As the costing work progressed during the first tranche reviews, that position became harder to maintain, except possibly in the highly urbanised counties of Avon and Cleveland.

Despite the amount of work devoted to estimating the recurrent costs and benefits of change, it was the cost of transition which attracted considerable publicity. The estimates made at various points in the review were based on differing assumptions and therefore are not strictly comparable; care is consequently needed in interpreting the data in Table 4.1. The earliest estimates, the 1992 ACC figures, were not widely circulated, perhaps because the counties regarded even the high assessment as too low to serve their cause. It was not until the autumn of 1993 that two estimates for the over-all cost of change for shire England became publicly available. The DoE had set up a Local Government Restructuring Finance sub-group on which county and district representatives sat. In the autumn of 1993, this sub-group received two documents which were intended to help the DoE in assessing the likely costs of change if the whole of England went unitary, using as their basis the emerging pattern from the first tranche reviews. Of course, the figures were made public but it was the counties' figure of £1.1 billion for transition costs which hit the headlines. However, with the December 1993 publication of the Commission's *Progress Report*, support was lent to the districts' somewhat lower assessment of the cost of change. Further support for the districts was forthcoming with the 1995 appearance of the Commission's report on the whole 1992–95 review process; the estimated cost of change throughout shire England had been somewhat reduced. In sharp contrast, by April 1994 the dis-

**Table 4.1**   Ex ante *estimates for aggregate transition costs in the event of all shire England becoming unitary (£ billion)*

| Date | Source | Transition cost | |
|------|--------|-----------------|---|
| August 1992 | ACC 1992, p. 4 | High (counties unitary) | 0.580 |
| | | Low (districts unitary) | 0.440 |
| Autumn 1993 | Rigg 1993 (county assessment) | | 1.100 |
| Autumn 1993 | Brooke 1993 (district assessment) | High | 0.897 |
| | | Low | 0.499 |
| | | Average | 0.698 |
| December 1993 | LGCE 1993, para. 96 | High | 0.780 |
| | | Low | 0.590 |
| April 1994 | ADC, *Local Government Chronicle*, 5 April, p. 1 | | 0.930 |
| March 1995 | LGCE 1995a, para. 178[a] | High | 0.738 |
| | | Low | 0.499 |

*Note*: [a]Figures for fifty proposed unitary authorities multiplied up for all shire England in proportion to population. Includes hybrid structures, for which transition costs differ from those for country-wide unitary solutions.

tricts' own assessment of transition costs had risen sharply and was only about 15 per cent below the counties' figure of £1.1 billion, leaving the Commission's estimates as the apparent anomaly, with distinctly lower figures.

Apart from the Commission's own work, it appears that only one over-all assessment of the probable ongoing costs and savings of a unitary structure was prepared, by the ACC in its 1992 document. The association estimated that a county-based system of unitary authorities would save £720 million annually, whereas a district-based structure would incur extra annual spending of £780 million. As a comparison with those figures, a tabulation has been made from the Commission's reports regarding the transition costs on the one hand and the ongoing costs and savings on the other expected to follow from the final recommendations forwarded to the Secretary of State, not all of which were implemented (Table 4.2).

Four counties in the first tranche have become all unitary – Avon, Cleveland, Humberside and the Isle of Wight – and for these cases the Commission estimated clear-cut savings which would fully justify the transition costs within a relatively short time. As a result of the accelerated review, the Commission recommended an all-unitary solution in four cases – Bedfordshire, Berkshire, Buckinghamshire and Dorset – of which only Berkshire actually became entirely unitary. For these four counties, it was estimated that there would be higher annual costs on a permanent basis, so that the cost of change would never be recouped. Elsewhere,

**Table 4.2** Ex ante *estimates accepted by the Local Government Commission for aggregate transition and ongoing costs/savings for unitary authorities (£ million)*

| | Ongoing costs/savings | | | | Transition costs | |
| --- | --- | --- | --- | --- | --- | --- |
| | Costs | | Savings | | | |
| | Low | High | Low | High | Low | High |
| Tranche 1: four all-unitary county areas implemented | | | 26.8 | 45.8 | 48.7 | 68.7 |
| Expedited review recommendations:[a] | | | | | | |
| all unitary | 8 | 18 | 3 | | 43.0 | 55.0 |
| hybrid | 3 | 38 | 9 | | 45.0 | 80.0 |
| Re-review recommendations implemented[b] | 6.7 | 44.5 | 5.2 | | 23.6 | 40.1 |

*Source*: LGCE (1997).

*Notes*: [a] Includes counties re-reviewed.

[b] See text for revised definition of transition costs.

hybrid solutions were recommended, with the strong balance of probability that ongoing costs would be higher than under the two-tier system, so that the cost of change would not be recovered. A similar assessment was made by the Commission in the 1995 review for those authorities proposed for unitary status with the remainder of the county remaining two tier.

Judging by these figures, it is virtually certain that, had all shire England gone unitary on a district basis, the result would have been a substantial increase in the running costs of local government compared with the no-change option. That was certainly the view which the Commission itself had reached by the end of the first tranche reviews:

> As a result of the detailed work done on indirect costs in each review area, it is clear to the Commission that a district-based unitary structure would be significantly more costly than the present two-tier structure. Therefore the transitional costs of moving to such a structure would never be recovered. At the other end of the scale, a single authority for the whole of an existing county area would be by far the most cost-effective solution in terms of overhead expenditure. In general, the Commission has found that the break-even point on indirect costs would be a unitary structure which would replace the existing structure of county plus district councils with about half the number of authorities. (LGCE 1993, para. 94)

Thus, on the basis of the first tranche studies, the Commission had confirmed the estimate made by the ACC the previous year that a district based solution would not be cost-effective and that the cheapest structure would indeed be based on counties. The Commission went on to observe that transition costs are difficult to estimate and that previous experience suggests they tend to be under-estimated.

During the review, there was some convergence between the ACC and ADC positions regarding transition costs. The ADC's opening case was that these would not be huge but with its £0.930 billion estimate in May 1994 it was within 20 per cent of the upwardly revised ACC figure of £1.1 billion. There was no such meeting of minds with regard to recurrent costs and savings. The submissions made by the counties and districts in the first tranche reviews are illustrated by the following aggregate figures for four county areas, for which twenty-five unitary authorities had been proposed – in effect, district-based unitary authorities. The districts themselves claimed annual savings of £23 million, whereas the counties argued that costs would rise by £46 million (Ernst & Young 1993a, p. 1). That relationship can be compared with evidence from the accelerated review. For twenty-four county areas, where estimates were made for identical sub-county unitary structures, the effect of which would have been to reduce the number of authorities from 199 to 117–22, or about 60 per cent, the competing cost estimates were as follows. In the case of transition costs, the estimates were reasonably close at £453 million on the districts' figuring and £574 million on the counties'. For recurrent expenditure, though, the comparable figures were an aggregate annual saving of £184 million according to the districts and additional expenditure of £105 million if the counties' estimates were accepted.

On the basis of the Commission's own assessment of ongoing costs and savings in relation to transition costs, there was little doubt that for unitary structures to be 'cost effective over time' the number of authorities would have to be reduced from the present number, to half or below. But, as we shall see in Chapter 7, the Commission's warning that actual transition costs were likely to exceed the *ex ante* estimates has in fact been borne out, and by a considerable margin above even the highest of the figures made public during the review. As for the conflicts of evidence about recurrent costs, at the time of writing it is still too early to make a full assessment. However, such evidence as there is suggests that the savings envisaged as a result of structural change have not matched the ADC's expectations.

### The 1995 re-review

The reconstituted Commission under the chairmanship of Sir David Cooksey was faced with a very tight timetable for conducting the further review of twenty-one authorities, to decide whether any or all of them should be recommended for unitary status in the manner that some cities such as Southampton and Nottingham had been, with the remainder of the county keeping the two-tier structure. Partly because time was pressing, partly because of the difficulties encountered previously in working along the lines of the Ernst & Young model, and partly on account of the nature of the task in hand, the Commission chose to approach the cost aspect of its work in a radically different way. The counties which might lose one or more districts were asked to calculate the transition costs they would have to meet and the magnitude of the subsequent *reduction* in indirect costs once they no longer provided services for the district(s) which might gain unitary status. Similarly, the districts were asked for their assessments of the transition costs they would face and the *increase* in indirect ongoing costs once they had taken over the county's functions. Once these estimates had been submitted, the timetable provided one week in which counties could comment on the districts' figures and vice versa. The Audit Commission was asked to examine the submissions, not so much to verify them as to make adjustments for consistency and to ascertain their 'reasonableness'. Given that clearance, the Commission obtained the aggregate figures for each review by adding the county and district estimates for transition costs and likewise adding the assessments of ongoing costs and savings to obtain a net ongoing cost/saving (LGCE 1995c, 1995d and 1995e). The merit of this approach is its simplicity but the Audit Commission's examination allowed considerable latitude in the interpretation of 'reasonable'. Summary data for the estimates accepted by the Commission are given in Table 4.2.

An important point to note is that the transition costs used for the 1995 re-review exclude some items which were included in the main review under redundancy costs; *all* redundancy, early retirement and other staff compensation costs were *excluded* from the 1995 analysis. This means that the transition cost figures are not comparable with the figures from the earlier review, and that the costs are significantly under-stated.

A further feature of the 1995 re-review is of some interest. The DoE had by this time become concerned about the mismatch between the transition costs which were estimated by authorities as part of their evidence to the Commission and the sums that were subsequently requested from the DoE for assistance with reorganisation costs where structural change occurred. Consequently, in making its recommendations the Commission was asked: 'To relate its estimates to the categories set out in the Department's arrangements for transition costs circulated on 2 December 1994' (DoE 1995, Annex A, para. 4). Clearly, the Department felt the need to put pressure on the system to limit the temptation for districts to propose unrealistically low transition costs and high recurrent savings, and for the counties to do the reverse.

Table 4.2 shows that the most optimistic assessment by the Commission was for annual savings of £5.2 million but with the possibility that ongoing costs would be increased by as much as £44.5 million. The balance of probabilities was evident, that reorganisation would increase rather than reduce local government costs. That assessment may be explored somewhat further by an examination of estimates which the counties made of their own costs and savings as compared with the estimates which the districts offered for those same costs and savings, and the symmetrical comparison of the districts' costs and savings as perceived by the districts and the counties. This comparison can be made for fifteen of the districts involved in the re-review and the aggregate figures are shown in Table 4.3. From this table, we can see that the counties and the districts came forward with very different figures for the costs of transition. Broadly speaking, the county figures are about twice those estimated by the districts; the two sides were as far apart at the end of the review as they had been earlier, if not further. In contrast, there was reasonable agreement regarding the reduction in the ongoing costs for the counties which would follow from the transfer of services to the districts; but that agreement did not apply to assessments regarding the increased costs that would

**Table 4.3**    *1995 re-review, fifteen districts in England: aggregates of estimated transition and ongoing costs (+) and savings (–) (£ million)*

|  | Counties | | Districts | |
| --- | --- | --- | --- | --- |
|  | *Own estimates* | *As estimated by districts* | *Own estimates* | *As estimated by counties* |
| Transition costs | +28.2 | +16.8 | +18.0 | +35.0 |
| Annual ongoing costs | –73.0 | –89.1/–83.3 | +92.2 | +124.8 |

*Source*: LGCE (1998).

*Note*: The figures are aggregates for fifteen districts for which comparable data are available. These are the submitted figures as adjusted by the Audit Commission. One district gave a range for the estimated annual savings for the relevant county.

face those districts on taking over the county functions. Perhaps the most interesting feature of this table is that, irrespective of the differences between the county and district estimates, the districts expected that reorganisation would add to costs and not yield long-term savings; the districts' own estimate of extra costs of £92.2 million each year would not be offset by their own figuring of the savings they expected the counties to make – savings which would not exceed £89.1 million annually. This is in marked contrast to the assessments made by the ADC and by individual districts early in the review, that a district-based structure of local government would yield annual savings fully sufficient to justify the cost of reorganisation.

## Conclusion

One of the oddities about the literature which has previously been published on the review in England is the minimal reference to the problems of evaluating the costs and benefits of change and the impact which the findings had on the thinking of the Commission. All through 1992–95, a serious and sustained attempt was made to address the evaluation of costs in a rational manner. To suggest, as Leach (1997) has done, that rationality ceased to characterise the Commission's work after the first tranche of reviews had been completed does less than justice to the work on costs, however imperfect that work may have been.

As the costing work progressed, it became clear that a universal district-based pattern of unitary authorities would undoubtedly cost more than the two-tier system. In order for a unitary structure to break even, the evidence showed that the number of authorities (counties plus districts) would have to be reduced by at least half. It also became clear that hybrid solutions would involve a small increase in annual costs, rather than a reduction. In making a judgement about appropriate structures, the costing evidence had to be weighed against the potential benefits of improved community identity, a matter to which we shall turn in Chapter 5. The evolving evidence on costs also had its impact on the thinking of the DoE.

As already noted, the 1992 *Policy Guidance* clearly expected that a structural change to unitary authorities should not incur higher costs and should in all probability lead to administrative savings. The Commission itself was: 'Not willing to put forward solutions that will cost significantly more than the present arrangements unless there are exceptional circumstances' (LGCE 1993, para. 95).

The revised *Guidance* issued in 1993 had contained some changes of wording which have been little remarked but which deserve to be noted. On costs, a new sentence was added, to the effect that the Commission: 'Is not precluded from recommending an option which would be marginally more expensive than the status quo if the extra cost would be outweighed by other considerations' (DoE 1993, para. 9). This amounted to a relaxation of the guidance for solutions to be 'cost effective over time'. This relaxation was taken a good deal further with the *Guidance* issued for the 1995 re-review. Having stated that a unitary structure can secure better coordination of services, the text continues by saying that: 'In some cases it can also result in reduced costs and bureaucracy' (para. 8). The document goes on:

> In relation to each review area, the Commission will need to seek and consider evidence on the costs and benefits of change (including both transitional and on-going costs and benefits) and set its conclusions in the context of this evidence ... It should provide in its reports an assessment of the quantifiable and non-quantifiable costs and benefits of change. (DoE 1995, para. 22)

This form of words sharply reduces the significance of costs and savings in the assessment of options, a change of status which is underlined by the absence of any reference to compiling costs and benefits over a fifteen-year period and applying to these tabulations a 6 per cent discount rate in a form of cost–benefit analysis, as specified in the 1992 *Guidance*. Responding to this shift in emphasis on the part of Government, the Commission in its advice to respondents for the 1995 re-reviews remarked that: 'It is open to the Commission to recommend an option that would be more expensive than the present arrangements if it believes that other considerations outweigh cost' (LGCE 1995e, para. 23).

The implication is beyond dispute. By 1995, the Government recognised that if the Commission were to be able to recommend any additional unitary authorities from among the twenty-one sent to it for re-review, this could only be done by increasing the cost of local government. The careful but deliberate rhetoric of 1992, which seemed *simultaneously* to promise both greater community identity and improved cost effectiveness as a result of structural change, had been quietly buried.

# 5

# Services, communities and public opinion

'Don't shoot the messenger.' Or: 'Nobody likes the man who brings bad news.'
(Sophocles, *Antigone*)

The previous chapter examined the problems of estimating the costs and benefits of structural change and it is now time to turn to other and related matters which were relevant, not only for the LGCE but also for the reviews in Scotland and Wales. Most of the material to be examined will be concerned with England, largely because there is a much bigger corpus of information than for the other two countries. However, in the case of both service provision and community identity, the issues were very similar across Great Britain and to avoid needless repetition material other than that which relates to England will be incorporated as appropriate. In contrast, though, the relevance of public opinion must be considered separately in each of the three countries; England will be discussed in the present chapter, while consideration of Scotland and Wales will be deferred to Chapter 6.

Some aspects of services have already been discussed in Chapter 4, at an aggregate level and concentrating on the central administration costs which might vary with different structures of local government. Thus the first section seeks to go rather further than we have done so far, to examine the evidence, both that which was offered in the review process and that which is otherwise available, regarding the probable impact of structural change on service delivery. We will then consider the issue of community identity, which was given prominence in the 1992 Act and also in the *Guidance* issued to the Local Government Commission, and the reactions of those who 'may be interested' in reform proposals; that is, public opinion.

## Services

The Commission was advised to assume that the standard and quality of services would not be affected by structural change, so that the main costing issue was focused on the circa 10 per cent of expenditure represented by central overhead costs. Similar assumptions were made in Scotland and Wales. The merit of this approach was that it eliminated from consideration the infinite possible range of proposals from existing and aspirant authorities regarding the ways in which they might reorganise front-line services in education, housing, social services, and so on. On the other hand, simplification of the problem in this way had the potential to hide significant impacts on service delivery, and a good deal of evidence and opinion was forthcoming on these matters.

As context, though, we need to bear in mind that the National Health Service and Community Care Act 1990 became fully operational on 1 April 1993. This Act transferred from the Health Service to local authority social services departments responsibility for the care of people entering private and voluntary residential and nursing homes and introduced the Care in the Community initiative. The associated transfer of funding represented a 32 per cent increase in the 1992/3 budgets of social services departments in England (Wistow *et al.* 1994, pp. 1–2). Consequently, these departments were under enormous pressure at the time local government structure was being considered, a fact which necessarily complicated any assessment of the potential impact of changing the local authority map.

### Economies of scale

In the early 1990s, it was widely assumed that if there were any economies of scale in service provision, they applied to the private sector firms from which local authorities were already buying services, or soon would be; consequently, the size of local authorities was not a material consideration. Despite the rhetoric of the 'enabling authority', in the early 1990s the significance of these external markets was in fact still comparatively modest. For example, in England in 1990/1, the expenditure of social services departments in the private and voluntary sectors amounted to 6.4 per cent of their total spending; the proportion was marginally lower in the shire counties, at 5.4 per cent (Wistow *et al.* 1994, p. 41). By the middle of the decade, Compulsory Competitive Tendering in Scotland affected 20 per cent of staff but just 10 per cent of expenditure (Midwinter and McGarvey 1995, p. 5). These figures are consistent with the view that in Wales the enabling role was 'secondary' to mainline activities (Boyne 1992). Consequently, at the time of the review it was quite clear that the direct provision of services remained an extremely important function of local authorities and could not be dismissed as of little concern for the consideration of structure.

In any case, from the very beginning of the review the Home Office made it clear that it at least was not persuaded of the irrelevance of scale. Both the police and fire services were protected from the review throughout Great Britain, as was made particularly clear in the *Guidance* given to the Commission. In respect of the police, it was stated that 'police forces would not be viable for areas smaller than their present boundaries'; the position for the fire services was stated to be that 'the optimum size of fire brigades is considerably larger than that of some district councils which may ... become unitary authorities' (DoE 1992b, Annex B, paras

32 and 33). For both these services, if the counties were broken up into unitary authorities there would have to be joint authorities to oversee them. Furthermore, the DoE also specifically drew attention to land use planning and transport as being matters that needed to be handled over areas that would exceed the territories of individual authorities and which would therefore need some form of cooperative working (the implicit assumption seems to have been that unitary councils would be based on districts). The force of these observations was subsequently underlined by the removal of trunk roads from the control of the new authorities established from 1996 in Scotland.

Similar governmental concerns were expressed for other services during the review. When the Commission published its draft recommendations for an area, the DoE undertook a consultation exercise within Government and then conveyed the reactions back to the Commission. An example is provided by a letter written in August 1994 reporting the results of the consultation on eleven sets of draft recommendations which had been published two months previously, many of which expressed a preference for unitary solutions:

> Concern was expressed that the reports do not explain clearly enough the impact of proposals on service provision, particularly in relation to the present county-level functions. Concerns have been expressed to us about public libraries, museums, arts services, trading standards and food law enforcement – and also the impact of the reorganisation on current local authority relations with other organisations eg the NHS. I am sure that these considerations have all been taken into account, but the final report should make clear how you see any difficulties being overcome and indicate where the scope for co-operative arrangements may need to be explored. (DoE 1994)

Thus from quite early on there was a clear contradiction in the posture of the Government; while scale economies in general were discounted, they were regarded as important with respect to certain services. In addition, as we have already seen for England and will identify in both Scotland and Wales, even the restricted examination of costs which focused on overheads very quickly revealed that there are some economies of scale for local authorities, such that a district-based solution would be more expensive, whereas unitary authorities at the scale of whole counties would save money.

In June 1993, Travers *et al.* published a study which endorsed the then conventional wisdom that scale economies for mainline services could not be detected, declaring that their existence was unproven. This report could easily be read to support the view that the size of an authority is not relevant in considering the structure of local government; that certainly was the interpretation placed on it when a pre-publication copy was circulated among Commissioners.

Examination of this study and of others shows a fundamental problem of research design in almost all the published cases (Boyne 1995). Many of the studies had adopted a univariate design, relating the chosen dependent variable (usually unit costs) to just one independent factor, normally the population size of authorities. Such a strategy ignores a whole host of factors that have a bearing on the cost of service delivery, including the quality of the service, the socio-economic circumstances of an authority and the sparsity/density of the population. Boyne is also critical of the general assumption that the statistical relationships are linear, ignoring the possibility that they may be U-shaped.

Boyne makes two distinctions which help to explain the indeterminacy of the evidence. By analogy with business studies, he points out that a local authority may be regarded as a firm, while the individual service units constitute the plants which comprise that firm. For some local authorities, unit costs are high because service delivery points are scattered and small, as with primary schools in sparsely inhabited rural areas; this does not mean that the local authority is inefficient. Some of these operational differences are captured in the SSA assessments and hence in central government revenue support grants and total expenditure, with an impact on unit costs averaged across an authority. Even if population size has little effect on the technical efficiency of service delivery within an authority, there may be other forms of efficiency which are associated with size, of which two are particularly relevant in the present context: redistributive policies within an authority and external bargaining costs. Small authorities will have little scope for the internal reallocation of resources; in addition, with many small authorities there will be higher transaction costs with external agencies, such costs being borne either by the local authorities or dispersed among the bodies with which they do business. In other words, the research problem is formidably difficult and Boyne comes to an unequivocal conclusion, as follows: 'Thus the new orthodoxy that there are no scale effects on local service delivery is unfounded and has no more empirical support than the old orthodoxy that large authorities are more efficient' (Boyne 1995, p. 221).

In this context, it is clear that something may be learned from the testimony that was received by the Commission during the years of the review, and it is to that body of information which we now turn, being the material submitted by national and regional organisations representing many of the professional interests concerned with local government. No equivalent distillation has been published for Scotland and Wales, though it seems clear that the messages conveyed were very similar.

Early in the review, the Audit Commission had taken the view that 'a district-based structure would be unlikely to be the best solution in terms of economy, efficiency and effectiveness' (LGCE 1995a, para. 74). More generally, the responses showed the following:

> There was a recurring anxiety that any new unitary authorities should be big enough to take a strategic view without which some functions of local government could never be effectively or conveniently performed. There was also anxiety that any division of existing county services would be detrimental. Since county councils account for nearly 70 per cent of local authority gross revenue expenditure and around 75 per cent of local authority staffing [in shire areas], it is hardly surprising that most of these views were concerned with the possible break-up of existing

county services. This led respondents to conclude either that the present two-tier structure should be retained, or that a unitary structure should comprise a small number of relatively large unitary authorities to replace a county council. (LGCE 1995a, para. 75)

The submission of the Joint Care Council was particularly interesting. The Council wrote on behalf of the four national associations of independent nursing home and residential care providers. It argued that:

> A move to a larger number of social services authorities would multiply community care plans, liaison and administration, and weaken efforts to achieve consistent and co-ordinated approaches to contracts, registration and other functions. The viability of the many small providers in the independent sector would be vulnerable to the additional transaction costs, which might also divert purchasing funds away from direct care provision. (LGCE 1995a, para. 103)

Clearly, it was deeply concerned by the external transaction costs identified by Boyne. The Trading Standards Administration went so far as to argue that there are scale economies in its field up to two million population, and that even county councils were finding it increasingly difficult to provide an effective service.

While some of the concerns contained in the submissions to the Commission could be dismissed as the special pleading of directly interested parties, many of the documents came from organisations whose members had no direct stake in employment by existing councils. There is in any case some corroborating evidence from the Department of Health, which was concerned about the potential impact on social services where structural change was taking place or would occur. To illustrate the scale of the task facing those in charge of the incoming authorities, the Department itemised the typical numbers of various client groups for an authority with a population of 200,000. While this figure was obviously used for illustrative purposes, by clear implication it was also used as a yardstick for judging what a 'smaller' authority might be. Below the suggested figure, an authority, lacking the necessary resources and expertise, would, in the judgement of the Department, have to enter into joint or collaborative ventures, the difficulties of which were emphasised (Department of Health 1996, paras 1.9, 2.14 and 2.15).

In the light of the above evidence, it seems more likely rather than less that there really are significant economies of scale in service delivery and that these were recognised at the time of the review within the Government and by those submitting evidence to the Commission. Such a conclusion is consistent with research findings for the education sector and for library services which became available in 1993 and 1994 (Midwinter and McGarvey 1994; Midwinter and McVicar 1993). It is also consistent with the evidence discussed in papers given to a 1995 seminar on the implications of reorganisation in Scotland for service delivery, a seminar which took place after the future shape of local government was known. Many of the papers on particular services expressed concerns about the probable impact of fragmenting the arrangements for service provision in

Scotland, echoing the concerns which were transmitted to the LGCE (Black 1995).

## Joint arrangements

In its *Guidance* to the Commission, the DoE clearly envisaged that unitary structures might be proposed in which the satisfactory discharge of functions could only be achieved if local authorities entered into joint arrangements with other councils, though ministers recognised the potential for problems with such arrangements: 'The Commission should consider recommending shared arrangements for some functions if a satisfactory structure seems unlikely to be achieved without them. Joint authorities do not benefit from the same direct accountability as individual authorities and a structure which does not require them is therefore to be preferred' (DoE 1992a, para. 14). Similar reservations were expressed in the Scottish and Welsh contexts, as noted in Chapter 6.

This recognition that a move to unitary authorities might imply the need for joint arrangements carried three sets of implications. In the first place, it laid a heavy qualification on the concept that there are no significant scale economies and hence on the idea that there need be no minimum size for local authorities. Second, it placed an onerous and impractical duty on the Commission: given the time and resources available, it was not possible systematically to examine the main services in each area and develop considered recommendations for joint arrangements in possible unitary structures. Third, the greater the number of joint arrangements that might be needed, the greater the dilution of accountability, which would be contrary to one of the ostensible reasons for reorganisation.

As a longstop in all of this, the 1992 Act gives the Secretary of State certain powers to impose joint authorities in the event that a council is failing, or may fail, in the delivery of a service. However, the wording of section 21 is inadequate. The provision only applies where there has been a structural or boundary change. The provision does not apply to London, the Metropolitan councils and the shire counties, where no structural change has occurred. Nor does the Act apply in hybrid counties, since the part of the county remaining with the two-tier structure is an area where no structural change has occurred, so that no direction can be given for joint service arrangements with a unitary authority (Chisholm 1995, pp. 565–6). This problem was first identified by Chisholm, who discussed it with Archie Gall at the Commission and, through him, the Treasury Solicitor who acted for the Commission. An analytical document was sent to the DoE in December 1994 but it was not until July 1995 that the Government acknowledged that the Act, despite its intentions, is a very limited instrument for imposing joint authorities. However, the key point is that the Government sought to make provision for the contingency that joint arrangements would be needed.

## *Overlap and coordination*

Time and again during the English review it was said that the removal of one tier of local government would eliminate the problems which arose from overlapping functions and would simultaneously provide opportunities for better coordination. In the author's experience, the two most commonly cited areas of overlap related to planning and to the respective roles of counties and districts for public health. As for the benefits of better coordination, the prime example quoted was that of housing (a district function) and social services (handled by the counties). The Scottish Office (1992a) made the same claim for housing and social services, and added leisure and recreation as a second instance. How valid were these claims?

Midwinter (1992) estimated that, in Scotland as a whole, the functions which overlapped between the districts and the regions accounted for 2.2 per cent of total expenditure. A separate estimate for a county and district in England put the proportion at just 1 per cent (Cheshire County Council and Congleton Borough Council 1994, para. 3). These figures are somewhat less than the range of 3.0 per cent to 6.0 per cent suggested by Chisholm (1995, p. 568), but even these higher figures still represent a very small proportion of total expenditure, suggesting that problems of overlap were not really that great. With respect to public health matters, the Institute of Trading Standards pointed out that of the seventy Acts relevant for county operations only one concerned the environmental health officers of districts (LGCE 1995a, para. 109).

The claim that unitary authorities would be able to integrate housing and social services would have been more convincing if the London boroughs and Metropolitan councils had been structured to combine these two services, but they were not. The 1993 issue of the *Municipal Yearbook* shows that, of the sixty-eight councils, fifty-five had separate directors for the two services; that is, 81 per cent of the total. In any case, the overlap of clients was actually quite small, one study showing that only 15 per cent of clients needed the services of *both* housing and social services (Cheshire County Council and Congleton Borough Council 1994, para. 19). This limited scope for coordination need occasion no surprise when it is remembered that people live in a diversity of accommodation: their own homes or with family members; renting from private landlords, local authorities or housing associations; in residential care; or are living in other circumstances. Consequently, the Chartered Institute of Housing was right to draw attention to the variety of ways in which the housing functions of councils could be combined with other responsibilities, the union with social services being just one option (LGCE 1995a, para. 82).

Planning was the other much-quoted area of dispute between districts and counties in England, also being noted by the Scottish Office (1992a). During the review of Hampshire, the author asked one district for concrete examples of the problems of working between the district and the county, not just in planning but generally. The response listed a number of specific instances, *all* of which related to planning issues. These matters of contention shared one fundamental characteristic: they were all issues in which local interests and concerns diverged from wider judgements about appropriate policies for the county as a whole. Vertical conflicts of this kind would not disappear with the creation of unitary authorities; they would change their manifestation to horizontal problems between authorities if the unitary councils were fairly small, or into problems of internal (and hence vertical) management within such councils were they to be large, or some combination of the two. The Scottish Office claim (1992a, p. 9) that in a unitary structure the planning problems of the two-tier arrangements would be 'eliminated' was nonsense.

When the GLC and the Metropolitan counties were abolished, considerable fragmentation of local administration occurred, and the post-abolition experience of joint working does not suggest that the new arrangements were a marked improvement on the previous county administration. In London, four issues have been particularly noted: transport and traffic management; strategic planning; catering for the homeless; and the sheer complexity of the bureaucracy needed to make things work (Travers *et al.* 1991). The authors concluded that matters could not be left as they were. Similar problems were identified in the former Metropolitan counties, along with the difficulties which arise from differing political control of authorities, leading to the conclusion that 'the evidence as far as the joint boards and committees is concerned is not particularly damning' (Travers *et al.* 1995, p. 45), which could be said to be damning with faint praise.

Removal of the county tier had in fact been accompanied by a significant increase in the *de facto* control of central government over the administration of the conurbations, especially in those areas of concern which are city-wide. This was particularly clear in the case of London, as recently documented by Newman and Thornley (1997), contributing to the call for an elected Assembly and also a mayor for the capital. The re-creation of an upper tier for London was put in hand by Labour following its general election victory in 1997, though the arrangements will be much scaled down from the former GLC.

During the review in England, it was clear that the creation of numerous small unitary authorities carried a serious risk that the fragmentation would lead to greater central control over councils. It was not at all evident that the benefits of removing one tier of locally elected administration would compensate for the creation of an unelected upper layer of administration, in the form of joint arrangements, and of increased central government control.

It was already apparent in the early 1990s that the world of service provision was becoming increasingly complex. For many of their activities, and especially for mainline services, local authorities were not local monopolists; they had to engage with a very large number of public and private agencies and with the public at large. An interesting study shows the scale of the network in which local authorities have to work, on the basis of assessments by a sample of three councils concerning the bodies which they regarded as *essential* players, this count providing the minimum measurement of the operational network. According to

Alexander (1991), for three councils these minimal networks comprised the following numbers of essential bodies:

A Scottish regional council                                      18
An English district council                                     15
An English district council economic development network        14

For the regional council, the constituent districts were collapsed into just one cell of the matrix identified. These figures amply confirm what was evident to many during the review, that while the removal of one tier of local government might simplify administration, the scale of that simplification would be comparatively small given the context of complex networks.

At the time of structural reform, the Government was pressing hard for the further privatisation of local government services and hence for an increase in the importance of formal contracts for the delivery of services. Drawing up and monitoring contracts is a skilled business, for which the range of prior experience is likely to be important. In principle, therefore, the quality of the contract arrangements might well be linked to the volume of contract work done by an authority and hence the reservoir of knowledge and experience. The present author concluded from this that there are likely to be some economies associated with the size of authorities and hence the volume of the contracting being undertaken, economies that would go beyond those arising from the bulk purchase of stationery, fuel, vehicles, and so on, which can be obtained by consortia of authorities operating joint purchasing arrangements. The expectation that a contract-driven system would be very complex, carrying associated costs, has been borne out by recent literature (e.g. Accounts Commission 1997; Charlesworth and Clarke 1995; Leach *et al.* 1996; Walsh *et al.* 1997; Wistow *et al.* 1994). Indeed, the very title chosen by the Accounts Commission, *The Commissioning Maze*, is evocative of the problems, while Walsh *et al.* explicitly call attention to the high cost of transactions. All of which indicates that the removal of one tier of local government might have rather little impact in raising the efficiency and effectiveness of local councils.

*Performance indicators*

With the Local Government Act 1992, a statutory duty was laid on local authorities to compile data on their performance, as specified by the Audit Commission for England and Wales and the Accounts Commission for Scotland. These data have become available since 1993/4, too late to have had any impact on the reform process. However, they do allow us to ask the following question: is there any evidence that the two-tier authorities performed less well than the London boroughs and the Metropolitan districts for the services for which they were respectively responsible? Scotland must be omitted from this comparison since the data are not comparable.

Even with that qualification, the data for England and Wales are problematic for all sorts of reasons. Boyne (1997) used the Audit Commission's 1995 publication of performance indicators and the pattern he found was clear-cut, namely that the differences in the average performance of the various classes of authority were small, much smaller than the range of performance for each class. Although Boyne does not apply a formal test, it is obvious that differences between the mean values are not statistically significant. From this, we can draw a robust negative conclusion: there is no evidence that the two-tier councils were performing less well than the London boroughs and Metropolitan districts. Deficient though the data may be, they offer no support for the assertion which was often made during the review in England that the two-tier structure had 'failed'.

## Conclusions

The framework set by the Government clearly indicated its reservations about the possibility of some services being delivered by small unitary authorities. Evidence which became available from respondents during the review pointed very clearly to the importance of local authority size for the delivery of at least some mainline services, and the LGCE itself came to the conclusion that, in general, a minimum population of 150,000 was required for a unitary council. In other words, scale economies could not be ignored, however difficult they may have been to measure.

Issues relating to service delivery, and especially to land use planning, quickly revealed the following obvious and surprise-free fact. To the extent that there was conflict between the tiers of local government, these conflicts represented differences either of interests or of political philosophy between a county and one or more of its constituent districts. These *vertical* conflicts were overt and could be fought out in an open political manner. To replace the two tiers with a large number of small unitary councils would convert the vertical disagreements into *horizontal* ones between neighbouring or nearby councils, with the potential for differences to be much more concealed and covert; some mechanism would have to be invented to achieve a resolution. If, on the other hand, the unitary authorities were to be large, the clash of priorities would largely become an *internal* matter within the authorities; some mechanism would have to be found to ensure that this was done properly, which would imply well-constructed systems of consultation and devolution. Here is a fundamental conundrum for which there is no simple answer.

The Commission very quickly discovered that for many important local authority functions, a district-based unitary structure would necessitate a significant number of joint arrangements of one kind or another, something that would inevitably incur costs and dilute accountability. With a smaller number of larger councils, forms of devolved service provision would be necessary. In both cases, the Commission itself had no power to ensure that proper solutions were found, having to content itself, in the main, with exhortation. That was another conundrum for which a simple solution was not available.

## Communities

The 1992 Act lays on the Commission a duty to consider the desirability of any change it recommends in the light of the need 'to reflect the identities and interests of local communities'. This requirement was amplified in the *Guidance* which was given to the Commission: 'The Commission should base its recommendations on communities and assess proposals from authorities, other organisations or individuals against the pattern of community identities. There will usually be widening circles of communities. The Commission should take account of the strength of identity associated with each level of community' (DoE 1992b, para. 6). Altogether, three and one half pages were devoted to spelling out the idea of a community index, which, it was suggested, the Commission should use.

From the wording of the Act, it is clear that Parliament intended the term 'community' to mean the community to which people feel they belong (the affective community); this is a radically different concept from the functional or effective community identified by commuter flows, the pattern of shopping trips, and so on, which had formed the basis for the Redcliffe-Maud and Wheatley recommendations nearly twenty-five years previously.

Anyone who knows anything about the geography of Great Britain will understand that communities defined in terms of a sense of belonging are likely to be quite small. Commissioners, dispatched to their respective English counties, quickly had this surprise-free fact confirmed for them. The Commission itself concluded that the proposed community index was of little utility and decided that the most efficient way in which to elicit the sense of belonging was to ask citizens. This was done in the first-stage polling of population samples in the review areas, before concrete proposals for local government structures were on the table for consultation. The pattern which emerged from these enquiries, undertaken by professional pollsters, was unequivocal. Many more people feel that they belong to the neighbourhood/village or town/nearest town than to either the district council or county council area (LGCE 1993, paras 80 and 81). These findings were subsequently confirmed by the fuller data obtained by MORI in the expedited review; Table 5.1 summarises the findings from all the surveys undertaken by MORI

**Table 5.1** *The sense of community identity in England*

| *Residents who felt they belonged to:* | *Very Strongly* <br> *(%)* | *Very or fairly* <br> *strongly* <br> *(%)* |
|---|---|---|
| Neighbourhood/village | 41 | 79 |
| Town/nearest town | 30 | 70 |
| District/borough/city council area | 18 | 56 |
| County council or county area | 17 | 52 |

*Source*: LGCE (1995a, p. 30).

throughout the review, the results being very similar to those obtained by the Red-cliffe-Maud Commission some twenty-five years earlier (Lord Redcliffe-Maud 1969, vol. 1, pp. 62–3).

These average figures mask some regional variations but nevertheless allow the following firm conclusion to be drawn. The strongest sense of community identity is with geographical areas which are substantially smaller than the districts which then existed, with the possible exception of clearly defined urban areas. Even then, with rare exceptions such as York, there was a manifest reluctance on the part of residents in suburbs beyond the city boundary to identify with the city.

The problem to be solved boiled down to the following: what degree of community identity could be achieved in drawing a map of local jurisdictions which would be large enough in terms of population or area to be viable? The idea that there is a pattern of 'natural communities' waiting to be discovered which could form the basis for a structure of local government proved to be an illusion. This was very clearly expressed in the conclusions reached by independent analysts of the MORI survey data, based on more than 46,000 questionnaires in over 200 districts:

> The principal implication of our analysis is that community identification, reformulated by us as 'attachment', provides a wholly inadequate basis for the construction of any feasible system of local government, at least at the levels of the presently-existing local authorities ...
>
> Our study provides powerful evidence in favour of community-based government at the parish level, but it suggests that beyond this, existing local authorities cannot claim to speak for, or embody, a larger sense of local community. Based on affective community, there is not a strong case for district- or county-based government. (Young *et al.* 1996, pp. 27-8; see also Game 1997, p. 74)

Consequently, unless unitary authorities were to be substantially smaller than districts, there was also a weak case for claiming that in general they would embody the sense of community identified in the Act.

For local government to be genuinely 'closer to the people', one must look to the internal organisation of principal authorities but the Commission had no jurisdiction in this matter, though it consistently made clear its support for fostering the role of parish and town councils. This has close parallels with the need in large cities for community-based planning at levels below that of the London boroughs (Nicholson 1996).

## Public opinion

In conducting its review of shire England, the Commission was obliged by the 1992 Act to provide information to, and to consult with, 'persons who may be interested in' proposals for an area; this obligation is made clear at three points in the Act. Consistent with this requirement was the *Guidance* issued by the DoE

(1992c), in which the importance of public opinion was underlined by reference to the encouragement of publicity in the media and, if necessary, formal opinion polling. The clear intention was that the process should be open and that it should be 'owned' by the citizens affected. This stance stands in stark contrast to the procedures adopted in Scotland and Wales (Chapter 6).

Throughout the review, the Commission took considerable pains to ensure that there was media publicity for the local reviews as they progressed, and by any reasonable standards those efforts must be judged a success; the files of newspaper cuttings and transcripts of television coverage were copious. Copies of draft recommendations and final recommendations were placed on public deposit and Commissioners held a large number of meetings with voluntary organisations, church groups, public figures, and so on. Formal polling was undertaken of sample populations in the review areas on behalf of the Commission. In addition, during the first tranche reviews, public meetings were organised by the Commission following the publication of draft recommendations, along with a limited leaflet distribution with the invitation to complete and return the tear-off slip recording opinions on the options put forward. These latter arrangements were modified for the accelerated review. The public meetings organised by the Commission were not repeated, partly because of the constraint of time and partly because the meetings held in the first tranche counties had proved to be a questionable way of gauging local opinion; there were clear indications that some meetings had been deliberately packed by supporters of a particular option. Nevertheless, public meetings were held which Commissioners did attend. To compensate for the reduced exposure of Commissioners, households received leaflets devised by the Commission and delivered by the Royal Mail, inviting responses which were then analysed by NOP. Though some mistakes occurred in the delivery of leaflets, the vast majority reached their intended destinations. The bald statistics for this unprecedented consultation programme are contained in the 1993 and 1995a publications of the Commission.

The first tranche public meetings were often bruising experiences for Commissioners. In many cases, it was clear that those actively opposed to the draft recommendations for the area had ensured a high turnout, so the atmosphere could be hostile. For the author, an abiding feature of the public meetings, of meetings with the voluntary sector and with others, was the cynicism expressed concerning the utility of the consultation process. Time and again, the view was expressed that whatever was said at the meetings or put in writing would have no impact on the final decision by the Commission, so that the consultation was regarded as a charade. When it was patiently explained that this was not the case, which was much easier once the review had progressed far enough for it to be possible to point to cases where the Commission had changed its mind, many individuals opined that whatever the Commission itself might think was immaterial, since the Government would impose its own wishes anyway. For many people, it was difficult to believe that the Act left the Secretary of State with limited discretion to modify recommendations, and that otherwise he had either to accept them or reject them.

This misapprehension, it must be said, was shared by some MPs (Chisholm 1997) and, according to an informant, even by ministers. In other words, it was quite clear that the currency of public discourse had been seriously devalued before the review had commenced. The Commission, to its credit, responded to the criticisms of structural proposals which were voiced. Regrettably, as Chapter 6 shows, ministers for Scotland and Wales chose to ignore important parts of the responses to the much more limited consultations in which they engaged, calling in question the purpose of the consultation exercises in those countries.

The Royal Mail household leaflet drop resulted in an 8 per cent response overall, or at least 10,000 for each county. In addition, there were several thousand individually written letters and other communications. These responses were analysed by NOP on behalf of the Commission, while in parallel a representative sample of some 1,200–1,500 residents in each county was polled by MORI. The key findings from this mass of information were made public in the two review documents published by the Commission (LGCE 1993, 1995a), and further details may be found in Game (1997). When faced with the abstract question of whether one or two tiers of local government should cover the respondent's area, those who supported the unitary concept outnumbered those in favour of two tiers by a margin of about 2:1. However, that support for the unitary concept did not translate into the endorsement of particular unitary structures when options were put forward converting concept into practice, as shown by Table 5.2.

In this table, the column for unitary structures records the aggregation of support for the unitary options put forward, which varied in number; consequently, the support for any one structure would be less than the figures shown. The modified two-tier column records support for what otherwise came be known as the

**Table 5.2**   *Responses to the Local Government Commission on structural options*
*(% support)*

|  | Unitary structures | Modified two tier | No change | Other and do not know |
|---|---|---|---|---|
| Accelerated review, direct responses, NOP analysis |  |  |  |  |
| Individuals | 32 | 22 | 40 | 6 |
| Businesses | 36 | 9 | 38 | 17 |
| Local councils | 21 | 19 | 52 | 8 |
| Local groups | 22 | 10 | 49 | 19 |
| National and regional groups | 11 | 9 | 46 | 34 |
| Schools and church groups | 6 | 4 | 79 | 11 |
| Total | 32 | 22 | 40 | 6 |
| All MORI polling of individuals | 27 | 11 | 38 | 24 |

*Source*: LGCE (1995a pp. 63–4).

'hybrid solutions', in which one or two authorities would become unitary councils while the remainder of the county stayed two-tier. Responses obtained during the accelerated review are sub-divided by category of respondent. Of the 1,293,382 responses analysed, 99 per cent came from individuals, dominantly as the return of the Royal Mail leaflets. The other 1 per cent of responses consisted of 11,908 submissions by various organisations. One of the striking features of the table is the fact that the direct responses of individuals were in line with the responses received from the various groups. Business groups were the most sympathetic to the unitary options put forward but even then the aggregate support for these options was only 36 per cent, with 47 per cent supporting no change or the modi-fied two tier. Among the individuals who responded, almost two-thirds wanted the status quo to be maintained or for it to be modified into the hybrid solution. In gen-eral, the MORI polling produced similar results, but with a larger proportion of respondents in the 'other and do not know' category. In sum, the Commission was left in little doubt in most areas that there was little support for the radical re-struc-turing of local government: 'In county after county the commissioners were con-fronted with apparently incontrovertible evidence of the slippage between people's majority support for the principle of unitary authorities in the stage one community identity surveys and their lack of enthusiasm for specific unitary struc-tures' (Game 1997, p. 85).

Unprecedented in its scale and scope, the consultation yielded pretty clear results and certainly had a major impact on the thinking of the Commission as it formulated its recommendations through 1993, 1994 and into January 1995. When it came to the re-review of twenty-one councils, conducted in the second half of 1995, the advice which was issued to the Commission placed less empha-sis on the sense of affective community and rather more on the functional, or effective, concept of communities. In any case, these areas were mainly reason-ably distinct settlements. Public opinion was a less significant factor, though far from negligible.

An imponderable in the weighing of public opinion was the impact of the cam-paigns which were waged by both counties and districts, campaigns which often became heated and in some cases led to allegations that public money was being improperly spent, something which was referred to the district auditor in a num-ber of cases. In general, the districts felt that the counties had an unfair advantage in terms of the resources they could deploy and the number of their employees – who were also residents and entitled to express their opinions in the consultation process. Whether this perceived imbalance really affected public opinion it is impossible to say.

One feature of the consultation process was widely misunderstood, especially in the first tranche reviews. The Commission had to put forward draft recommen-dations for consideration and many people took the view that these initial propos-als would be the ones to which the Commission would adhere when formulating final proposals. It is true that some Commissioners saw things in this light and regarded their role as being to 'sell' the draft recommendations, and the omission of the status quo option in almost all the first tranche reviews and in some of those conducted in the expedited programme of 1994 reinforced that impression. From the beginning, other Commissioners took the view that the formulation of draft recommendations was a means of eliciting further information which had not been available in the initial stages, as a means of testing the situation, and as the review progressed this attitude became more general in the Commission.

One of the propositions made in support of unitary authorities is that members of the public find the two-tier structure confusing. However, the Commission reported no evidence to support this claim. Personal experience during the review led the author to the following conclusion. In so far as citizens are confused by the two tiers, this confusion merely reflects the much wider problems that people have in knowing who is responsible for what, an inevitable consequence of the general fragmentation of local service delivery which the Government was actively promoting. An organisational solution to this problem was already being implemented in the early 1990s in a number of local authorities, in the form of improved methods for handling enquiries, joint arrangements between a county and some of the districts within its borders, and joint one-stop-shop information centres and the like, which could either put the enquirer in touch with the relevant local authority officer or point them in the right direction to tackle another agency. This impression, that the difficulties of the two-tier system were exaggerated and that citizens face a much bigger set of problems in finding their way through the network of agencies, is consistent with the evidence collected by the Widdicombe Committee (1986), that in general people were at that time satisfied with their local authorities. It is also consistent with the findings of a study commissioned by the DoE itself: 75 per cent of respondents were satisfied or very satisfied with their county council and 82 per cent with their shire district authority; the comparable figures for the Metropolitan councils were 70 per cent and 72 per cent for the London boroughs (Lynn 1992). If there were serious confusion about the two-tier structure, we would expect the satisfaction level for the shire authorities to have been lower than for the conurbation unitary authorities. As for Scotland, there was clear evidence that the electorate did in fact have a remarkably shrewd idea about the respective roles of the districts and regions (Midwinter 1992). In sum, the argument that the confusion caused by the existence of two tiers was serious proved to be rather tenuous.

## Members of the legislature

The attitudes of individual MPs clearly influenced the course of events. Conservative backbench MPs became increasingly concerned about the turmoil which the review was engendering in England and early in 1994 these concerns were publicly articulated by Sir Marcus Fox, Chairman of the influential 1922 Committee. Even ministers, most notably Douglas Hurd, pressed for the retention of the counties (Wilson 1996; Young 1994). These rumblings of discontent almost certainly reflected MPs' awareness that their constituents were unhappy with the prospect of radical change, and in this sense the attitudes of the parliamentarians were a reflection of wider public attitudes. It also reflected anxiety in Conservative circles that the dismantling of the county council system was opposed by many of their own councillors and would amount to the seemingly gratuitous destruction of important political power bases in local government.

How influential the unease among Conservative members of the House of Commons may have been is hard to tell from the outside but some strong inferences may be made. In its final recommendations for the counties in the expedited review, the Commission proposed an all-unitary solution in four cases. Of these, the Secretary of State accepted only one, Berkshire, with the amendment that there should be six councils and not the five put forward by the Commission. Berkshire was a rather special county, in that it had lost substantial territory in 1974, to become an elongated area with Reading at its waist: in addition, until very late in the day the County Council had pushed for its own demise, though to be replaced by a smaller number of councils than the Commission recommended. Reflecting this situation, public opinion was more positive for change than was common elsewhere, while the Commissioner responsible was ardently in favour of small unitary authorities. However, the consideration which almost certainly swayed the Secretary of State in favour of an all-unitary outcome was the public support of the county's MPs, including John Redwood, lately in charge of the review in England and translated to the Welsh Office to oversee structural change there. In the other three counties, John Gummer rejected the all-unitary option, opting either for no change or for a hybrid solution. One of the eventual no-change counties was Somerset, where all the Members of Parliament were Conservative and were against the proposed unitary structure; one of these MPs, David Heathcoat-Amory, had publicly threatened to resign his ministerial office if change were to be implemented. In making his decisions, Gummer sought to achieve a greater degree of 'rationality' in the final outcome by giving unitary status to significant towns such as Luton and Milton Keynes, to create a general pattern of hybrid solutions where there were major cities and no change where larger urban areas were absent. Berkshire does not really fit that pattern and is generally regarded as a somewhat maverick outcome of the review, to explain which it is necessary to look at the impact of individual MPs. More generally, there is little doubt that towards the end of the review it was pressure from Members of Parliament which helped persuade the Secretary of State to opt for minimal rather than maximal change when faced with the recommendations that arrived on his desk. It is also probable that the hardening of attitudes in the House of Lords played its part in persuading the Government to accept only limited change. During the course of the review in both Hampshire and Kent, the author was made aware of the opposition to change of individual members of the Upper House, confirming the assessment of Young (1994, p. 92).

## Conclusions

Three basic conclusions may be drawn from the preceding discussion. First, the idea that scale economies are irrelevant in deciding the structure of local government is manifestly wrong, however difficult it may be accurately to assess their significance. Second, 'natural communities' suitable as the basis for viable units of principal local authorities throughout the country do not exist, though there are some cases where there is a good approximation. Third, although politicians across the political spectrum had convinced themselves of the merits of the unitary principle, and although the public had been willing to endorse the concept in the abstract, translating the idea into concrete proposals caused very large numbers of people to change their minds. The evidence on this is overwhelmingly clear in England. In Scotland and Wales the consultation process was much less open and was conducted without the mass participation of the public; even so, it seems clear from the evidence cited in Chapter 6 that attitudes there were rather similar to those in England.

Numerous commentators took the view that the LGCE allowed itself to be over-persuaded by the expression of public opinion, thereby failing to support unitary solutions which ought to have been recommended. That view ignores the fact that the 1992 Act enjoins the Commission to ensure that 'persons who may be interested in the review' of an area would be informed that the review was to take place, would then explicitly be given the opportunity to comment on the draft recommendations and, finally, would be notified that final recommendations had been submitted to the Secretary of State and could be inspected locally. These statutory provisions were amplified in the *Procedure Guidance* issued to the Commission, which made it abundantly clear that the Government wanted the English county-area reviews to have maximum publicity, with the fullest possible participation, including public meetings and opinion polling. The response from the public may not have been what the Government wanted but the Commission discharged its obligations, and took heed of the reactions which were elicited.

From a personal perspective as a member of the Commission for the main review, the author considers that the weakest part of the Commission's work reviewed in this chapter lay with questions of service delivery and the implications of local authority size, not with the testing of public opinion, which in many ways was a model which sets a standard for the future. The weakness on service delivery stemmed from too much reliance on the costing work described in Chapter 4 and inadequate attention to the evidence submitted to the Commission about individual services. That in turn reflected the fact that this evidence arrived in dribs and drabs throughout the review, such that the documents lost their impact. But equally important, although the main documents were circulated to Commissioners, the volume of material was considerable and took a deal of digesting, for which there were not the resources until the main review work was over. The compilation which was included in the report on the 1992–95 structural review (LGCE

1995a), in which the author played a considerable part, was not available at the time decisions were being taken.

# 6

# Parliament legislates for Scotland and Wales

From scenes like these old Scotia's grandeur springs,
That make her loved at home, revered abroad:
Princes and lords are but the breath of kings,
'An honest man's the noblest work of God.'
(Robert Burns, *The Cotter's Saturday Night*)

Viewed superficially, the procedures adopted in Scotland and Wales, and the resulting all-unitary outcomes, compared favourably with the experience in England. However, closer examination shows that the reality was a good deal more complex (Boyne *et al.* 1995). To aid clarity of exposition we will initially consider the reform process in the two countries separately. Attention will then be turned to an issue which relates to both countries: the absence of an independent commission. It is convenient to begin this discussion with events in Wales. But first there is a general point to make.

The Government explicitly set about introducing unitary local government throughout both Scotland and Wales, and did so on the basis of arguments in favour of the structural change which were similar to those we have already rehearsed in the case of England. The two-tier structures were held to be confusing for citizens and to lack local accountability as a consequence. Removal of one tier of local government would yield economies in administration, remove frictions and would make possible the integration of local government services, all leading to better value for money. The counties were held to be remote bureaucracies; in addition, there were held to be continuing loyalties to some former (small) counties and also to major urban centres. The Scottish Office (1991, para. 13) drew attention to the increasing need 'to establish a complex network of external links with a range of powerful public sector bodies'. The conclusion was then drawn that it was the two-tier structure which presented 'real obstacles to local government in meeting the challenge of change', rather than any other consideration, either internal or external to individual councils.

## Wales

As early as 1976, the Labour Party in Wales had embraced the concept of unitary authorities. Ten years later, three of the four party groups were in favour of structural change, only the Conservatives holding to the view that this was not needed. It was not until the DoE initiative in 1990 that the Welsh Conservatives showed an interest in structural reform (Boyne *et al.* 1995; Jones 1986). However, prior to that David Hunt had been appointed Secretary of State for Wales in May 1990 and immediately initiated private discussions with local authority representatives about the issues which were of concern to them. Two matters dominated the requests made to him: the ending of the Poll Tax and the introduction of unitary local government (Lord Hunt 1999). The request for a unitary structure of local authorities was consistent with the position of the Labour Party, which dominated Welsh politics at that time. Thus, despite his earlier reservations about structural change (Griffiths 1996, p. 66), Hunt was willing to see whether a consensus could be achieved. Consequently, immediately after Heseltine's announcement on 5 December 1990, he convened a meeting of the Assembly of Welsh Counties (AWC) and of the Council of Welsh Districts (CWD), a meeting which was held in January 1991, being the first publicly acknowledged one to consider structural options. In the eyes of one observer, 'This initial meeting was of great significance because it was on the basis of this low-key and preliminary discussion that David Hunt was to rest his claim to consensus [for change]' (Thomas 1994, p. 49).

The CWD, following the lead of the ADC in London, had, in 1990, published a version of *Closer to the People* and had been actively promoting the case for all thirty-seven districts to take over county functions. It fairly quickly adjusted this position, to press for twenty-seven authorities, some as existing districts and some by amalgamation. In line with the ADC, the CWD argued that these councils would better reflect community identities than the two-tier arrangements and would, in the changed and changing world of service delivery, be able to operate cost effectively.

Following up the January meeting, the AWC next month submitted a document to the Secretary of State which demonstrated how little real consensus there was between the two tiers (AWC 1991). Though this document accepted the possibility of unitary structures, that acceptance was highly conditional. In the short term, the AWC argued, there should be some tidying up of the existing two-tier arrangements. Then, in the medium term: 'If it is accepted that the institutions of government in Wales are in need of radical review' there should be an elected Council for Wales, with central government powers devolved to it from the Welsh Office. If such a body were to be created, the counties continued, it would be appropriate to remove one tier of local government – the districts – to convert the eight counties into unitary authorities. Under these circumstances, the existing community councils should be enhanced, with some powers devolved to them. The counties then and subsequently pressed the case that the creation of more than eight unitary authorities would give rise to serious problems of fragmentation in service delivery, with the need for joint arrangements, and that a move to a unitary structure should only occur in the context of an elected Council for Wales (e.g. AWC 1992b). In their account of the Welsh review process, Boyne *et al.* (1995, p. 8) do scant justice to the counties' position when they state: 'In April 1991, the two associations confirmed their agreement on the single-tier principle' (see also Griffiths 1996; Hambleton and Mills 1993).

June 1991 saw the publication by the Welsh Office of a consultation document. Ruling out an independent commission, and also implicitly ruling out the status quo, this document offered three options for an all-unitary structure in Wales, consisting respectively of thirteen, twenty and twenty-four councils. A clear preference was expressed for the twenty-council option but it was evident that the Welsh Office had not come to a final conclusion. Indeed, not only were comments invited but the hope was expressed that consultations would lead to a consensus on the way forward. In an apparent attempt to achieve agreement, the Secretary of State established the Welsh Consultative Council for Local Government (WCCLG), on which both the districts and (reluctantly) the counties agreed to sit, with equal representation. This body, serving as a substitute for an independent commission, was Chaired by the Secretary of State. By the time the WCCLG was established, the focus of debate was on the number of unitary authorities to be established, not whether reform was needed and, if so, in what context.

The magnitude of the differences between the counties and the districts may be illustrated in the following manner. The WCCLG set up a sub-group to assess the financial and other implications of reform. In February 1992, this sub-group considered two documents, one from the counties and one from the districts, giving details of their respective estimates of the financial implications of various unitary structures by comparison with the two-tier arrangements. Table 6.1 summarises the ongoing costs/savings estimated by both sides, for between eight and twenty-seven unitary councils, and shows clear agreement on one thing – that with eight authorities there would be annual savings in excess of £30 million, equivalent to about 1.5 per cent of *total* annual spending. There was also agreement that as the number of authorities increased annual savings would become smaller. However,

**Table 6.1** *Wales: estimates of annual ongoing costs (+) and savings (–) comparing unitary structures with the status quo (£ million)*

| Number of unitary authorities | County estimates | District estimates |
|---|---|---|
| 27 | +21 | –9 |
| 24 | +14 | –12 |
| 20 | +3 | –17 |
| 13 | –14 | –24 |
| 8 | –33 | –32 |

*Sources*: AWC (1992a, p.5); CWD (1992, p. 4).

there was a sharp divergence over the rate of this decline. According to the districts, even with twenty-seven councils there would be annual economies of the order of £9 million; in contrast, the counties estimated that with twenty authorities there would be extra costs and that these would rise to £21 million if there were to be twenty-seven councils.

The Welsh Office published no analysis of the submissions it received in response to the 1991 consultation document, nor indeed at any point in the review process. According to Thomas (1994), the most common plea which was put to the Welsh Office in the summer and autumn of 1991 was for there to be an independent commission. This was something for which the AWC pressed, only to be mocked by the CWD for alleged prevarication and delaying tactics; the Labour Party in the House of Commons also argued for the establishment of a commission. It is quite clear that throughout the review process there were cross-cutting currents which militated against the achievement of consensus. Individual counties and districts had their own agendas to pursue; business and other interests did not speak with one voice; and the Welsh Labour Party, which in 1989 had opted for between seventeen and twenty-five unitary authorities, found itself in an ambivalent position as the authorities which it controlled fought for survival. At the same time, the Labour Party could also watch the Conservatives being heaped with opprobrium for eliminating one tier of local government, which could be viewed as an important step to the establishment of an elected body for Wales, to which the Party was committed. In sum, the basis for a generally agreed way forward did not pre-exist and was not created in the consultation process.

With a general election imminent Hunt announced in March 1992 that he was minded to proceed on the basis of between twenty-three and twenty-five unitary authorities, expressing a preference for the lower figure (Griffiths 1996; Thomas 1994). He was evidently toying with the idea of some councils as small as 20,000 or 30,000 population, though subsequently, it seems, pressure from within the Welsh Office and from Cabinet colleagues persuaded him to set a higher population threshold (Griffiths 1996, pp. 68 and 74).

When a White Paper was finally published by the Welsh Office in March 1993, it proposed the creation of twenty-one new principal authorities. The document gave no justification for the proposed structure, beyond the claim that there was widespread support for the principle of a unitary structure and that the twenty-one councils, once in place, would be broadly cost neutral. No evidence was offered regarding the level of support which had been elicited for the options which had been set out in 1991. While acknowledging concerns about the capacity of the smaller authorities to deliver the full range of services efficiently, the White Paper did little more than promise that the legal constraints which limited trading between local authorities would be relaxed. Yet in the 1991 consultation document the following had been said about service provision:

> Some local public services are better managed and coordinated if they cover large geographical areas and large populations. Similarly, some services are resource-intensive but are needed by relatively few people, though they are important to them.

These strategic or specialist services – such as transport planning or personal social services – are delivered at county level under present arrangements. They benefit from strategic planning and targeting of resources.

There is a range of options available for ensuring that the quality and efficiency of these services will be maintained or improved with the introduction of unitary authorities. For example, some services might need to be provided by several councils acting together to form joint boards for specific purposes, or cooperating in other ways. Councils could also contract out services to other agencies or organisations. Groups of councils could formulate joint strategies for dealing with common problems or challenges.

Cooperative arrangements would need to be set up with care, as such mechanisms could be a source of that friction between authorities, blurred accountability and extra cost which the introduction of unitary authorities is intended to remove. (Welsh Office 1991, paras 5.1–5.3)

It is precisely matters of this kind which the AWC went to considerable trouble to bring to the attention of the Secretary of State. With the appearance of the 1993 White Paper, it was clear that these submissions had been largely ignored as the protestations of self-serving vested interests (Thomas 1994).

Introducing the proposal for twenty-one councils, the Welsh Office cited work by consultants on the probable level of transition costs and of the ongoing costs/savings. Touche Ross (1993) had worked on an option for twenty-three councils and these results were cited as follows: 'The Government's consultants have advised that under a 23-authority structure services could be delivered at broadly no extra cost to the current system, and that savings are possible' (Welsh Office 1993, para. 6.8). No estimate was offered regarding the magnitude of the possible savings, this depending on the policies adopted by the new bodies, and it is clear that the Welsh Office considered that structural reform on its own would leave recurrent expenditure little changed. For a structure of twenty-three councils, the Touche Ross study had shown that the aggregate cost of transition would be in the range of £66 million to £153 million at 1992/3 prices, figures very similar to those it obtained for structures in the range of fifteen to twenty-seven authorities. It is quite clear that the Welsh Office had concluded that if there were to be more than twenty or twenty-one authorities, recurrent expenditure would be increased and that such an increase could not be justified. Equally clearly, it did not expect that with twenty-one councils there would be annual savings to recoup the transition costs.

In this context, a CWD study published in October 1993 makes interesting reading. The CWD had revised its estimates for both transition and ongoing costs and now reckoned that the cost of change for twenty-three authorities would be £67 million, close to the lower Touche Ross figure and way below the counties' assessment that the costs would amount to £202 million. The districts also reckoned that with twenty-three councils there would be annual savings of £17 million (cf. Table 6.1). In other words, the districts were taking a much more optimistic view of the benefits of change than the Welsh Office.

There is a further point to make about the costings. The figures given by the Welsh Office explicitly excluded certain items of expenditure, namely: the costs of shadow authorities; winding up the affairs of existing authorities; rationalising information and technology systems; and, in some cases, building or acquiring accommodation for the new councils (Welsh Office 1993, para. 6.10). Consequently, irrespective of the accuracy of the figures for the items covered, the figures prepared by Touche Ross must be treated as under-estimates of the cost of change. This qualification was not included in the explanatory and financial memorandum which accompanied the Bill proposing twenty-one councils when this was presented to Parliament, the transition costs being given as lying in the range of £65 million to £150 million.

To draw a map of communities as the basis for local government areas is a difficult matter, no less so in Wales than elsewhere. One of the problems is that the concept of 'community' is imprecise; another problem is that community identity and party political affiliation are apt to be closely related. By choosing to conduct the review himself, the Secretary of State was open to the suspicion of gerrymandering. In addition, since Parliament had the opportunity to amend proposals laid before it, the suspicion of partisan advantage would inevitably point in that direction as well. Boyne *et al.* (1995) cite Monmouth and Pembrokeshire as two areas which traditionally had voted Conservative and which the Government wished to keep separate. In addition, we may note two areas which were mentioned to the author by a senior officer in the Welsh Office, Conwy and the Vale of Glamorgan. Thus, the first aspect of partisan advantage was the attempt to create some councils which the Conservatives could reasonably hope to control. In addition, though, by breaking up the county structure, it would be likely that the minority Opposition parties would have improved prospects in some parts of Wales, thereby weakening the over-all significance of the Labour Party (Boyne and Law 1993). But, in so far as the Opposition parties, including Labour, went along with the idea of creating relatively small unitary councils, they were themselves complicit in the gerrymandering process (Boyne *et al.* 1995, pp. 29 and 59–60; Griffiths 1996).

Gerrymandering has a significance which runs beyond the possibilities of providing partisan advantage in the control of local authorities. The structure of local government provides the framework for the Parliamentary Boundary Commissions when they undertake their periodic reviews of parliamentary constituencies. In creating a new structure of local government in Wales, as in Scotland, a new framework was being put in place which could potentially affect the pattern of representation in Parliament at a later date. The political stakes were high (Butler and McLean 1996).

After the publication of the 1993 White Paper, Redwood replaced Hunt as the Secretary of State, taking over the unitary proposals of his predecessor and converting them into the Bill to be laid before Parliament. In the process, the boundaries of eight of the proposed unitary authorities were modified, though the number of councils remained unaltered. Some of these changes were minor but others were more substantial. Then, during its passage through Parliament, the Bill itself was modified, most notably by splitting Mythyr Tydfil from Blaenau Gwent in a deal between the Government and the Opposition, thus increasing the number of authorities to twenty-two (Griffiths 1996, p. 71).

The changes which occurred to the unitary structure of local government from the time of the 1993 White Paper to the signing of the Act are summarised in Table 6.2. Although the population range remained virtually unaltered, the distribution of authorities in that range had changed. The number of smaller authorities had increased, a direction of change which is consistent with the other evidence pointing to the role of partisan advantage as an important ingredient of the reform process. Indeed, Boyne and Law (1993), having reviewed the evidence amassed during the consultation exercise, could find no link between that evidence and the White Paper proposal for twenty-one councils. They came to the conclusion that the only posssible explanation for the proposed reforms lay in the opportunity for greater power to be vested in the Welsh Office and in the break-up of powerful Labour-controlled authorities. A rather similar assessment was made by another observer one year later: 'The conclusion is that the closed and exclusive nature of the Local Government Review process in Wales was not intended to achieve a consensus between the two tiers of local government but was to allow the Conservative government to impose its own agenda' (Thomas 1994, p. 59).

There is little doubt that the reform process in Wales was tainted by the suspicion of gerrymandering. However, attempts to gerrymander assume that past

**Table 6.2** *Scotland and Wales: population size distribution of unitary authorities*

| | Scotland | | Wales | |
|---|---|---|---|---|
| Population range | White Paper | As enacted | White Paper | As enacted |
| Under 30,000 | | | | |
| (all Scottish Island Councils) | 3 | 3 | | |
| Under 70,000 | 0 | 1 | 2 | 3 |
| 70,000–100,000 | 7 | 8 | 2 | 4 |
| 100,001–150,000 | 5 | 10 | 11 | 10 |
| 150,001–200,000 | 3 | 2 | 3 | 2 |
| 200,001–250,000 | 2 | 3 | 2 | 2 |
| 250,001–300,000 | 3 | 0 | 1 | 0 |
| Over 300,000 | 5 | 5 | 0 | 1 |
| Total number of councils | 28 | 32 | 21 | 22 |
| Smallest (mainland) (000) | 76.0 | 48.9 | 66.7 | 59.5 |
| Largest (mainland) (000) | 620.0 | 623.5 | 295.4 | 306.5 |

*Sources*: Scottish Office (1993, pp. 23–5); Welsh Office (1993, p.9); *Regional Trends*, vol. 31, (1996, p.239) for the 1994 populations of authorities as enacted.

voting patterns are a good guide to future intentions. In the event, when elections were held for the shadow authorities few candidates standing as Conservatives were elected and the Party failed to gain control of a single council. Subsequently, the Conservatives also lost all parliamentary representation at the time of the 1997 general election, though there had been no change in the parliamentary constituencies following the re-drawing of the local government map.

The shadow councils finally took control of the new unitary authorities on 1 April 1996. There are two features of the Act which brought them into being which deserve special notice, one concerned with intra-authority decentralisation and the other with inter-authority cooperation. With regard to the former, nine sections of the Act are devoted to community councils, including section 14, which sets out the powers of the Secretary of State to direct a new principal authority to consult with its community councils on matters that are of mutual interest. In addition, the Secretary of State was given the power to direct a new authority to prepare decentralisation schemes for the delivery of services within its boundaries. However, this last power was time limited, expiring on 1 July 1996. Taking the two provisions together – the explicit role accorded the community councils and the possibility of directions for decentralisation schemes – it is clear that the Government recognised that at least some of the new councils consist of several distinct communities. This throws some interesting light on the rhetoric that unitary authorities should be based on identifiable communities.

The second feature of interest is the provision in the Act for joint arrangements between councils. If the Secretary of State should be concerned that one or more authorities were failing, or were likely to fail, to exercise specified functions satisfactorily, then a direction could be issued specifying the manner in which the particular service or services should be delivered. Subsequently, if the situation remained unsatisfactory, a direction could be given to set up a joint board. These provisions were time limited, in that no new directions for either stage could be made after 31 March 1999. Clearly, though, the Government was concerned that during the transition period some councils might not be able to discharge some functions adequately. Section 25 of the Act does keep the promise to relax the rules regarding the ability of councils to enter into contracts with one another for the supply of particular services, thereby permanently widening the range of options for councils to organise service delivery (see Griffiths 1994).

To conclude this account of the reform process in Wales, there are two further matters to mention. The first of these concerns the dynamics of the debate within Wales. It will be recollected that the districts very quickly resiled from their position that there should be thirty-seven unitary authorities; in contrast, the counties were adamant that the number should not exceed the number of counties; that is, eight. Alan Barnish, who was Chief Executive of Powys County Council from 1990 to 1993, has this to say about the stance of the counties:

Perhaps the most significant observation I would make is that the AWC was quite inept in its dealings with the Secretary of State. Throughout the whole process the AWC refused to move from its position of 8 unitary authorities. This was the case even when it was evident to everyone that 13 or 14 was the absolute minimum and around 20 the most likely outcome.

In taking this rigid stance, the Counties effectively excluded themselves from the debate. The result was that the arguments in favour of somewhat larger unitary authorities (than eventually emerged) were never really tested.

My assessment is that there was support amongst civil servants and some sympathy by the Secretary of State for around 16 or 18 unitary councils. This could never really move forward as a serious proposition without advocacy by the AWC. The AWC turned down the opportunity on numerous occasions to take a more flexible approach. As a negotiating tactic it failed miserably, as obviously the Secretary of State was never going to entertain just eight unitary councils. (Barnish 1999)

The second concluding comment has already been alluded to but deserves explicit recognition. As the Welsh Office worked up its proposals for structural reform, there was, apparently, considerable discussion thereof in the 'Whitehall Village':

Drafts of the white paper and bill were circulated to other departments, most significantly the Department of the Environment and the Scottish Office. Comments of those other departments and differences of view were communicated to relevant ministers and ultimately resolved in cabinet committee where the Welsh Secretary was merely one of a number. This is the most secret recess of the policy process and one can only infer from the known twists and turns of Welsh Office statements where the Whitehall blocks were placed. David Hunt in 1992 was publicly supportive of new authorities as small as 20,000 or 30,000 population, Meirionnyd and possibly Radnorshire. The white paper set a floor at 70,000 population with Cardiganshire. Many believed that the Whitehall network of other departments and ministers had sought such a floor to set some consistency between Wales, Scotland and England. There were officials in the Welsh Office who would have welcomed such an input. (Griffiths 1996, p. 74)

As an officer of the CWD at the time, Griffiths was very close to the events he describes and the 'floor' of 70,000 is consistent with the evidence in Table 6.2 regarding the Welsh Office proposals. At the time, Redwood was the Minister at the DoE reponsible for the review in England. He confirms that the inter-departmental consultations did occur, noting that there was pressure for the threshold to be set at 100,000 or even 150,000, but that he personally argued for a lower figure, the better to obtain units of local government based on natural communities (Redwood 1999). Discussions in the 'Whitehall Village' would have taken place prior to the publication of the Welsh White Paper in March 1993. This would therefore have been after the DoE issued its original guidance to the LGCE in July 1992 and before the revised version was issued in November 1993. Both versions contain the following phrase: 'There need be no maximum or minimum size for the area or population covered by a unitary authority' (DoE 1993, para. 11). In other words, the public position of the DoE in 1993 belied the conclusions which had been reached within Government. The discrepancy can be explained in part by the problem that the Government might have faced if the guidance to the LGCE had been amended and a council had sought judicial review on the grounds that the discretion of the LGCE had been compromised. Nevertheless, the discrepancy shows just how far rhetoric and reality diverged, and there is little doubt that this contributed to the difficulties faced by the LGCE when it made public in December 1993 its own conclusion that a population of 150,000 should be taken as indicative of the lower threshold for an English unitary authority (LGCE 1993, para. 41).

## Scotland

From the mid-1970s onwards, the Scottish National Party and the Liberals characterised the recently reformed two-tier structure in Scotland as remote and bureaucratic, advocating its replacement with unitary authorities. The Labour Party initially dodged the issue, regarding the structure of local government as a matter for a future Scottish Parliament, but towards the end of the 1980s came to the view that structural reform would be desirable. However, common to all the Opposition parties was the view that reorganisation should only occur as part of a wider constitutional settlement with a Scottish Parliament as its centrepiece. Conservative ministers, having implemented some reallocation of functions between the tiers following the 1981 Stodart report, were not interested in structural reform, not least because of the potential link with the establishment of an elected body for Scotland. However, Stodart's report had expressed sympathy for the unitary concept and, following dismal local election results in 1987, Conservative grassroots activists began to press for change and the party leadership paid some attention. Work was initiated in the Scottish Office in 1988, leading to the opinion in that quarter that a unitary structure would be advantageous. Manifestly, though, when Ian Lang, as Secretary of State, decided to follow the lead given by Heseltine in England, he misjudged the level of agreement for change (Boyne *et al.* 1995; McVicar *et al.* 1994; Midwinter 1992).

The first consultation paper was issued by the Scottish Office in June 1991. This document confined itself to the principles and criteria to be employed in drawing up a unitary structure of local government, and was pitched in very general terms. For example, it was proposed that a unitary structure of local government should be within the democratic tradition; that is, that councillors should be elected. Only passing mention was made of the possibility that the two-tier structure could be retained: it would require a convincing case to be made 'in a particular area' (Scottish Office 1991, p. 10). It was claimed that the Wheatley Commission had acknowledged the advantages of a unitary structure, even though it had recommended a two-tier system. While it is true that this Commission had indeed recognised the attractions of the unitary concept, it was emphatic about the impossibility of devising a workable system and the Scottish Office document made no attempt to show why circumstances had changed so dramatically that the Wheatley report could legitimately be cited in support of the unitary principle (see

Midwinter 1992). In contrast to the Welsh consultation document, the Scottish Office paper focused entirely on general issues and offered no actual structures for consideration, to show how principles might be converted into practice.

Numerous responses were elicited by the consultation document, which responses were summarised in a Scottish Office (1992b) publication. This document claimed that two-thirds of respondents endorsed the unitary concept, a claim that was forcefully challenged in an independent study of the submissions by the Unit for the Study of Government in Scotland at the University of Edinburgh (McCrone *et al.* 1992). This analysis excluded the submissions made by local authorities, and led to the following conclusion:

> Even allowing the most generous definition of 'support' for the Government's proposals, less than half (48.6%) of submissions favour one-tier authorities. This figure falls to 34.5% if we exclude those who support single-tier but are critical of the Government's proposals. Among submissions which do not come from Conservative Party members and affiliates, only 27.4% uncritically support the Government's position. (McCrone *et al.* 1992, Summary)

All of the Scottish local authorities were members of the Convention of Scottish Local Authorities (CoSLA). Although there were inevitable differences between authorities notwithstanding the dominant position of Labour in local politics, CoSLA (1992) was able to submit a robust document to the Scottish Office. CoSLA argued that the prior issue for consideration was the establishment of a Scottish Parliament, and that the only proper way to consider the structure of local government in Scotland was by means of an independent commission, both views that were widely shared. It noted the absence of popular support for change and took strong exception to the proposal to remove police, fire and water/sewerage responsibilities from the jurisdiction of local authorities. In sum, CoSLA argued that the Government had not made the case for change (see also Midwinter 1992).

Despite the manifest unpopularity of the proposal to create unitary authorities in the absence of provision for an elected body for Scotland, and without an independent commission, the Scottish Office (1992a) came forward with a commitment to change and four illustrative options for unitary structures throughout the country – fifteen, twenty-four, thirty-five and fifty-one councils – and invited comments. On this occasion, the Scottish Office did not publish any analysis of the responses received. To fill the gap, CoSLA again asked McCrone *et al.* (1993a, 1993b) to provide an independent assessment. As previously, this examination excluded the responses from the local authorities. Altogether, 3,289 documents were analysed. Only 15 per cent of respondents offered a view on a preferred unitary structure for the whole country, the other responses being either at a more general or a more particular level. The unitary option which attracted the most support was for 35 councils, 146 respondents favouring this proposal. The least favoured possibility was for 51 authorities, with only 65 supporters. Not one of the options gained as much as 30 per cent support among the 15 per cent of replies offering an opinion on a nation-wide structure of unitary councils. Put another way, of the total replies received, fewer than 5 per cent favoured the most popular of the four structures offered. As the authors noted: 'While there is some support for single tier authorities and for smaller units of local government, this is out-weighed by hostility to the government's proposals' (McCrone *et al.* 1993a, p. 3).

The Opposition parties, and especially Labour, dominated Scottish local gov-ernment at this time. There were serious conflicts of interest between the regions and many of the districts, which made it difficult for Labour to mount a unified and vigorous response to the Government's proposals. CoSLA also found it difficult to maintain a united front. This situation had close parallels with Wales. Unlike Wales, though, there was relatively little dialogue between the Scottish Office and the representative body for local authorities, CoSLA. It appears that the Scottish Office made little attempt to engage CoSLA in a serious effort to find common ground and, indeed, for much of the time CoSLA had a policy of non-cooperation.

The Government did attempt to respond to some of the criticisms by proposing to widen the scope of the Scottish Grand Committee, that group of MPs which rep-resents Scottish constituencies in the House of Commons (Secretary of State for Scotland 1993). Published in March 1993, under the provocative title *Scotland in the Union: A Partnership for Good*, the document served to inflame rather than to soothe Scottish sensibilities and did little to aid the reception of the White Paper which followed in July (Scottish Office 1993). This document proposed the main-tenance of the three island councils and the creation of twenty-five mainland uni-tary authorities, making a total of twenty-eight altogether. Introducing these proposals, the Secretary of State noted that consultation had extended over two years and made the following claim: 'The responses over that time have revealed substantial support for the creation of unitary authorities across Scotland – within local government, among professional and other representative organisations and, most important of all, among the general public' (Scottish Office 1993, Foreword by Ian Lang, p. iii). That assertion was far removed from the reality.

The 1993 White Paper also claimed that with twenty-eight councils substantial benefits would be obtained: 'Enormous advantages in service provision, in terms of integration and efficiency, will accrue simply from having the same authority responsible for all local government services in its area' (Scottish Office 1993, para. 3.1). The only evidence adduced in support of this contention was in the form of costings for the transition and for the subsequent savings in ongoing costs, based on the work of the consultants Touche Ross. Transition costs were put at £120 million to £196 million, while ongoing savings were estimated to lie in the range of £110 million to £330 million over the first five years, with the middle of the range likely to be £200 million (Scottish Office 1993, paras 5.6 and 5.7). The last figure translates into an expected annual saving of £40 million.

The Touche Ross report had been submitted to the Scottish Office in October 1992 and was then made public with apparent reluctance (CoSLA 1993). The Scot-tish branch of the Chartered Institute of Public Finance and Accountancy (CIPFA) issued its own assessment of the Touche Ross figures in March 1993, concluding as follows: 'CIPFA concludes that the Touche Ross report does not properly assess the likely costs of reform and a rigorous, independent study into the financial implications of change should be implemented' (CIPFA 1993, p. 11). Equally critical were separate evaluations by McQuaid (1993) and Midwinter (1993a, 1993b). The Treasury became involved because of its concern that the Scottish Office had under-estimated the costs of reorganisation (Black 1996, p. 10) but this concern apparently had as little effect as the publicly voiced criticisms, as we shall see.

CoSLA attempted to obtain clarification from Touche Ross on a number of issues but with limited success. On the basis of work done by individual authorities and an examination of the Touche Ross assumptions, CoSLA (1993) put forward its own assessment of the impact of reform on recurrent costs. This work used the consultant's figures for seven of the eleven cost headings identified (noting that this did not necessarily mean endorsement of those figures), and substituted alternative figures for the other four headings – central administration and corporate services, financial services, planning and economic development, and libraries. It was for these services that CoSLA was most in disagreement about the assumptions used by Touche Ross. Table 6.3 shows the effect of these modifications. This table shows the familiar trend, that if there were to be a small number of unitary authorities there would be significant annual savings, and that these savings decline as the number of authorities increases. However, CoSLA maintained that the Touche Ross figures over-stated the savings if there were to be fifteen councils and under-stated the extra annual costs should there be fifty-one authorities.

Early in 1994, CoSLA published further work on the costing of change, repeating and extending its previously expressed criticisms. On this occasion, it came forward with figures for the total costs of transition, which it put in the range of £375 million to £720 million; it did not identify any compensating annual savings. One of the major reasons for the CoSLA figures for transition costs being so much higher than the Touche Ross estimates lies in the treatment of redundancy costs, another being property. The fundamental point made by CoSLA was that even if in aggregate the number of staff would not be changed by reorganisation and the amount of property required remained constant, there would inevitably be problems of mismatch, with consequential redundancy and property costs (CoSLA

**Table 6.3**  *Scotland: estimates of annual ongoing costs (+) and savings (–) comparing unitary structures with the status quo (£ million)*

| Number of authorities | Touche Ross estimates | Touche Ross amended by CoSLA |
|:---:|:---:|:---:|
| 51 | +57.6 | +184.3 |
| 35 | −54.7 | +67.5 |
| 24 | −119.9 | −4.2 |
| 15 | −191.9 | −81.5 |

*Source*: CoSLA (1993, pp. 8–9).

1994). Even accepting this basic point, the upper end of the range of costs identified by CoSLA did seem very large, an impression confirmed by the evidence from England (Table 4.1) when it is remembered that the population of shire England was about 30.7 million, whereas that of Scotland was approximately 5.1 million.

So far as can be judged, the CoSLA figures were ignored by the Scottish Office. Even so, and despite the deficiencies of the Touche Ross data, it seems reasonably clear that these latter played an important role in persuading the Scottish Office that it would be unwise to base a unitary structure on the existing fifty-three districts in mainland Scotland, thereby pushing it to the White Paper proposal for twenty-five mainland councils, giving a total for Scotland of twenty-eight authorities. However, note that the cost figures contained in the 1993 White Paper were carried forward unaltered to the explanatory and financial memorandum which accompanied the Local Government etc. (Scotland) Bill when it was published, despite the criticisms which had been forcibly expressed.

In proposing twenty-eight unitary authorities for all Scotland, the Scottish Office signalled its awareness that there would have to be more collaboration between councils in the provision of services than hitherto:

> Under the existing two-tier structure, some authorities provide services or parts of services jointly with other authorities. It is expected that some of the new authorities will consider the merits of joint arrangements of one kind or another and the Government are firmly of the view that all of the new councils should take full advantage of opportunities to share expert advice and specialist facilities with other councils. It is expected that the new authorities will also have to consider, to a greater extent than in the past, the possibilities of providing services or parts of services in conjunction with other authorities. (Scottish Office 1993, para. 3.2)

In offering this advice to the prospective new councils, the Government was confirming what had been explicitly recognised in the 1992 consultation paper, that even with as few as twenty-four unitary authorities joint arrangements would be needed for virtually all the mainline services except housing and education. In other words, there would be an unelected upper tier of local government (Kerley and Orr 1993). To make such inter-council cooperation possible, the 1993 White Paper promised that the legal framework in Scotland would be modified. The parallels with Wales are compelling. It is quite clear that the Government expected the move to unitary structures to create certain inefficiencies for which the remedy would dilute the advantages claimed for making the structural change.

It is also noteworthy that in proposing twenty-eight councils, the Government had abandoned any credible claim to the authority of the Wheatley Commission. This Commission noted that, whereas a number of witnesses had pressed the unitary case, nobody had vouchsafed a map translating that case into concrete proposals, and it itself had tried to do so and had failed. In so far as the evidence from witnesses was helpful, it had pointed to about twenty councils for Scotland, sub-stantially fewer than the number proposed by the Government (Wheatley 1969, Chapter 22).

From very early in the whole process, there were widespread suspicions that the Government would attempt to gerrymander (Alexander and Orr 1994). Some of the responses to the 1991 consultation paper are revealing of grassroots Conservative thinking, as instanced by the Eastwood Conservatives, who said that boundary changes 'should, where possible, give a Conservative electoral advantage' (McCrone *et al.* 1992, Appendix 2). With the unveiling of concrete proposals, the suspicions of gerrymandering noted by Boyne *et al.* (1995, pp. 19 and 57) focused on Berwick and East Lothian, East Renfrew, Eastwood, South Ayrshire and Stirling, the last of these being the constituency of Michael Forsyth. To make it possible for Stirling to be kept distinct, a senior officer at the Scottish Office pointed out that it was necessary to create a number of rather small local authorities around it. The same individual also drew attention specifically to Clackmannan, East Dumbartonshire and Falkirk as areas where the Conservatives wished to have local authorities that were winnable.

Some of the gerrymandering occurred in the preparation of the White Paper and some subsequently. Although the Bill which was published provided for twenty-eight councils, the same number as in the White Paper, there had been a number of boundary adjustments. As proposed in the Bill, the boundary for East Renfrewshire was defined in extreme detail, relying in part on minute topographical features and even upon Ordnance Survey grid coordinates. By the time the legislation emerged from the parliamentary process, this authority had been reconfigured and it was now Angus which displayed the same level of detail for its definition. More important, Parliament increased the number of councils by four. As Table 6.2 shows, the net effect of these changes was almost to double the number of councils with populations under 100,000, with a compensating reduction in the number of larger authorities.

An account of the committee stage of the Scottish Bill in the House of Commons shows that structural amendments were fought out in a partisan political manner. These battles were complicated by the inclusion in the Bill of highly contentious proposals for the water industry, on which Labour wanted serious discussion and therefore desired to limit the time spent considering structural and boundary matters. On the other hand, the Conservatives were happy to filibuster their own Bill 'to avoid debate on more contentious and politically dangerous issues such as water' (Boyne *et al.* 1995, p. 59). National commentators were scathing about the legislation which emerged as the Local Government (Scotland) Act 1994: 'This was partisan redistricting, and neutral commentators raised their eyebrows at some of the new Scottish districts (*sic*). The boundaries of East Renfrewshire seemed to have been drawn to maximise the probability of Conservative control of the local authority, and not for any articulated geographical reason' (Butler and McLean 1996, p. 14).

To the extent that gerrymandering did occur, it was not sufficient for the Conservatives to win control of a single unitary authority when in due course elections were held for the new councils which came into being on 1 April 1996. In only one case, East Renfrewshire, did they come close to a clear majority of council-lors and in general their candidates fared very badly indeed. More damaging, per-haps, was the complete elimination of parliamentary representation with the 1997 general election.

Although the Scottish Act mentions community councils, the concern is almost entirely with their creation, maintenance and abolition; with one exception, no duty is laid upon the principal councils to consult with them. Section 23 of the Act requires *all* the new councils to prepare and implement a decentralisation scheme, in the preparation of which community councils are to be consulted. From the wording of the Act, it is clear that these decentralisation schemes were intended to be a permanent feature of local government throughout Scotland, a requirement that is considerably stronger than the provisions in the Welsh Act. As in Wales, so in Scotland, the provision for decentralisation schemes and reference to commu-nity councils imply the recognition that many of the new councils' boundaries do not equate with identifiable communities but embrace some or many distinct localities.

The Scottish Act makes provision for the establishment of joint boards for the discharge of specified services; in Wales, this provision was time limited but this is not the case in Scotland. Furthermore, where a joint board is established between two or more authorities in Scotland, that board 'shall be a body corporate and shall have a common seal' (section 62A(5) of the Act). This provision high-lights the problem of accountability when joint arrangements are put in place.

A senior academic observer summed up the Scottish reform process in terms that are amply borne out by the evidence which has been discussed above: 'In determining the new power structure, it is clear that the interests of the Conserva-tive Party were paramount considerations' (Midwinter 1995, p. 109). The rhetoric used in favour of structural change was far removed from the realities.

## Why was there no commission for either Scotland or Wales?

The review of local government in England was undertaken by an independent commission, charged to make recommendations to the Secretary of State, which he could implement with or without modification by laying an affirmative order in Parliament, or he could reject the recommendations. Despite the strong pressure that was evident in both Scotland and Wales in favour of a commission, the deci-sion was taken to proceed without a commission, a decision which caused con-siderable resentment in both countries. Why this difference of approach?

To answer this question, we need initially to consider the reasons that were given by Government for dispensing with a commission. For both Scotland and Wales, it seems that ministers had genuinely persuaded themselves that there was a consensus in favour of a unitary structure and that the 'only' issue was its precise configuration. On that premiss, there was little to be gained by sharing the presumed popularity of the changes with the Opposition parties, while at the same time delaying the whole process. In addition, and made explicitly clear in the case of Wales, it was believed that the two countries were small enough, and by impli-cation simple enough in their geography, for it to be realistic that civil servants could assist ministers in the task of devising structures for the respective territo-ries. Ministers were clearly not attracted to the idea of a roving commission on the English model, but that was not in itself a reason for having no commission; had a commission been established, it could have been required to consider the entire country in making its recommendations all in one go. In Wales, it was claimed that preliminary discussions had clarified the issues and that this made a commission unnecessary, while in Scotland the parallel assertion was that the 1969 Wheatley report had covered most of the ground and that its rejection of the unitary princi-ple had been overtaken by changes in service delivery and other events. Neither of these claims stands up under scrutiny. Finally, in the Scottish case it was argued that, because the Wheatley recommendations had in any case been substantially modified when it came to legislating for change, it was in reality proper for Par-liament to be closely involved.

This last point was put explicitly by Ian Lang as follows: 'It is Parliament which will, rightly, make the final decisions about local government reform, and months of Parliamentary consideration of the reform Bill lie ahead. The precise final outcome is anyone's guess, but I have no doubt it will be a structure of local government which is right for Scotland' (Lang 1994, p. 23). This passage is instructive. The paper would have been written after the Scottish Office had come forward with proposals for a total of twenty-eight councils, yet it displays an acute awareness that the final outcome might differ very considerably, suggesting that the White Paper proposals were not self-evidently the 'best' for Scotland. In addi-tion, by implication, we are asked to believe that the parliamentary consideration of the Bill would be based on matters of high principle, not low politics. The improbability of this being the case had been signalled by John Major as Prime Minister as early as 1991.

At the time that structural reform was being proposed in 1991, the Conserva-tives had few Scottish and Welsh MPs – eleven out of seventy-two in Scotland, and eight out of forty in Wales. In addition, they controlled only three of the Scot-tish districts, just one Welsh district, and not a single Scottish region or Welsh county. In other words, in both countries the Conservatives were politically mar-ginalised. The biggest of the local authorities in existence was Strathclyde region, with about one half of the population of Scotland and powerful enough to present a serious challenge to central government; this authority was considered by Major to be a 'monstrosity' (Hayton 1993, p. 8) and it had never been controlled by the Conservatives since its creation in the mid-1970s. Senior officers at both CoSLA and the Scottish Office agreed that its dismemberment was to be, in effect, a re-run of the politically inspired abolition of the GLC and the Metropolitan counties in England. Given the low political ebb of the Conservatives in Scotland, there was clear potential for partisan gain by re-structuring local government into smaller units: 'This partisan motivation for reform was most clearly stated by the prime minister [John Major] in his first address to the Scottish Conservative Party in May 1991' (Alexander 1992, p. 60). For confirmation, bear in mind the public pledge by Allan Stewart, a Minister at the Scottish Office, that suburban areas around Glasgow would not be incorporated into that city to form a Greater Glasgow (Hayton 1993, p. 9). Such an expansion, however desirable it might be functionally, would mean the incorporation into a Labour-dominated city of areas such as Bearsden which were thought likely to vote Conservative.

The other major factor that seems to have weighed with ministers was the expectation that if there were to be commissions in Scotland and Wales it would be very difficult to prevent local government reform being linked with the introduction of elected bodies for the two countries. Such a prospect was anathema to the Conservatives.

The alternative question to ask is why was it that the Government chose to use a commission in England? Between the time of making his announcement on 5 December 1990 that there would be a wide-ranging review of local government structure in England and 21 March 1991, Heseltine had consulted on the form that the English reform process should take. On the basis that there was no 'blueprint' for change, he opted for a rolling review programme, area by area. That formula reveals the lack of consensus on the need for change and, if change were needed, what it should be. The absence of agreement among ministers has been confirmed to the author in interviews and was clearly evident among Conservative MPs. During the passage of the Bill, Labour tabled an amendment to require the LGCE to come forward with all-unitary proposals; this amendment was defeated by the Conservative majority. As one senior Conservative backbencher observed to the author, he would not have voted for the Bill if he had thought it would mean wholesale change instead of the more limited task of sorting out 'problem' areas, a view that was clearly widely held by his colleagues. If the Bill had proposed a blueprint for change in England, sufficient MPs might have voted against for the legislation to be in jeopardy in the Lower House, and the upper chamber might well have proved unwilling to comply with its passage.

Such calculations did not apply for Scotland and Wales, where the Conservatives held very few parliamentary seats. An English majority in the House of Commons could impose a solution with no fear of a backbench revolt. This being the case, there was no short-term need to establish commissions to reconcile the inevitable conflicts of interest and evidence. The conclusion seems to be inescapable, that the difference in the treatment accorded to England on the one hand, and Scotland and Wales on the other, cannot be ascribed to considerations of principle concerned with the good governance of the country. The decisions rested on political calculations.

## Conclusion

It is quite clear that, when Heseltine announced the review of local government structure in England, the implications for Scotland and Wales had not been thought through. It is equally clear that divergent policies were pursued in the various parts of Great Britain, a fact which reduces the force of claims that the reforms were based on clear principles. It also seems to be the case that though it was the English initiative which triggered change in Scotland and Wales, there was then a reciprocal effect upon the course of events in England. In the first place, the fact that ministers for Scotland and Wales fairly quickly decided upon an all-unitary outcome in their respective jurisdictions put pressure on the DoE and its ministers to push for a similar outcome in England. With the departure of Heseltine from the DoE after the 1992 general election and his replacement by Michael Howard, assisted by John Redwood, the scene was set for deliberate attempts to use the 1992 Act for England to achieve a generally unitary outcome, and to do so by attempting to 'influence' the LGCE, instead of pursuing the 'no blueprint' approach.

Then, in 1993, as the LGCE's final recommendations for the first tranche areas began to show that unitary outcomes were improbable in substantial parts of shire England, the Government had a somewhat different problem. Evidence was accumulating that structural reform of local government was not the popular undertaking which had been envisaged and pressure was mounting in the summer for the Government to call off the English review. The Government considered this option and also the possibility of converting the review into an 'opt in' process for reform under specified rules. Either course of action would in itself have been a humiliating U-turn. But if policy had changed in this way in England, ministers for Scotland and Wales would have been in a difficult position if they had persevered with the preparation of the Bills for their respective jurisdictions. Indeed, if ministers had pulled back from reform in England, it is not certain that the parliamentary votes could have been mustered to force reform through for Scotland and Wales, though Lord Lang (1999) is clear that he would have wished to proceed. Thus the commitment of the Scottish and Welsh ministers to unitary structures undoubtedly contributed to the decision which was taken to soldier on in England but to do so on a sharply accelerated timetable and with the benefit of revised guidance to the LGCE intended to result in generally unitary outcomes.

If one needs confirmation that it was predominantly political considerations which determined the policy of creating unitary authorities which are smaller than the pre-existing counties and regions, and contributed to the decision of the Government to persevere despite all the difficulties, one need look no further than a remark by the Secretary of State for Education in October 1994. At that time, the Government was encouraging schools to opt out of local authority control but the rate at which this was happening was falling short of ministerial wishes. The Secretary of State noted that the uncertainties arising from the splitting up of education authorities would be as effective as any more direct scheme to encourage opt-outs (Chisholm 1995, p. 566). In other words, structural reform was then being perceived as a means for achieving a specific policy goal that was proving hard to realise in other ways.

The refusal to have independent commissions in Scotland and Wales rankled in both countries with many people and organisations. This discontent was compounded by the way in which the consultation process was tightly managed and controlled, with limited and/or slanted revelation of the results therefrom, and an apparent disregard for what the responses had shown. The impression was created that irrespective of evidence and arguments, the Government would proceed more or less regardless in both Scotland and Wales. To argue, as the Government did, that it would be Parliament which would ultimately make the decisions, while legally accurate, fuelled the anger. It meant that English MPs would determine the outcome in Scotland and Wales. Furthermore, there was scepticism about the quality of that parliamentary scrutiny, a scepticism amply confirmed by Boyne *et al.* (1995) and Griffiths (1996). Griffiths provides a particularly telling glimpse of the fundamental inadequacy of the committee stage of the Welsh Bill. The Conservative representation on the committee included nine MPs for English constituencies: 'A sullen silence was usually maintained by these members and much constituency correspondence was undertaken' (Griffiths 1996, p. 65).

In the short term, the Government got its way and local government was radically re-shaped in Scotland and in Wales. Initially, the Government had thought that the reforms would improve its popularity ratings but in the event hostility to the reforms outweighed support, especially in Scotland. Few electoral dividends have been reaped so far by the Conservatives. Indeed, the manner of the reform process probably contributed to constitutional developments which the Conservatives opposed, for the following reason. One observer of the Welsh reform commented that: 'If consensus can be said to exist, it lies in local government's acceptance of the political legitimacy of the authority of the Secretary of State' (Thomas 1994, p. 60). With the benefit of hindsight, it seems clear that the way the structural reform of local government was handled in both Scotland and Wales contributed to the erosion of the general acquiescence to (English) political authority and thus augmented the pressure for elected bodies in both countries.

The estimation of the costs of change and of the longer-term impact on expenditure proved no easier in Scotland and Wales than in England. Common to all three countries is the clear picture from the imperfect evidence that large unitary authorities, at the scale of whole counties, would have yielded cash savings, and that conversely a district-based solution would be more expensive. Beyond that common ground, however, there was considerable divergence between counties and districts in Wales, and between the Scottish Office and CoSLA in Scotland, a precise re-run of the divergent opinions evident in England. There is, however, a major curiosity. In proposing twenty-one councils in Wales and twenty-eight in Scotland, the respective ministers were looking to an almost identical percentage reduction in the number of local government units, to somewhat under half. In both countries, the lower estimate of the transition cost to these new structures was about £23 per person but the upper limit of £38 in Scotland was substantially exceeded in Wales, where the figure was about £52. Perhaps more interesting, the Welsh Office was not in the least confident that this investment would be recouped through recurrent savings, regarding the proposed change as broadly cost neutral. In contrast, the Scottish Office took the emphatically optimistic position that twenty-eight authorities would result in annual savings of about £40 million. It could be argued that this reflects the larger average size of the councils which were proposed in Scotland than in Wales – about 180,000 population compared with about 140,000 – but that simple explanation ignores the impact of the size distribution and other variables, and also ignores the criticisms that were directed at the work of Touche Ross, in particular by CoSLA. At this stage of the argument, we will do no more than note that in the light of the English and Welsh estimates for recurrent costs/savings, the Scottish Office ones look decidedly optimistic. That said, it is clear that the estimates of costs and savings had an important impact on the review process in Scotland and Wales, just as they did in England, by pushing the recommendations away from district-based solutions. In all three countries, the argument that districts could take over the county/region functions and could generate savings in comparison with the two-tier structures was found to be wanting.

The promoters of the unitary concept argued that abolition of the large and 'remote' counties and regions would bring local government closer to the people and make it possible to base local authorities on communities. Despite this, the legislation for both Scotland and Wales makes provision for the decentralisation of administrative arrangements within the new councils, and for improved consultation with community councils. This implies that ministers and Parliament recognised that in many cases, if not generally, it is impossible to draw a map of communities that translates into a viable pattern of local government units. Many, if not most, unitary authorities are in fact an amalgamation of distinct communities at the scale of the parish, community or town, just as is the case for the districts in England, as the LGCE reported. The simple rule of thumb should surely be reversed: it is desirable that local authority boundaries *do not pass through* communities, to ensure that a whole community is included in one authority. The more sophisticated rule, but horribly difficult to put into practice, is to seek some aggregation process so that communities which are similar in their characteristics and needs are grouped together, but that would require a completely different approach from that adopted in the 1990s.

Given that legislative provision was made to ensure that the new Scottish and Welsh councils are adequately responsive to the variety of concerns and interests within their borders, one has to ask whether the problem of the perceived 'remoteness' of the counties and regions could not have been addressed by means other than their abolition? The clear answer is that 'yes' this could have been done, had there been the will to identify precisely what the real problems were and to find appropriate remedies. As it is, the provisions in the two Acts amount to the quiet burial of one of the reform's major strands of rhetoric, actively promoted by the district associations of England and Wales and adopted by the Government: the idea of making local government more accessible to the people merely by changing the structure of principal authorities.

The legislation for England, Scotland and Wales shows concern for the impact of structural change upon the capacity of the new authorities to deliver services. In all three cases, provision is made empowering the relevant Secretary of State to order the setting up of joint arrangements, though the form of this provision differs in each case. A general and continuing power exists in Scotland; a general but time-limited competence was conferred in Wales; and in England a curiously muddled and limited provision was made which in practice can only be used in a small number of cases where structural reform has actually occurred, and which does not apply in areas untouched by structural change (Chisholm 1995, pp. 565–6). It is of course arguable that there should be reserve powers vested in appropriate ministers, but if this is to be done there are cogent reasons why the provisions should be similar across Great Britain. That aside, the fact that the Government felt it necessary to include these safeguards in all three pieces of legislation does suggest that there were some reservations about the possible impact of structural reform on the effectiveness of the new authorities, and this in turn throws interesting light on the claim made by the Scottish Office that the proposed structure of twenty-eight councils would yield 'enormous advantages in service provision'.

From the evidence reviewed in this chapter, it is clear that the process by which the new authorities were brought into existence in both Scotland and Wales left a great deal to be desired. We have already seen that the process in England was also a difficult one, subject to considerable criticism. In the concluding chapter of this book, we will address some of the issues for the governance of the country which arise from these experiences, including the role of central government and the utility of independent commissions. Meantime, we will merely note that in all three countries there were serious failures by central government but that the nature of those failures differed. On the other hand, however wanting the processes may have been, we should not assume that the outcome, in the form of the structures actually put in place, is defective. Judgement on that question must be suspended pending an examination of the evidence to date on how well the new arrangements are working, a matter considered in Chapter 8. Prior to that, however, we will examine the information which exists regarding the actual costs of structural change, as compared with the estimates of expected costs with which we have been dealing so far.

# 7

# The actual costs of reorganisation

> The transitional costs of reorganisation are difficult to estimate, and past experience
> suggests that they tend to be underestimated. (LGCE 1993, para. 96)

Now that structural change has occurred, it is possible to enquire what the reorganisation has actually cost, as compared with the *ex ante* estimates reported in earlier chapters. A certain amount of information is available from government sources but these sources suffer from various defects and cannot be accepted at face value as a comprehensive account of the reorganisation costs which have been incurred. There are two basic reasons for this: the data are incomplete for the cost headings which they cover; and important cost elements are omitted. For these reasons, the material must be handled cautiously and with the exercise of judgement.

For ease of presentation, attention will first be given to the evidence about reorganisation costs in England, with Scotland and Wales treated next. For all three countries, the starting point will be the officially available data; supplementary intelligence will then be considered, including the author's own survey of local authorities in England. Once the picture has been built up for what the actual costs have been it will be possible to compare the *ex post* evidence with the *ex ante* estimates which have already been reported.

## England

### Official data

The official data on the actual costs of change are for the amounts which the Government has authorised local authorities to *borrow* to defray expenses. These are known as Supplementary Credit Approvals (SCAs) and the view taken by Government has been that the sums borrowed would be repaid out of the annual savings expected to accrue from reorganisation. The SCA data relate to a fairly narrow concept of the transition costs, the main components being the costs of

changing computer-based information systems and costs associated with the provision of accommodation, and redundancy and related personnel costs (but
excluding pension liabilities). However, the rules that have been applied to the
counties have been more restrictive than those applying to the other authorities, in
that the counties could not request an SCA for costs associated with IT and accommodation costs, it being assumed that in all cases these would be zero. In effect,
the SCAs are intended to meet the overhead costs associated with structural
change, but do so imperfectly.

The starting point for our examination will be the SCA data as published, but
from the outset it must be emphasised that the information suffers from a number
of defects beyond the narrowness of the cost concept embodied in the figures.
Some authorities have not asked for and have not received an SCA allocation, so
the SCA data do not tell the whole story. In addition, there were differences
between the assessments which local authorities made of their needs and the
amounts which Government was prepared to sanction, the latter generally being
the lower figure.

Under the SCA system, a local authority could receive permission to borrow in
the year immediately prior to reorganisation and for three years thereafter.
Because change occurred first in the Isle of Wight, in April 1995, and was not
completed until April 1998, the transition costs will be spread across the period
from 1994/5 to 2000/01, though the great bulk of the costs has fallen in the three
years 1996/7 to 1998/9 (see Table 7.1). At the time of completing the text for this
book, initial allocations had been made for the year 1999/00 for the sum of £52.1
million, though the DETR had set aside a sum of £100 million, on the basis that
any under-spend would be added to the overall total of the Revenue Support Grant

**Table 7.1** *England: supplementary credit approval costs of reorganisation (£ 000)*

| | Year | | | | | | |
|---|---|---|---|---|---|---|---|
| | *1994/5 outturn* | *1995/6 outturn* | *1996/7 outturn* | *1997/8 outturn* | *1998/9 mid-year review* | *1999/00 initial allocation* | *Total* |
| SCA bids | | | | | | | |
| All-change counties | | | 69,841 | 70,802 | 27,876 | | |
| Hybrid-counties | | | 113,620 | 173,333 | 87,476 | | |
| Total | | | 183,461 | 244,135 | 115,352 | | |
| SCAs allowed | | | | | | | |
| All-change counties | 3,514 | 45,600 | 44,238 | 41,323 | 29,227 | 10,773 | 174,675 |
| Hybrid counties | | 5,631 | 57,473 | 110,202 | 88,887 | 41,342 | 303,535 |
| Total | 3,514 | 51,231 | 101,711 | 151,525 | 118,114 | 52,115 | 478,210 |

*Sources*: Bids: *Hansard* written answers. 4 November 1996, cols 339–40; and 29 June 1998, cols
78–82. Allocations: DETR Local Government Reorganisation Costs Scheme, via the Internet.

for distribution to local authorities in general. No allocations were available for the final year, 2000/01. Taking these two points together, it is evident that in the analysis which follows there will be some under-estimation of the actual costs of change.

Because the costs of change are spread over a number of years, the figures for each year ought in principle to be adjusted to a common base to eliminate the effects of inflation. On the other hand, the rate of inflation was comparatively low over the whole of the relevant period, while, as will be seen, there are large uncertainties about the data and the estimates that can be made from them for the magnitude of the actual costs, as distinct from the officially ackowledged costs. Therefore, in the ensuing discussion all the primary data are quoted from the relevant sources without inflation adjustment; they amount to costs at current prices. By following this procedure, the reader who wishes to trace the data back to source can do so quite readily. In the later stages of the enquiry it will become necessary to adjust for the effects of inflation so that proper comparison can be made between England on the one hand and Scotland and Wales on the other, and also so that the *ex ante* evidence can be compared with that available *ex post*.

The Department of the Environment, Transport and the Regions responded very helpfully to requests for information. Initially, figures were supplied in the form of copies of *Hansard* but towards the end of 1997 the SCA figures were put on the Internet in a consolidated form, and this has been the main official source on which reliance has been placed. However, although *Hansard* is a rather chaotic source, some useful information is contained there regarding the bids for SCAs made by authorities, information which is not available on the Internet, and use has been made of this as appropriate.

Table 7.1 summarises the SCA data for the entire period from 1994/5 to 1999/00. In assessing SCA applications, the DETR operates a three-stage process – an initial allocation, a mid-year review and then a record of the outturn – and this process is reflected in the table, for the bids made and for the SCAs granted. In other words, there is an iterative adjustment as the situation unfolds. However, it must be remembered that the SCA permissions given may not actually be used and the DETR has no information regarding the scale of non-use. Thus the SCAs granted amount to permissions which may or may not be taken up if an authority finds that it can fund the expenditure from other sources. Nevertheless, the SCA data show the magnitude of the costs which the Government has been willing to acknowledge.

For reasons which are set out more fully in Appendix 2 and Appendix 3, the figures in Table 7.1, including the grand total of £478.2 million, must be treated with caution since some authorities made no request for an SCA, or had their bid rejected. On a conservative estimate, these 'missing' SCAs amount to 5.6 per cent of the published total. More important, the arcane rules which apply to local government finances cause some serious problems in assessing the significance of the SCAs. In summary terms, if an SCA is used for capital purposes, such as accommodation and IT expenditure, no further permission is needed from the DETR.

However, although councils cannot normally borrow to fund recurrent expenditure, a dispensation may be granted in the form of a 'capitalisation direction'. Therefore, to use an SCA for staff costs, which are treated as recurrent costs, a local authority must obtain this second form of permission. If that were the end of the matter, there would be no problem, since all the capitalisation directions would be a sub-set of the SCA data and could be ignored. Unfortunately for our purpose, capitalisation directions may also permit a local authority to use some of its Basic Credit Approval (BCA) and/or unused capital receipts to finance the cost of reorganisation. To the extent that capitalisation directions are used for this purpose, this will be permission for expenditure which is *additional* to the permission embodied in the SCA data.

Appendix 2 shows that the impact of the capitalisation directions is almost certainly sufficient to account for at least the 5.6 per cent of 'missing' SCAs and that, on certain assumptions, the sums involved could amount to 42 per cent; applied to the aggregate SCA in Table 7.1, we would have a range of from £505 million to £679 million. The lower figure, which is based on the 'missing' SCA entries, is the absolute *minimum* figure for the actual costs of reorganisation. The upper figure must at this stage be treated as a provisional estimate to be checked against other evidence.

The next step is to compare the bids which local authorities made for SCAs against the allocations authorised by the DoE and DETR. There is no doubt that some councils made extravagant requests in the early years and the DoE asked several to re-submit their bids. Using information published in *Hansard* (1996, written answers, 22 January, cols 84–5 and 4 November, cols 339–40), it is possible for a sample of authorities to compare the aggregate of the bids before and after the revision process for the year 1996/7. In aggregate, the councils had reduced their bids from £221.5 million to £156.6 million. If the latter figure is compared with the figure of £183.5 million shown in Table 7.1, it will be seen that the sample of authorities is a very large proportion of those granted SCAs. The revised bids amounted to 71 per cent of the original bids and were in turn scaled down in terms of the allocations actually made, which amounted to 55 per cent of the £183.5 million revised bids. The following year, the Department agreed 62 per cent of the bids and by 1998/9 was willing to accept a slightly higher figure than had been requested.

Clearly, the DoE exercised substantial downward pressure on the transition costs it would accept in 1996/7 but despite this pressure councils were still putting in bids for SCAs that were a good deal higher than the Department would allow, implying a continuing gap in the respective assessments. That gap disappeared in 1998/9. These figures are open to three interpretations. According to the first, the excessive claims made by local authorities early in the transition period have been adjusted to the realistic levels adopted by the Department. On the other hand, because SCAs are permissions to borrow, carrying the implication that future income must be found to repay the debt, local authorities would have a strong incentive to keep their requests to a reasonable minimum; for this reason, the first interpretation seems somewhat improbable, other than for the small number of councils which did indeed submit overly ambitious requests. A more probable explanation is somewhat more complex. Many of the new unitary authorities wished to establish adequate accommodation and IT facilities from the very beginning but were forced to forego their aspirations for efficient resources, reducing capital expenditure in the short run at the expense of higher recurrent commitments in the medium term. This view would be consistent with the Government's desire to present the structural change as being cost effective. Consequently, in order to keep the accepted costs of change as low as possible, councils were forced to come into line with the DoE whether or not the allowed SCAs actually met their real costs. Given the nature of the whole process, it is not altogether surprising that it took time for local authorities to come into line.

The third possibility is that over time the DoE itself moved its assessments towards those made by the local authorities. In 1996, Colin Myerscough of the Department held a number of meetings around England to explain the basis on which the SCAs granted thus far had been calculated. He was faced with widespread criticism from the counties, the districts and the new unitary authorities; criticism that the DoE assessments were unrealistically low. It seems probable that this experience had an impact on the process, both in dampening the expectations of councils and in persuading the Department to be more generous, with this change feeding through in time for the 1998–9 bid and allocation procedure.

It seems reasonable to suppose, therefore, that there were solid grounds for local authorities to submit bids which were in excess of the sums which the DoE was willing to countenance. With that in mind, we may take the aggregate of the bids for the three years shown in Table 7.1 and compare that figure with the amount which was granted for the same years; the SCAs allowed equalled 68 per cent of the sum requested. Expressed another way, the sum allowed would have to be up-rated by 46 per cent to give the sum which councils considered they needed. If that ratio is applied to the entire sum of £478.2 million SCAs granted, the total cost of reorganisation would be £698 million, which is a slightly larger figure than that derived from the SCA and capitalisation direction data

## Survey of local authorities in England

In February 1998, letters were sent by the author to all the new unitary local authorities in England, the districts which were about to become unitary authorities and the counties involved, enquiring about the costs of transition. Of the seventy-two authorities contacted, forty responded with usable information. One authority was able to supply information for the county, one of the four which by that time had ceased to exist, thereby giving information for forty-one of the seventy-six relevant authorities; this is a response rate of 54 per cent. Information was sought regarding the SCAs for which authorities had bid in each year and the use of reserves to fund transition costs. Some of the respondents also supplied data for the SCAs granted and for expenditure out of the revenue account.

The quality of the information supplied appears to be good. Many of the returns include information on the actual SCA allocations and these figures can be compared with the published DETR data. The correspondence is almost perfect. However, two authorities were omitted from the analysis because the DETR data on SCAs granted do not allow one to be sure of the relevant sum, with the consequence that Table 7.2 summarises information from thirty-nine councils, or 51 per cent of the total. That these are reasonably representative of the English local authorities involved in reorganisation is shown by two facts. Over the five-year period, the 51 per cent of authorities obtained 47 per cent of the SCAs awarded by the DoE/DETR; and the SCAs allowed to them represented 67 per cent of their reported bids, this latter proportion being very similar to the proportion of 68 per cent already noted as the over-all proportion.

**Table 7.2**  *Survey of English authorities regarding their use of reserves and revenue to finance transition costs, 1994/5 to 1998/9 (£ 000)*

| Value of SCAs requested | Value of SCAs granted | Reported expenditure from reserves and revenue |
|---|---|---|
| 336,254 | 225,955 | 85,072 |

*Source*: Author's survey, see text. The value of SCAs granted was obtained from the DETR; see Table 7.1.
*Note*: Data for thirty-nine authorities: sixteen counties and twenty-three districts/unitary authorities.

The key fact which we can derive from Table 7.2 is that the £85 million which local authorities reported as having been drawn from reserves and/or the revenue account to cope with the costs of reorganisation is equivalent to 37.6 per cent of the value of the SCAs allowed by the Department. Some of the £85 million reported will have required the issue of capitalisation directions but the amount involved is not known. However, from the survey returns it is absolutely clear that authorities had difficulty in identifying the full expenditure incurred which was additional to their allotted SCAs, a position amply confirmed by the interviews which the author conducted. Although the information in Table 7.2 undoubtedly under-states the actual use of funds in addition to the SCAs, it is likely to be the most accurate assessment available of expenditure needs in excess of SCA allocations; nevertheless, the 37.6 per cent increase represents the *minimum* degree of up-rating from the SCA allocations which is needed to obtain a realistic estimate of the actual costs.

## Assessment

The first assessment, based on capitalisation directions, suggested that the *maximum* that should be added to the SCA data is 42 per cent. A somewhat higher figure was estimated from the comparison of council bids and allocations, and a marginally lower one from the survey returns, this last figure being a *minimum* figure. In the light of this information, it seems reasonable to propose that the SCA allocations should be increased by 40 per cent to obtain an estimate of the cost of reorganisation, and this figure will be used henceforth. On this basis, a total of £699 million has been spent on the reorganisation in England.

## Scotland and Wales

Whereas in England the Government has reckoned that the costs of reorganisation for individual authorities would be spread over four years, the equivalent period in Wales has been six; the Scottish Office, in contrast, has restricted the period to just three years. It is not clear why there has been this different treatment.

The Welsh system of local government finance bears some resemblance to that which is used in England so that, as Table 7.3 shows, SCAs have been the main source of government provision for the costs of reorganisation. These, along with some special grants and a small amount for miscellaneous matters which are not directly the concern of local authorities, add to a total of £108.7 million, this figure representing the officially acknowledged cost of the change.

As in England, councils asked for a larger sum of SCAs than they were awarded, these additional requests amounting to at least £32.3 million (Local Government Association for Wales 1997). If we accept that figure, then the Welsh Office allocations represent 73 per cent of the total sum for which a case was made, a ratio which is comparable with experience in England. On the evidence already examined for England, this suggests that the Welsh local authorities were being realistic in their requests. However, that direct comparison ignores the fact that the Welsh Office made special grants of £19.5 million, which had no parallel in England. Therefore, we should deduct this sum from the £32.3 million of addi-

**Table 7.3** *Wales: official costs of reorganisation (£ 000)*

|  | 1994/5 outturn | 1995/6 outturn | 1996/7 outturn | 1997/8 outturn | 1998/9 outturn | 1999/00 provisional | Total |
|---|---|---|---|---|---|---|---|
| SCAs |  |  |  |  |  |  |  |
|   IT/premises | 1,378 | 17,895 | 20,374 | 7,090 | 700 |  | 47,437 |
|   Revenue costs |  | 4,919 | 23,358 | 10,114 | 773 | 1,500 | 40,664 |
|   Total | 1,378 | 22,814 | 43,732 | 17,204 | 1,473 | 1,500 | 88,101 |
| Special grant |  | 17,550 | 1,950 |  |  |  | 19,500 |
| Staff commission, etc. | 260 | 601 | 200 | 1 |  |  | 1,072 |
| Total | 1,638 | 40,965 | 45,882 | 17,205 | 1,473 | 1,500 | 108,663 |

*Source*: Welsh Office (1999a).
*Note*: The greater part of the revenue costs is accounted for by staff compensation.

tional SCAs requested, so that £12.8 million should be added to the overall figure in Table 7.3, giving an aggregate of £121.5 million.

Table 7.4 sets out the officially acknowledged reorganisation costs for Scotland. In this case, the figures represent the sums made available in the annual financial settlements and therefore they amount to grants, not permissions to borrow. In this sense, the Scottish councils have been treated more generously than their counterparts elsewhere. On the other hand, the Scottish Office has assumed that substantial savings have resulted from the creation of the unitary councils and that these savings started in their first year, 1996–7. This means that the financial provision has been based on the net figures.

**Table 7.4** *Scotland: official costs of reorganisation (£ million)*

|  | 1995/6 | 1996/7 | 1997/8 | Total |
|---|---|---|---|---|
| Shadow authorities | 41 |  |  | 41 |
| Capital allocations | 15 | 70 | 20 | 105 |
| Total transition costs | 56 | 70 | 20 | 146 |
| Assumed savings |  | 30 | 40 | 70 |

*Source*: Scottish Office (1999).

The Scottish Office estimates of £146 million gross and £76 million net costs over the period to 1997/8 may be compared with an estimate prepared by the Convention of Scottish Local Authorities and the Scottish branch of the Chartered Institute of Public Finance and Accountancy (CoSLA/CIPFA 1996). This careful piece of work concluded that for these three years the actual cost of change would amount to £281 million, this figure being virtually double that allowed as the gross cost by the Scottish Office, and nearly four times the net figure which has been used for funding purposes.

The CoSLA argument that the official figures seriously under-estimate the expense of reorganisation has received support from two quarters. Shortly after the 1997 general election, Malcolm Chisholm, responding on behalf of the new Secretary of State to an MP's question about the costs and savings associated with structural reform over the period from 1995/6 to 1999/00, had this to say:

> The previous administration made certain assumptions in setting the last three local government finance settlements and the planned figures for the next two years. The government do not endorse those assumptions, but we are committed to live within the existing public expenditure control totals for this year and next. Within those totals we have, however, allocated an additional £89 million for schools in 1998/9 to reflect the priority we attach to education. My right hon Friend has made it clear that this will be the only change of substance to the forward expenditure plans for local government current expenditure in 1998–99. (*Hansard* 23 July 1997, written answers, col. 608)

In other words, the incoming administration had examined the financial ledger which it had inherited and had decided that it could not accept the entries for the assumed costs of reorganisation, which it regarded as too low, but that because the Government as a whole was committed to an over-all figure for public expenditure the dubious figures would have to stand. The sum of £89 million relates to the year immediately following the three years which the Scottish Office recognised as the transition years, but taken in the context of the figures in Table 7.4 gives some idea of the scale of the under-estimation which the Labour administration judged to have occurred.

It could be argued that Chisholm's response was based on political point scoring rather than real analysis and that therefore his assessment could be dismissed. However, a senior civil servant in Scotland confirmed to the author his doubts about the assumed annual savings and hence the validity of the net costs used by the Scottish Office. More important, the Controller of Audit to the Accounts Commission (1998) has reviewed the transition period, noting both the official and the CoSLA estimates of the cost of change. From the tenor of the document, it is clear that he regarded the CoSLA estimate to be much more plausible than the figures used by the Scottish Office:

> I offer no view upon the accuracy of the various estimates of the costs of reorganisation, but it is difficult to avoid the general conclusion that the actual costs were significantly greater than the estimates provided for by The Scottish Office. It is striking that, in 1995/96, The Scottish Office made no explicit provision for redundancy costs incurred by the outgoing councils whereas these councils, according to CoSLA figures, incurred severance costs of some £80m in that year. (Controller of Audit to the Accounts Commission 1998, para. 7.2)

There is little doubt that the Controller of Audit did not believe the figures used by the Government and that he had considerable confidence in the information compiled by the local authority association. This suggests that the costs of reorganisation in Scotland will have been of the order of £281 million, as estimated by CoSLA.

## Comparisons: England, Scotland and Wales; *ex ante* and *ex post* estimates

We can take the analysis another step forward by converting the estimates for aggregate costs into costs per person, so that comparisons may be made between the three countries. For this stage of the enquiry, we will initially go back to the total figures shown in the tables which record the officially acknowledged costs of reorganisation (Tables 7.1, 7.3 and 7.4). Population figures for mid-1996 have been used as the basis for calculation; the totals for Scotland and Wales, and the populations of the unitary authorities in England. The results are set out in Table 7.5.

**Table 7.5**   *Great Britain: officially acknowledged reorganisation costs, 1994/5 to 1999/00*

|  | Transition assistance (£ million) | Population mid-1996 (000) | £ per person |
|---|---|---|---|
| **England** | | | |
| Five all-change counties | 174.7 | 3,310 | 52.8 |
| Twenty hybrid counties | 303.5 | 4,932 | 61.5 |
| Total | 478.2 | 8,242 | 58.0 |
| **Scotland** | | | |
| Gross costs | 146 | 5,149 | 28.4 |
| Net costs | 76 | | 14.8 |
| **Wales** | 108.7 | 2,912 | 37.3 |

*Sources*: Tables 7.1, 7.3 and 7.4. Population data for England and Wales from *Finance and General Statistics* and for Scotland from the *Annual Abstract of Statistics*.
*Note*: The population shown against the hybrid counties is for the unitary authorities.

The over-all official cost of change has been £58 per person in England, with a somewhat higher cost in the hybrid county areas and lower in the five counties which have experienced complete change. This lower figure of £52.8 is the near-est equivalent to the experience in Scotland and Wales, where substantially lower sums are recorded. Given that the Scottish costs were provided in the form of grants, whereas borrowing permissions were the main instrument in Wales and the sole official funding in England, we would expect a ranking in the order shown – highest in England and lowest in Scotland. However, the range in *per caput* costs is very large and it does not seem plausible to suggest that the differences in reor-ganisation process and of the relevant powers of local authorities could be ade-quate to explain them. The author has discussed earlier versions of these figures with a number of people and nobody has been able to offer a convincing explana-tion based on the objective facts of the reforms.

However, at this stage in the discussion some account must be taken of the impact of inflation, since most of the costs for Scotland and Wales occurred some-what earlier than in England. It would be possible to convert the annual figures to a common year by deflating them by an index of prices but, looking ahead to the comparison of *ex ante* and *ex post* data, an alternative and approximate approach has been adopted. It will be recollected that in previous chapters we have assem-bled the available *ex ante* estimates of the cost of reorganisation and in doing so have been able to record the year in which the figures were published. It is not always possible to establish the year which has been used as the basis for the esti-mates without considerable research labour. Therefore, annual adjustments for price changes would introduce a spurious degree of accuracy in a context in which the rate of inflation has in any case been quite low. Examination of Tables 7.1, 7.3

and 7.4 shows that, to a reasonable approximation, reorganisation costs in both Scotland and Wales were centred on 1996, whereas the central point for England was 1997. Over the period from 1992 to 1997, inflation first fell and then rose but the variation was not huge (Table 7.6). So it will be assumed that the aggregate costs for England represent costs at 1997 prices, whereas those for the other two countries are in 1996 prices.

**Table 7.6**   *Index of retail prices (annual averages)*

| | |
|---|---|
| 1992 | 126.1 |
| 1993 | 133.5 |
| 1994 | 138.5 |
| 1995 | 140.7 |
| 1996 | 144.1 |
| 1997 | 152.5 |

*Source*: *Annual Abstract of Statistics.*

Returning to the figure of £52.8 per resident in the five all-change English counties, we may treat this as being a figure in 1997 prices. On the basis of the Retail Prices Index, this represents a cost of £49.9 in 1996 prices and it is this figure which should be compared with the equivalent *per caput* costs for Scotland and Wales shown in Table 7.5. Even if the inflation adjustment should be double that which has been applied, it is absolutely clear that the contrast between the acknowledged costs in England on the one hand and Scotland and Wales on the other cannot be accounted for in this way. For the moment we will set aside the question of why there should be such large differences between the countries until we have conducted a further exercise, to estimate the probable magnitude of the actual costs of reorganisation in Scotland and Wales.

The basis for this estimation is simple. It has been assumed that the official cost information is fuller and more reliable for England than for the other two countries, an assumption that seems entirely reasonable in the light of the evidence presented thus far. Even so, the English data need to be increased by 40 per cent, as already described, and that adjustment has been made to the reported cost per person for the all-change counties of £52.8, giving a cost per person of £73.92. This adjusted figure has then been multiplied by the populations of Scotland and Wales respectively to give estimates for those countries in 1997 prices, as shown in Table 7.7, with the equivalents in 1996 prices using the scaling procedure described above. The table also shows what the costs in England would have been had the whole of shire England been reorganised, again using the five all-change counties as the basis of estimation. With these estimates of the probable actual costs, we are now in a position to assess the accuracy of the *ex ante* estimates.

**Table 7.7**   *Great Britain: author's estimates of the actual measured costs of reorganisation (£ million)*

|  | 1996 prices | 1997 prices |
|---|---|---|
| England |  |  |
| actual reorganisation | 632 | 669 |
| if all shire England reorganised | 1,298 | 1,374 |
| Scotland | 360 | 381 |
| Wales | 203 | 215 |
| Total for actual reorganisation | 1,195 | 1,265 |

*Source*: See text and Table 7.5.

### Comparison of ex ante *and* ex post *estimates of reorganisation costs*

It will be recollected that Table 4.1 shows the various *ex ante* calculations that were made during the structural review, assuming that the whole of shire England would be reorganised. Those estimates, adjusted for inflation, may be compared with the figure of £1,374 million shown in Table 7.7, a figure which is taken to be in 1997 prices. In 1992, early in the review, the counties came forward with estimates that were clearly far too low – £532 million to £701 million in 1997 prices. A year later, the county estimate had become a single figure, £1,256 million, which proved to be very close to, though nevertheless below, the costs actually incurred. In the same year, the districts came forward with a range of costs, from £570 million to £1,024 million, a range that does not straddle the actual costs and carries the implication that costs would be limited to somewhere near the middle of the range, or about £797 million, barely half the outcome. By 1994, in the light of the accumulating evidence, the districts accepted that the lower end of the range was unlikely and settled for a single figure; although in nominal terms this had been increased from 1993, adjusted for inflation to 1997 the sum remained at £1,024 million. In other words, the district assessment remained lower than the counties' by a substantial margin and amounted to no more than three-quarters of the costs actually incurred.

The Local Government Commission also proved to be seriously in error. Paradoxically, its 1995 figures are lower than those offered in 1993. In both cases, the Commission signalled the uncertainties attached to the estimation process by giving upper and lower limits but in neither case did the higher figure come close to the actual costs. In 1993, the Commission estimates put the upper limit at £891 million, with a lower figure of £674 million; two years later, these figures had become £800 million and £541 million respectively. In giving a range, the Commission made it clear that the actual costs would be somewhere between the upper and lower limits, maybe about £785 million according to the earlier figures or £670 million on the basis of the 1995 estimates.

These comparisons show that the initial estimates by both the counties and the districts were grave under-estimates but that with the passage of time their estimation became more realistic. The most accurate figure to be produced was the 1993 county estimate; although this was realistic, it was nevertheless an under-estimate. The LGCE estimates proved to be less reliable than those of the local authorities, and this is a serious matter because it was on the basis of the work done by Ernst & Young that the Commission made its own judgements and then recommendations.

For Wales, the *ex ante* estimates reported in Chapter 6 were all issued in 1993. The Welsh Office carried forward its own figures to the explanatory and financial memorandum which accompanied the Bill when presented to Parliament, with modifications for the change in the number of authorities proposed; the range was put between £65 million and £150 million. The lower end of this range was endorsed by the districts, whereas the counties put the cost of reorganisation at £202 million. Up-rated to 1996, these costs become £70 million to £162 million in the case of the Welsh Office, and £218 million on the basis of the counties' figure. These estimates are to be compared with the figure of £203 million shown in Table 7.7 for actual *ex post* costs in 1996 values.

There can be no doubt that the district estimate was seriously low and that the total estimated by the counties was reasonably close to, though somewhat above, the actual costs. As for the Welsh Office, its range does not straddle the aggregate cost that has been incurred, though the upper figure is not unreasonably conservative. However, the implication of the official estimate was that costs were likely to be near the mid-point, or £116 million, which would be a serious under-estimate of the actual situation.

As in Wales, so in Scotland, the official cost assessments were published in 1993. The Scottish Office put the gross cost of reorganisation at £120 million to £196 million, figures which were carried forward to the time when the Bill was laid before Parliament. Converting these figures to 1996 prices, the official *ex ante* estimates for gross costs were £129 million to £211 million; these estimates fall a long way short of the estimate shown in Table 7.7, that the actual gross costs amounted to about £360 million. The other *ex ante* costing which we have reported was that of CoSLA (1994), the range being put at £375 million to £720 million which, converted to 1996 values, is equivalent to £390 million to £749 million. The lower of these two figures is close to, though somewhat above, the estimate of actual costs of £360 million. The higher figure is clearly a considerable over-estimate of the costs. On the other hand, estimates prepared by CoSLA and CIPFA (1996), showing reorganisation costs of £281 million, appear to have been conservative.

It should be remembered that the CoSLA estimate of £281 million has received support from the Controller of Audit to the Accounts Commission. Furthermore, CoSLA did not identify offsetting annual savings, so that its gross figure is simultaneously its estimated net cost, from which we may make the following categorical statements. First, the Scottish Office under-estimated the gross costs of reorganisation by a seriously large margin. Second, at this stage of the enquiry, the strong balance of probability is that this error was compounded by the assumption that there would be offsetting annual savings, so that the net costs would be substantially less than the gross figure. If we may anticipate Chapter 8, there is little evidence that the assumed savings have in fact materialised, confirming the assessment made by the Controller of Audit. Hence, finally, the net cost figures used by the Scottish Office and included in the explanatory and financial memorandum which accompanied the Bill when it was presented to Parliament gave a misleading picture in suggesting unreasonably low transition costs.

### Implications of the ex ante/ex post comparisons

The serious under-estimation of transition costs by the Local Government Commission, the Scottish Office and the Welsh Office raises some important issues. In England, it is clear that the LGCE misjudged the realities despite employing the services of Ernst & Young. As a member of the Commission for most of the review period, the author was well aware that Commissioners generally considered costings to be a matter for the professionals and that there were also widespread doubts about the validity of the figures which were being used, with worries that they were being put too low. With the enormous pressure on individual Commissioners, it was impossible to become sufficiently familiar with the arcane issues to challenge the assessments that were coming forward. In retrospect it is, of course, a matter of judgement whether the decisions to which the Commission came would have differed had more realistic costings been available but it is quite clear that in general unitary structures would have seemed less attractive. It is the author's opinion that fewer recommendations would have been made for the creation of unitary authorities. Had that been the case, the history of the review might have been very different, with the focus much more explicitly upon the large cities in a review structured along lines closer to the abortive proposals in *Organic Change* (DoE 1979).

Something that cannot be gainsaid is the irrelevance of the requirement in the *Procedure Guidance* issued to the LGCE for the costs and benefits of structural options to be calculated over a fifteen-year period, discounted at 6 per cent per annum and with the likely margins of error specified. To its credit, the Commission refused to take this guidance seriously but, given that the process was spelled out in this way by the Government, who was fooling whom?

In both Scotland and Wales the Government also seriously misjudged the financial implications of reorganisation, especially in Scotland, and this despite the professional advice which it commissioned. It is a matter for speculation what impact there would have been had that advice produced more realistic assessments, or if the opinions of CoSLA in Scotland and the counties in Wales had been taken more seriously. As reported in Chapter 6, it does appear that however imperfect the official costing data were, they did cause both the Scottish Office and the Welsh Office to move away from very small unitary authorities. Consequently, it is reasonable to infer that, had more realistic intelligence been used, the effect would have been, at the very minimum, to reduce the number of councils that would have been created. There would probably have been a similar effect in England.

Two other issues arise from the findings, of which one has already been mentioned, namely the differential treatment of transition costs in the three countries of Great Britain. However one may assess the data, there is no doubt that councils in England have been treated more generously, or less harshly, than in Wales and especially in Scotland, and that the differences go far beyond that which can be accounted for by differences in the objective local government circumstances facing councils. To explain the pattern which has been revealed, one has to turn to other considerations. An obvious starting point is the fact that at the time of reorganisation the Conservatives had minimal significance in local government in both Scotland and Wales, as had been the case for quite some time. In England, on the other hand, the Conservatives traditionally played an important role at both the county and the district levels, and though their electoral fortunes were at a low ebb they could reasonably expect to regain their importance. Of equal significance, the Government had few MPs elected for constituencies in Scotland and Wales, depending on those elected in England. Under these circumstances, it does not take much imagination to suppose that ministers could see the political benefits of trying to be realistic in the assessment of reorganisation costs in England. By the same token, they would have been under less pressure in Scotland and Wales.

However, there is another reason which may have been more important. It is habitual for major Bills to be accompanied by a brief explanatory and financial memorandum, as a matter of factual information for the benefit of the legislature. In the case of the Local Government Bill which became the 1992 Act for England, there was no such financial information; since the Bill provided for a process leading to an uncertain outcome, it would have been impossible to give realistic figures. For Scotland and Wales, where specific proposals were put forward, there was a financial statement giving estimates of the cost of reorganisation, as we have already noted. Seen from the viewpoint of the Government, it was manifestly desirable that the actual costs should fall within the range which had been specified at the time the Bills were laid before Parliament. From the preceding discussion, we have seen that the officially acknowledged costs of reorganisation lie squarely within the respective ranges which had been indicated to Parliament before the event – almost exactly in the middle of the range in the case of Wales, and towards the lower end in Scotland. It seems highly probable, therefore, that in these two countries there has been an element of the self-fulfilling prophecy in the way in which the Government handled the provisions for the transition, thereby holding down the amounts which would officially be recognised. Because the specific constraints in England were looser, it was practicable to be more realistic and it seems likely that this combination of circumstances provides an important part of the explanation for the differential treatment of the three countries. The change in political control at Westminster which occurred in 1997 will have had little impact on these dynamics, since by that time the general pattern had been established and, as we note in Chapter 8, the incoming Labour administration was pledged to maintain for two years the public spending limits which had been set by its predecessor.

This leaves to last the question which is the most important of all. There is no doubt that the information supplied to Parliament substantially under-stated the real costs of reorganisation, though we have every reason to suppose that the figures were provided in good faith. An obvious question, for which there is no answer, is the attitude which MPs would have taken to the legislative proposals for Scotland and Wales had the costing data been more realistic. The more general point is that for Parliament to legislate in a rational manner in the best interests of the nation, it is not merely desirable but is in fact essential for it to be provided with accurate details of the financial implications of the Bills which are being considered. Manifestly, this was not the case when the structural reform of local government in Scotland and Wales was being considered. This particular case is not an isolated event; the Layfield Committee complained about the inadequacy of the financial assessments which accompany proposed legislation as long ago as 1976 (pp. 42–3).

It might be thought that we have now exhausted the examination of reorganisation costs but that would be a mistake. It will be recollected from Chapter 2 that the major cities claimed they could take over the functions of the counties with minimal cost and disruption, so it would be appropriate to see whether that claim has been borne out in practice. In the second place, we have so far concentrated exclusively on the quantitative information which is available but this material ignores the fact that substantial transition costs have been incurred which have been excluded from consideration, even in the survey conducted by the author. These two matters are addressed in the succeeding paragraphs.

## The Major Cities

Early in the review process, eleven cities made claims which seemed to be extravagant concerning their ability to take over responsibility for county functions at minimal cost of change. All eleven cities have in fact become unitary authorities and, for the nine which are in England, data are available for the value of the SCAs which have been allowed. Assuming that the claims which the cities made in 1991 are accepted, we would expect that these SCA data would show a much lower cost of reorganisation than has been the general experience.

The nine cities in question are: Bristol, Derby, Hull, Leicester, Nottingham, Plymouth, Portsmouth, Southampton and Stoke-on-Trent. Information is available for the SCAs granted to these cities and also the counties in which they were formerly included. There is a problem in assigning the county SCA information between two cities if only one is included in the above list, as is the case with Plymouth and Torbay in Devon. In these cases, the county SCA has been allocated among the cities in proportion to the value of the SCAs allowed to the two urban authorities. This approximate procedure gives an aggregate SCA for the nine cities of £107.2 million, for city populations which totalled 2.376 million. Consequently, the value of the SCAs per city inhabitant was £45.1, which is lower than the average figure shown in Table 7.5 of £58; in fact, the proper comparison is with the average for England excluding these nine cities; that is, £63.2. In other words, the SCA data show a transition cost for the Major Cities which is nearly three-quarters of the cost elsewhere. While one would expect the costs for the Cities to be below costs in other parts of the country because the Cities are comparatively large unitary authorities, the difference is much smaller than one would suppose from the claims made in 1991.

This evidence leaves one with a choice between two conclusions. It may be the case that the Major Cities, and the Association of District Councils with whom they cooperated, genuinely believed the case which they put forward early in the review process. Or it may be that their claims were made tendentiously. Neither conclusion flatters the authorities concerned.

## The unquantified costs of reorganisation

The Chief Executive of a county which was relinquishing two districts was asked whether he could put a figure on the actual costs of change beyond those identified for SCA purposes. His response was immediate and unequivocal, and ran more or less as follows:

> I do not know how much the transition process is costing and I do not wish to know. In order to know, I would have to ask my senior colleagues to keep detailed records and they have more important things to do. Besides, if they knew the demands made on their departments, they would be knocking at my door for more resources. Since I do not have the funds for this purpose I do not want them making requests.

In other words, he was turning a Nelsonian eye to the problem and the costs had to be absorbed somehow in existing budgets.

Conversations with senior officers in other authorities, both counties and inheriting unitary councils, have shown unanimous support for the position taken by the Chief Executive quoted above. From a management viewpoint, the policy of not knowing the magnitude of these 'hidden' costs is entirely rational. There was a job to be done and the last thing anybody would want would be squabbles over non-existent resources. From the point of view of the inquisitive researcher, it is frustrating to learn that there is a category of information that does not exist, even though the headings which are relevant are easily identifiable (Lloyd 1996).

If these unquantified costs of change were trivial, the absence of information would not matter much. However, from conversations with senior officers, it is clear that authorities involved in the transition – both counties 'losing' one or more districts and districts becoming unitary authorities – have felt themselves to be under great pressure, resulting in long hours of work well above the normal duties of staff and councillors, fully confirming the asssessment made by the Social Services Inspectorate (1996). In one English county involved in the main review, the mini-review in 1995 and the subsequent transition of a district to unitary status, senior officers clearly felt that a total of about five years had been 'wasted', in the sense that little policy development work had been done. The picture painted in one district preparing to become a unitary authority was that the 'hidden' costs of change probably equalled the amount formally acknowledged in the SCA which had been granted.

While it is probable that this particular council was unusual, there can be no doubt that the unquantified costs of reorganisation have been considerable. There were the opportunity costs of the time and energy which were diverted from development work and the taking forward of initiatives because the immediate problems of transition had to take priority. On a conservative estimate, this policy 'stand-still' period cannot have been less than two years in the generality of cases. There was the very large amount of unpaid overtime and there were the human and practical costs associated with the uncertainties which necessarily attended the process of staff appointments and transfers, uncertainties for which the staff commissions in the three countries had no real remedy – nor indeed could they have been expected to. In some cases, there were even threats of legal action arising from disagreements regarding staff transfers. Some of the relinquishing authorities, possibly the majority, sought to minimise the number of individuals who would be made redundant by making short-term appointments whenever they could. Cambridgeshire was one such council and was successful in its attempts to minimise redundancies in this way but the achievement was in part off-set by the ramifying implications of having staff on short contracts in jobs which are normally filled on a permanent basis. By reducing redundancies, local authorities were able to avoid pension costs which do not appear in the officially recognised costs of reorganisation; these pension payments are a significant element in the sum of 'hidden' costs.

Other uncertainties and their attendant costs arose with the transfer of assets, with the most bitter and contentious case probably being the break-up of the county-wide museum and art gallery arrangements in Leicestershire as a consequence of the creation of Leicester as a unitary authority and the failure to agree continuing joint provision. Where counties or regions ceased to exist, difficulties could arise because there was uncertainty regarding the scale of the financial assets or liabilities which would be bequeathed to the successor councils; Strathclyde Regional Council ended its life with substantial net debts, while Denbighshire inherited debts the size of which has been serious in relation to its resources.

The process of disaggregation inevitably implies the risk that the spatial distribution of fixed assets and associated staff may not match the operational needs of the new authorities, or of the continuing counties in England. Under these circumstances, joint arrangements may provide a temporary solution, and indeed may offer an option for the long-term future, but the probability is that in the medium term it will be necessary to close some facilities and to open others so that operational needs can be more effectively met. Although such costs may be directly attributable to reorganisation, they will not be identifiable as such. An example which clearly provides the potential for these costs to be incurred is York. The new unitary authority has 25 per cent of the children resident in the former county council of North Yorkshire but has 35 per cent of the residential accommodation for children (Craig 1999; Craig and Manthorpe 1996). A mismatch on this scale invites a proces of adjustment.

Another hidden cost to note has arisen from the disaggregation of the assessments which are made by the Government of the spending needs of authorities, these assessments being the basis for decisions on the scale of revenue support grants on the one hand and the capping of total expenditure on the other. To cushion the change, special transitional, or damping, arrangements were put in place in both Scotland and Wales, and to a lesser extent in England. Even so, there were serious perturbations as some authorities were faced with lower revenue resources than had been expected.

Interviews with numerous officers in relinquishing authorities and in councils which were inheriting functions yielded a unanimous conclusion, that the hidden costs were significant. The same point was made in several of the returns made in response to the author's survey of transition costs which has been reported above. While it would be wrong to emphasise these burdens unduly, it would be equally wrong to ignore them. On the basis of the subjective information available, it seems unlikely that these unrecorded costs in England could have been less than 10 per cent of the value of the SCAs granted, and possibly as much as 25 per cent, and it is probable that the situation in Scotland and Wales has been no different. At all events, there is no reasonable doubt that the cost estimates reported in Table 7.7 as being the best available are themselves an *under-estimate* of the true costs of reorganisation for the local authority system. Additional and unquantified costs have been incurred by bodies which work with local government, such as the health authorities and the voluntary sector; the problems faced by the latter have been examined by Craig and Manthorpe (1999).

## Conclusion

That there was serious under-estimation of the costs of reorganisation on the part of the Government, of the Local Government Commission for England and of the districts cannot be doubted. The precise magnitude of that misjudgement is clearly open to debate but there is also no doubt that whatever refinements may be made to the analyses reported above the broad orders of magnitude would be unaffected. The counties in England and Wales, and CoSLA in Scotland, came the nearest to providing an accurate prediction of the actual costs of reorganisation. During the review process, it was too easy for those who were ardently in favour of unitary solutions to dismiss the county and CoSLA figures as being the product of self-serving vested interests, and therefore as being worthless. While nobody would suggest that the counties and CoSLA were disinterested, the retrospective evidence is that they did an honest and professional job, and did so from the basis of a good understanding of what was involved. Interviews conducted with some of those closely involved with the county costing work made it clear to the author that a serious attempt had been made to arrive at a reasonable approximation to the truth.

The lobbying which was undertaken by the districts, especially in the early part of the whole process, was based on a serious under-estimate of the costs of reorganisation, and the decisions taken by the LGCE and by Government were also based on assessments which, it is now evident, were seriously flawed. It is a matter for speculation whether different decisions would have been forthcoming had the costing been more realistic. Given that the cost data did play a significant part in the decision process, the probability is that the outcome would have differed in some degree.

There is no realistic doubt that the official provisions for the cost of reorganisation have been considerably more realistic in England than in Scotland and Wales, and particularly in Scotland. The scale of the under-provision in Scotland and Wales was such that it undoubtedly contributed to the extreme financial pressure under which councils have operated in the immediate post-reform period. Local authorities in general were finding that funding pressures were severe but it was evident beyond any reasonable doubt from the columns of the local government press that the difficulties were greatest in Scotland. Although that crisis in Scotland (Midwinter 1998) arose primarily from the level of the general grant settlement and the imposition of capping, the under-funding of reorganisation was on a scale to compound the problems.

Despite the errors of judgement regarding the cost of reorganisation on the part of those taking the decisions, it may be the case that the benefits derived from the re-structuring have been sufficiently large to justify the upheaval in England, Scotland and Wales which cost at least £1,265 million (Table 7.7, 1997 prices). Thought of as an investment, such an outlay ought to have generated a substantial return; in purely financial terms, that return should perhaps be something like £126.5 million annually, though of course there are other non-monetary benefits to consider as well. So the task for the next chapter is to consider the post-reform situation, asking the question whether the postulated financial and non-financial benefits have been commensurate with the cost of the change.

# 8

# How well are the new arrangements working?

He that will not apply new remedies must expect new evils; for time is the greatest innovator. (Francis Bacon, *Of Innovations*)

So far as the general public is concerned, it is absolutely clear that where structural change has occurred it has done so with minimal disruption. The media have not been filled with horror stories, of services suddenly withdrawn from individuals or of major policy changes which have caused public anxiety. Every one of the individuals interviewed during the research for this book confirmed that the highest priority during and immediately after the handover period was to achieve a 'seamless' transition and, virtually without exception, this has been achieved. For example, the Chief Inspector of Social Services in Wales, reporting on the years 1996 to 1998, had this to say: 'I am pleased to report that, for the majority of service users, change was achieved without serious disruption or negative consequences to services for the majority of service users. All change brings uncertainty, and it is a measure of the commitment and success of service providers, that they have been able to manage the change so well' (Social Services Inspectorate for Wales 1998, pp. 1–2). There was similar praise for the management of the transition from HM Chief Inspector of Schools in Wales (1998) and for social services in England (Social Services Inspectorate 1997).

The availability of collated performance indicators allows one to enquire whether the picture reported for education and social services has been repeated across the spectrum of services provided by councils. In the case of Wales, the Audit Commission found that there had been some deterioration:

> In most services the new councils did less well than their predecessors. In some cases, such as inspecting food premises or processing council tax benefit claims, the new councils did significantly less well than their predecessors ...
>
> While improvements have been made in some areas, this appears in some cases to have been achieved at the expense of other services. This pattern may result from positive choices made by the new councils to change priorities, or it could be the unintended by-product of a period of considerable change. (Audit Commission 1998a, pp. 2–3)

The Audit Commission (1998b) has also reported on the performance of authorities in England. In this case, the year 1996/7 was the first year for thirteen unitary councils and the second for the Isle of Wight. No comment is offered regarding the achievements or failings of these new authorities in comparison with areas where no change had occurred or was imminent but inspection of the data suggests that there is no discernible difference, implying that where change had occurred it had not impacted adversely or positively on services. Finally, the Accounts Commission (1998) makes no observations regarding the impact of change in Scotland, implying a reasonably seamless transition, a view confirmed for Scottish schools by HM Inspector of Schools (1999). The general picture presented by these official documents is that the new authorities in Great Britain have, with the help of the relinquishing councils, got off to a good start, though there seems to be some doubt in the case of Wales.

At this immediate and practical level, it is quite clear that the councillors, officers and employees involved in structural change are to be commended for the success with which the transition has been effected. However, that conclusion is merely the starting point for assessment of the new structures, not the sum and completion of that account. After all, one of the justifications for structural reform was that there should be, even would be, an improvement in the performance of local authorities in terms of economy, efficiency and effectiveness. However, in seeking to identify whether this has actually been the case, two exceedingly difficult problems must be faced. The first of these is the certainty that it will take time for any benefits to become evident, probably of the order of five years. Consequently, it could be argued, the present study has been undertaken too soon. The second problem is much more fundamental. In the period prior to structural reform and thereafter, local government has been in flux for all sorts of reasons, including the imposition, and now partial relaxation, of universal capping, the introduction of Compulsory Competitive Tendering and its replacement by Best Value, and the Care in the Community initiative which, it was announced in 1998, is to be radically reviewed. With these and numerous other changes, it is impossible to construct a formal analytical model which would allow one to control for the impact of the major variables and to isolate the effect of structural change taken in isolation. For this reason, we are driven to employ a less rigorous approach, to piece together available information in the light of judgement.

In publishing performance data for England, the Audit Commission (1998b, 1999) distinguishes four groups of authorities – the new unitary councils, the counties and districts of the two-tier areas, the London boroughs and the Metropolitan councils. The massive sets of information are difficult to summarise but the over-all picture is quite clear in some important respects. In the first place, there is considerable variation around the average performance for each group of authorities, and the differences between the mean values are generally small. There is nothing in the data to suggest that the districts and the counties perform less well than the other authorities; in the field of education, the indicators suggest that the counties do better than the conurbation authorities. This geographical pattern for schooling relates, at least in part, to deprivation associated with the inner cities and areas within some conurbations, though it may also be linked to policies pursued by the councils. The key point in the present context is that in so far as there are serious problems in the school system they are concentrated in areas which were exempt from structural reform in the 1990s (Office for Standards in Education 1998).

We can go beyond these bald comparisons in the following manner. One of the benefits claimed for creating unitary authorities was the expected improvement in the economy and efficiency of service delivery. Some estimates of the expected ongoing savings have been given in previous chapters but we do not have adequate data to estimate what the magnitude has been in practice. However, we can begin our further enquiry by considering how large those *ex ante* estimates of savings might be in comparison with changes in actual expenditure over a period of years, comparing areas in which structural change occurred in the 1990s with areas where there was no change. This historical view will give us a context in which to consider the other information which is available.

In examining these historical data, two points should be borne in mind. First, the expenditure of authorities is intimately affected by the combination of local circumstances and the decisions taken by individual councils, and by the policies of central government as mediated through the SSA assessments, capping rules, controls on capital expenditure, and so on. Therefore, the sole interest of historical data in the present context is to establish whether the variations which have occurred over time in expenditure per person as between the groups of authorities identified have been large or small relative to the cost impact which might be expected from reorganisation. Second, it will be remembered from previous chapters that the most optimistic assessment which was made for ongoing savings for any of the proposed structures approximating that which has been put in place was that of the Scottish Office; its estimate of £40 million annual savings was equivalent to about 0.7 per cent of estimated net expenditure by councils; that is, total spending, not just indirect costs. If such savings were realised, they would represent a one-off reduction in the costs of operation, not a percentage reduction to be applied year on year. For our purpose, therefore, in considering the historical data it is that figure of 0.7 per cent change in costs which provides a useful reference point.

## Historical expenditure data

The aggregate expenditure of a local authority for each of its residents cannot be taken as a measure of the efficiency with which it functions, since expenditure is affected by a multitude of factors, as already noted. Nor can one infer that if the expenditure per person of one group of councils is either rising or falling relative to other councils that the authorities in question are becoming less or more efficient. However, the question that can be asked is whether there have been large or small changes in the relative expenditure of authorities, and how such changes compare with the savings that were supposed to flow from structural reform.

To explore this question, a simple concept has been adopted. The local authorities of Great Britain have been classified as shown in Table 8.1. For each of the seven primary groups, time-series data can be constructed for aggregate expenditure per person. One of the groups can be selected as the reference group, and the *per caput* expenditure of the other six can then be expressed as a percentage of the reference group, year by year, to create a time series of relative outlays which is not affected by inflationary changes in the value of money. To apply this concept, it is necessary to have data for individual English authorities and for the whole of Scotland and Wales for a number of years. For the figures to be meaningful, the definition of aggregate expenditure must be reasonably consistent from one year to the next. Data which meet these criteria are published by the Chartered Institute for Public Finance and Accountancy for England and Wales, and separately for Scotland. In fact, two sets of data are published, one for estimated expenditure and another for outturn figures. Advice from the Institute of Public Finance, an offshoot of CIPFA, suggested that the former set is the more appropriate for time-series work because the definitions employed have been more consistent (Clarke 1997). Therefore, use has been made of the annual publication *Finance and General Statistics* for England and Wales, and *Rating Review: Estimates of Income and Expenditure* in the case of Scotland.

**Table 8.1** *Local authority groupings for the purpose of examining expenditure time-series data*

| No structural change in the 1990s | Structural change in the 1990s |
|---|---|
| London boroughs | Five all-change counties |
| Metropolitan councils | Twenty hybrid English counties |
| Fourteen English two-tier counties | Scotland |
| | Wales |

CIPFA offers several options for the definition of total expenditure in England and Wales. The most inclusive is Gross Revenue Expenditure but this includes mandatory payments such as student awards and is in any case not available consistently. It was judged that the most useful figure to take would be Total Expenditure on Services. This total differs a little from the Aggregate Net Expenditure used for Scotland.

A two-stage analysis must be undertaken for England and Wales. The first allows comparison between five groups of authorities – London, the Metropolitan councils, non-Metropolitan England, Scotland and Wales. At this level of analysis, the expenditure data include precepts for the fire and police services and the passenger transport boards. The second stage is to examine non-Metropolitan

England by aggregating county areas in the following manner. There are those counties where there was no structural change in the 1990s, the five counties which have ceased to exist and the remainder where a hybrid solution was the outcome of the review (one or more unitary authorities and the remainder of the county staying two tier). For individual counties, districts and unitary authorities, the tabulated information excludes precepts other than at the county level, therefore omitting fire, police and transport precepts. Data have been tabulated for each of these groups back to 1981/2. Though it would be possible to create a longer time series, to do so would require tedious manipulation of the published figures for which the marginal return seemed to be small.

The outcome of this two-stage tabulation is presented in Table 8.2 and Table 8.3. In the first of these, the Metropolitan areas of England for any year have been taken as representing 100 while in the second the 14 no-change counties have been selected as the reference group. Both tables show some striking changes in relative expenditure. Table 8.2 records a substantial decline in expenditure per person in both London and Scotland relative to the Metropolitan areas of England in the period since 1985/6. In contrast, non-Metropolitan England has maintained a

**Table 8.2**    *Great Britain: estimated total expenditure by local authorities (£ per person; English Metropolitan areas = 100)*

| Year | London | Shire England | Scotland | Wales |
|------|--------|---------------|----------|-------|
| 1998/9 | 120.2 | 81.4 | 127.2 | 98.2 |
| 1997/8 | 123.1 | 83.4 | 130.0 | 84.1 |
| 1996/7 | 124.4 | 82.7 | 135.9 | 100.3 |
| 1995/6 | 124.9 | 81.1 | 137.0 | 100.9 |
| 1994/5 | 129.1 | 82.3 | 139.9 | 104.7 |
| 1993/4 | 131.7 | 82.6 | 142.5 | 100.2 |
| 1992/3 | 131.1 | 83.0 | 139.9 | 98.6 |
| 1991/2 | 130.3 | 82.5 | 143.6 | 98.0 |
| 1990/1 | 137.1 | 83.2 | 147.1 | 97.3 |
| 1989/90 | 132.5 | 82.3 | 149.7 | 96.4 |
| 1988/9 | 135.1 | 80.6 | 147.7 | 92.8 |
| 1987/8 | 140.6 | 79.8 | 150.3 | 92.5 |
| 1986/7 | 145.3 | 80.0 | 152.7 | 92.9 |
| 1985/6 | 146.2 | 80.7 | 155.1 | 94.8 |
| 1984/5 | 142.7 | 78.9 | 136.0 | 95.8 |
| 1983/4 | 139.0 | 79.7 | 136.8 | 96.0 |
| 1982/3 | 137.8 | 80.7 | 138.4 | 96.4 |
| 1981/2 | 134.2 | 81.6 | 147.1 | 97.1 |

*Sources*: *Finance and General Statistics* and *Rating Review: Estimates of Income and Expenditure*.
*Note*: For England and Wales, Total Expenditure on Services has been used; in the case of Scotland, it is Total Net Expenditure.

remarkably constant position, at about 80 per cent of the Metropolitan expenditure. The position in Wales has been less stable, with spending generally at or a little below parity with the conurbations and with a sharp downward perturbation in 1997/8.

Table 8.3 shows that within non-Metropolitan England the three groups of county areas have generally maintained their relative positions. Compared with the no-change areas, the group comprising the five abolished counties has had a very stable level of expenditure per person, though there was a major downward fluctuation in 1997/8. Relative expenditure in the hybrid counties has been falling slightly since 1986/7, with a substantial dip also in 1997/8.

The conclusion is inescapable, that the scale of even the highest of the *ex ante* estimates of recurrent savings from reorganisation is very small in relation to the actual changes which have occurred, changes which have arisen from a multiplicity of causes. The converse proposition is that if the new structures are in fact more costly than the pre-existing two-tier arrangements, it is probable that any such increment would also be too small to detect at this aggregate level. Clearly, if the agenda had seriously been to achieve savings in local government expenditure, structural reform would be a low priority in comparison with the other measures that Government has actually taken or might take.

**Table 8.3**  *Shire county areas in England: estimated total expenditure on services*
*(£ per person; fourteen no-change counties = 100)*

| Year | Five county areas replaced by unitary authorities | Twenty hybrid county areas |
|------|---------------------------------------------------|----------------------------|
| 1998/9 | 115.6 | 103.5 |
| 1997/8 | 109.3 | 96.5 |
| 1996/7 | 114.2 | 101.5 |
| 1995/6 | 114.1 | 101.8 |
| 1994/5 | 114.2 | 102.5 |
| 1993/4 | 113.0 | 103.0 |
| 1992/3 | 113.5 | 103.2 |
| 1991/2 | 114.8 | 103.2 |
| 1990/1 | 114.7 | 105.5 |
| 1989/90 | 113.3 | 103.6 |
| 1988/9 | 116.2 | 105.4 |
| 1987/8 | 116.7 | 105.9 |
| 1986/7 | 117.2 | 106.6 |
| 1985/6 | 116.7 | 106.1 |
| 1984/5 | 118.1 | 106.4 |
| 1983/4 | 118.9 | 106.4 |
| 1982/3 | 119.7 | 106.8 |
| 1981/2 | 114.5 | 105.4 |

*Source: Finance and General Statistics.*

This aggregate conclusion finds striking confirmation at the level of individual services in the range of unit costs and in the changes thereof over time (Department of Health 1997). The average weekly cost in England for elderly residents in local authority homes was £283 in 1994/5, with a range from under £100 to over £400 (the quality of the care must have varied considerably). Over the decade from 1984/5 to 1994/5, average costs in real terms rose by 38 per cent, with some authorities finding that costs in their residential units had risen by over 100 per cent; a handful of councils had nevertheless succeeded in reducing expenditure per resident. As overhead costs amounted to only 13–14 per cent of total expenditure for social services, the great bulk of the variation arose from differences in front-line spending, mainly staff costs. The clear implication is that, to achieve improved efficiency and better services, there is a great deal that can and should be done which has got nothing to do with the possible gains from a unitary structure.

## Financial constraints on councils

By any reasonable standards, the mid-1990s was a period in which local authorities were placed in very difficult financial circumstances, as part of a national drive to limit public expenditure. Problems were particularly acute in Scotland, with the general 'fiscal paradox of large spending reductions and tax increases simultaneously' (Midwinter 1998, p. 57). Indeed, Midwinter records that some 6,700 full-time equivalent posts had been lost in Scottish local government, substantially in excess of the 1,800 maximum that had been forecast by ministers as a consequence of structural reform. Similar problems, though somewhat less severe, have been faced in both England and Wales.

In addition to the general financial pressure, major issues arose in disaggregating the assessments which the Government makes of the spending needs of counties and regions for the purpose of determining revenue support grants. As a result, some of the new authorities gained quite favourable settlements while others, such as Leicester, were faced with the need to reduce expenditure and at the same time to cut the level of Council Tax. These disaggregation problems were sufficiently severe for special damping arrangements to be put in place to spread the transition over a number of years, primarily in Scotland and Wales.

The net effect of the general financial stringency and the problems of disaggregation is to render any rigorous and tidy comparisons of 'before' and 'after' quite impossible. These difficulties of analysis have been compounded by the change of administration which occurred with the 1997 general election and consequential policy changes.

## The 1997 general election

The year 1997 marks an important watershed in British politics. After eighteen years in power, the Conservatives were replaced by Labour, commanding a massive majority in the House of Commons. Initially, this change in political control at Westminster was marked by continuity with respect to local government rather than immediate radical initiatives. This was particularly true of finance, since the incoming administration accepted for the first two years the spending plans which had been put in place by its predecessor. However, it was not long before the impact of the political change was felt, with a strong push for general modernisation of the local government system. Universal capping has been ended, though the relaxation in control may be more apparent than real, and Compulsory Competitive Tendering is being replaced by the concept of Best Value, with potential implications for the previous drive to convert councils into enabling authorities (DETR 1998). In 1999, Scotland elected its new Parliament, which will have a major role in the governance of that country; the Welsh equivalent, an Assembly, has lesser powers. A new London-wide authority, including an elected mayor, was in the process of being established at the time this book was completed, while new Regional Development Agencies (RDAs) took up their duties in England in April 1999.

The over-all impact of these changes cannot be assessed at this stage but two features stand out. In both Scotland and Wales, the new elected bodies have powers in respect of expenditure and decisions which had hitherto been exercised through the Scottish and Welsh Offices, so that there has been a downward devolution from London. The existing unitary structure of local government has been taken as a given, at least for the present. The RDAs in England are not elected bodies and in effect are agents for devolved central government activities, with no immediate implications for the structure of local government. However, if or when the Government proceeds to convert the RDAs into some form of democratic control, the issue of local government structure may come to the fore. In Opposition, the Labour Party had said that the elected regional assemblies would only be introduced where unitary local government was in place, implying a process for converting the remaining two-tier areas. So far, the Government has shown no eagerness to proceed with these assemblies in England and in any case if they would genuinely involve devolution from Westminster and Whitehall that would imply the downward transfer of an upper tier of government rather than the creation of a new one.

Beyond a peradventure, the context in which local government operates has been substantially changed by the general election of 1997, a fact which makes it difficult to tease out the effects of structural change treated in isolation. In addition, the Conservatives have been forced to re-think their attitudes to local government. At the time of the structural reform, the replacement of the two-tier structure by unitary councils in Scotland was presented as providing an appropriate structure for the functions undertaken by local authorities. Since the election, the Scottish Conservatives have proposed that local authorities should lose certain functions. There have been serious problems with loss-making Direct Labour Organisations (DLOs) and the Conservatives propose that they should all be privatised (*Local Government Chronicle*, 19 February 1999, p. 6). A consultation paper which was circulated in late 1998 made the more radical proposal that the entire council housing stock in Scotland should be transferred to community ownership over a period of ten years, saying: 'Because councils have such a poor record for delivering good quality housing we would not wish councils to be involved with the management of the agencies to which houses would be transferred' (*Local Government Chronicle*, 27 November 1998, p. 7). Finally, the manifesto published for the 1999 election to the new Parliament proposed that all schools should be removed from local authority control and given into the care of local school boards (*The Telegraph*, 9 April 1999). These proposals could be interpreted as evidence that the Conservatives now consider that the functions of local authorities in Scotland should be adjusted to the structure of councils introduced in 1996; if that is the case, it sits oddly with the claim which was made that reorganisation would yield very large benefits, and demonstrates the limited basis on which the reforms were considered.

Of considerably greater significance is the evolution of Conservative thinking in England, which seems to be going in the opposite direction. The party has much greater strength in local government than is the case north of the Border and at the first annual conference after the 1997 general election a sharp change in attitudes was signalled (Calpin 1997), reinforced early in 1998 by William Hague, the Party's leader: 'For too long we have treated local government, local government elections and local councillors as though they didn't matter. We spent far too much time reorganising local government and not enough time campaigning for it' (*Municipal Journal*, 27 February 1998, p. 7). A little over a year later, the deputy leader gave the Rab Butler memorial lecture to the Adam Smith Institute, in which he explicitly argued that there are clear limits to the role of 'free' markets for the provision of important services such as health, welfare and education: 'We must stop behaving as if we are only true to ourselves when we are applying the free market paradigm to anything or everything' (Lilley 1999). This speech triggered some angry responses from within the party and at the time of completing this book it was not clear what the outcome of the debate would be. However, it is clear that important parts of the political rhetoric which justified structural reorganisation are being reassessed in Conservative circles, reinforcing Hagues's comments about local government. These changing attitudes are consistent with an interesting evaluation of trends in the body politic since the general election: 'Cautiously, hesitantly, and in a fragmented way, the values of public service are beginning to be rebuilt' (Terry 1999).

## The enabling authority?

It appears that there are no comprehensive data which allow one to monitor progress towards the concept of local authorities as enablers rather than providers. Consequently, we must rely on patchy and incomplete information for the situation as it was in the late 1990s, for comparison with the limited information assembled in Chapter 5. For the purpose of this enquiry, it is convenient to treat the main service headings separately.

### Social services

There is no doubt that in recent years there has been some decline in the absolute number of residential units, for both the young and the old, run by local authorities, and also the number of residents housed therein. In proportionate terms, the number of residents in the social services sector housed in local authority institutions has declined much more dramatically. Employment in what may be called social services in the independent sector now equals or exceeds social services employment in local authorities (Social Services Inspectorate 1997, para. 34). On the face of it, these facts imply great strides towards the enabling authority.

That interpretation would be too simple. Over the period 1984/5 to 1994/5, the expenditure of local government social services departments in England rose by 61 per cent in real terms (Department of Health 1997, p. 3). Much of the apparent privatisation of the social services arises from the transfer of funding that has taken place since 1993/4 from the social security budget of central government to the budgets of local authorities, as part of a reorganisation of care delivery, especially for the elderly living in residential units. The scale of this transfer is evident in data for England. Between 1984/5 and 1992/3, social security expenditure on residential care for the elderly rose tenfold in constant values, from £200 million annually to £2 billion. This figure of £2 billion can be compared with the total expenditure of social services departments on all their activities of £7.5 billion in 1994/5, the year after the transfer from the social security budget began.

Thus, in the social services field, the enabling role consists very largely, though not entirely, of taking over the management of arrangements with the independent providers, rather than the loss of existing direct provision. This is shown by employment data for England over the period 1986 to 1996, set out in Table 8.4. A similar situation is evident in Scotland; expenditure on community care was £286 million in 1995/6, of which £203 million was money which had been transferred from the Department of Social Security and the National Health Service, mainly in respect of residential care. Nevertheless, a 1997 survey found that, measured by value, 46 per cent of residential care was provided by local authorities; they were also responsible for 92 per cent of domiciliary care. Few of the authorities surveyed envisaged that there would be any large-scale change in the position (Accounts Commission 1997), though another survey suggested that there

**Table 8.4** *Staff employed by social services departments in England (full-time staff equivalents; 000)*

| Year | Total | Domiciliary services | Day care | Residential care | Social work, other | Senior staff, administrative, support |
|------|-------|----------------------|----------|------------------|--------------------|---------------------------------------|
| 1996 | 234 | 55 | 31 | 68 | 42 | 37 |
| 1995 | 234 | 57 | 31 | 69 | 41 | 36 |
| 1994 | 238 | 59 | 31 | 72 | 41 | 35 |
| 1993 | 233 | 58 | 30 | 74 | 38 | 32 |
| 1992 | 235 | 58 | 30 | 79 | 39 | 30 |
| 1991 | 237 | 59 | 29 | 83 | 38 | 29 |
| 1990 | 240 | 60 | 31 | 88 | 35 | 28 |
| 1989 | 239 | 60 | 29 | 89 | 35 | 26 |
| 1988 | 236 | 60 | 29 | 88 | 34 | 26 |
| 1987 | 232 | 60 | 28 | 88 | 32 | 26 |
| 1986 | 224 | 57 | 26 | 87 | 31 | 24 |

*Source*: Social Services Inspectorate (1997), Table 5.
*Note*: Rows do not necessarily add to the totals shown on account of rounding.

may be greater resort to the independent sector in the future than the Accounts Commission thought likely (Craig and Manthorpe 1998a).

This evidence suggests that progress towards the enabling authority has been slower than the rhetoric of the early 1990s would have led one to believe. Confirmation of that conclusion is to be found in a White Paper issued in March 1997 by the Conservative administration, shortly before the general election, in which certain proposals were made for both England and Wales. Although local authorities would retain the power directly to provide residential care, it was stated that legislation would be introduced to alter the terms on which this could be done: 'The need to retain directly managed residential homes is likely to become increasingly rare. The law will therefore place a strong and clear onus of proof on authorities wishing to retain existing residential homes or to open or acquire new care homes' (Department of Health and the Welsh Office 1997, para. 2.30). If enacted, such a requirement would have made it possible to force local authorities to relinquish their stock of residential units for both young and old persons. The fact that the Conservatives felt the need to take such draconian powers implies that the full realisation of the enabling authority would otherwise have been unlikely. With the 1997 change of Government, the proposed legislation was not brought forward.

The funding arrangements for residential units for the elderly are complex and are tilted in favour of the independent sector (Department of Health 1999; Sutherland 1999). The continuing unequal financial treatment of the public and independent sectors would suggest that local authorities will wish to pass the management of residential units to the independent sector, a view that is reinforced by the apparently higher costs of running public sector homes (*Economist,*

20 March 1999, p. 37). However, profit margins have become so low in the private sector that homes are being closed, a process that will probably continue as new employment legislation forces an improvement in the wages and conditions of private employment. A contributory factor has been the widespread practice of local authorities to make spot purchases of places in the independent sector rather than providing core funding. Thus, although councils may wish to divest themselves of residential units because capital controls make it difficult or impossible to carry out the necessary upgrading of facilities, it is not at all certain that agencies in the independent sector will continue to wish to take over the responsibility (Tidball and Robinson 1999). The really critical issue will be the nature of the Government's response to the Sutherland Royal Commission on the care of the aged and the decisions to be taken following the review of the benefits system which was in hand at the time of writing.

## *Education: schools*

The fundamental innovation which the Conservatives introduced into the public school system was the insistence that local authorities devolve a high proportion of their education budget to individual schools for management at that level. In the period up to 1997, there was never any question of privatising state provision and requiring local authorities to act as purchasers in the market. In fact, it was a matter of seeking to remove schools from local authority control by encouraging them to opt for Grant Maintained (GM) status, funded directly by central government. Initially, there were considerable financial inducements, buttressed by a biased system for making the election to transfer, and from 1990/1 it looked as though large numbers of schools would opt out of local authority control. In fact, as Table 8.5 shows, by 1994/5 the rate of change was declining and by 1996/7 had become very slow indeed. Virtually all the secondary schools which became grant main-

**Table 8.5**  *Public sector mainstream schools: total number and number grant maintained*

| Year | England | | Scotland | | Wales | |
|------|---------|-----|----------|-----|-------|-----|
| | Total | GM | Total | GM | Total | GM |
| 1996/7 | 3,569 | 652 | 403 | 1 | n.a. | n.a. |
| 1995/6 | 3,594 | 642 | 405 | 1 | 228 | 11 |
| 1994/5 | 3,614 | 622 | 406 | 1 | 227 | 11 |
| 1993/4 | 3,629 | 554 | 408 | | 227 | 10 |
| 1992/3 | 3,773 | 262 | 412 | | 229 | 4 |
| 1991/2 | 3,847 | 130 | 419 | | 229 | 2 |
| 1990/1 | 3,897 | 50 | 424 | | 230 | |
| 1989/90 | 3,976 | | 429 | | 231 | |

*Source: Annual Abstract of Statistics 1999, Table 6.1.*

tained are located in England, with only minimal uptake in both Scotland and Wales. Indeed, as of January 1999 there were only two such schools in Scotland, one of which had requested to transfer back to its local authority (*Local Government Chronicle*, 22 January 1999, p. 2). Although primary schools are much more numerous than secondary schools, the absolute number opting out has been smaller, with again virtually all being in England.

Thus even under the Conservative administration, the rate of opting out fell far short of the scale which the Government had envisaged and which the LGCE was advised to expect. In the belief that the role of councils would diminish to the point of vanishing, many argued that the education sector should be disregarded in the structural review. In the light of Table 8.5, it is clear that this radical approach to the relevance of the education sector was misplaced. In any case, with the change of political control in Westminster in 1997, the opt-out has been put into reverse. With effect from 1999, the GM schools in England and Wales became Foundation schools under local authority control; and legislation may be introduced in the Scottish Parliament to rectify what now seems the anomaly of a single GM school in that country. Furthermore, the accumulating evidence shows that the problems which exist in the education sector have roots in the post-war egalitarian ideology of comprehensive education, the manner in which schools have been managed, some aspects of innovations in teaching methods and a whole host of other factors including finance, all of which have little or nothing to do with the map of local authority boundaries (*Economist*, 10 April 1999, pp. 34–6).

*Housing*

From the early 1980s, there has been a continuing decline in the significance of public housing in the over-all housing stock. It was deliberate policy on the part of the Government that council tenants should have the right to buy their rented houses on favourable terms and for local authorities otherwise to transfer their stock to housing associations. In addition, local authorities have been forced to cut back their own building programmes. As a result, local authorities now account for about 16 per cent of the housing stock in both England and Wales, down from 22–3 per cent a decade ago (Table 8.6). Scotland differs, in that local authorities were much more important providers of housing and the rate of transfer has been slower than elsewhere in Great Britain. That difference may disappear with the announcement that the Government wants one-quarter of the council stock in Scotland to be transferred to community ownership in a period of three years; indeed, Glasgow has decided to transfer its entire holding of dwellings (*Municipal Journal* 1999, 26 February, p. 9 and 19 March, p. 9). The fundamental reason for these transfers lies in the financial constraints placed on local authorities: to up-grade Glasgow's stock was estimated to cost £1.2 billion which, under the restrictive public sector borrowing rules, would take thirty years to finance but probably no more than six years in the independent sector.

In sum, the housing sector does show signs that the role of local authorities will

**Table 8.6** *Great Britain: stock of dwellings by tenure (000)*

| December | Owner-occupier | Private | Rented Housing association | LA/New Town | Total |
|---|---|---|---|---|---|
| England | | | | | |
| 1997 | 14,033 | 2,304 | 1,008 | 3,353 | 20,699 |
| 1990 | 13,171 | 1,906 | 613 | 3,944 | 19,634 |
| 1987 | 12,264 | 1,899 | 5.12 | 4,403 | 19,078 |
| Scotland | | | | | |
| 1996 | 1,330 | 152 | 98 | 666 | 2,246 |
| 1990 | 1,088 | 126 | 65 | 845 | 2,124 |
| 1987 | 922 | 147 | 54 | 943 | 2,067 |
| Wales | | | | | |
| 1997 | 892 | 106 | 49 | 203 | 1,250 |
| 1990 | 840 | 91 | 24 | 226 | 1,181 |
| 1987 | 782 | 93 | 20 | 253 | 1,148 |

*Source*: DETR, Scottish Office and Welsh Office (1998, p. 122).

become minimal or non-existent in the near future. For this sector, privatisation has been real. Although this may fit the concept of the local authority as an enabler, it does not fit with the argument that uniting county and district functions in unitary authorities would make the integration of housing and social services easier. To the extent that there are advantages in having both services controlled by one authority, the reality has been that housing has been moving out of local authority control altogether, making the structural argument irrelevant.

## Direct Service Organisations

Periodically, the Local Government Management Board has conducted surveys to ascertain the scale on which certain services are contracted out in England, services such as the cleaning of buildings, refuse collection and catering. These are services for which the Direct Services Organisations (DSOs) must compete with independent operators to secure contracts. The latest survey shows that, in 1998, 68 per cent of these contracts by value were won by the DSOs. For the more 'managerial' services, the proportion ranged upwards from 76 per cent for construction and property services to 88 per cent for legal matters and 93 per cent in the case of housing management (LGMB 1998, pp. 3 and 16). The data are also presented in terms of the number of contracts, by which criterion the proportion won by the DSOs is lower than it is by value. We may infer that for large contracts the in-house bids are fully competitive with the bids submitted by the independent sector but that the independent sector has an advantage for small contracts. This in turn throws some interesting light on the existence or otherwise of scale economies and the ability of local authorities to capture them; we may infer that large councils with large contracts are fully able to reap scale economies but that smaller authorities find that costs are higher and that they cannot match the independent sector so effectively. How far this conclusion applies in Scotland and Wales is a moot point, given the serious losses which the DSO and DLO organisations have incurred, but it may be that the small size of many of the new councils is a relevant factor; CoSLA certainly takes the view that inter-authority cooperation and/or mergers will be necessary to achieve economical working (*Local Government Chronicle*, 25 September 1998, p. 7).

It is clear that local authorities remain the primary providers in the fields covered by the DSOs, despite the manner in which the rules for Compulsory Competitive Tendering were drawn up to favour the independent sector. The introduction of Best Value practices probably heralds a more level playing field in the future. It seems abundantly clear that the process of contracting out in the DSO field has gone much less far than the Government had expected in the early 1990s. In fact, we are witnessing the long-standing continuation of the mixed economy of provision (Ascher 1987).

## Joint arrangements

It will be recollected that the relevant legislation for both Scotland and Wales gave the Secretary of State the power to direct two or more local authorities to set up joint arrangements for the discharge of specified services if this were considered to be necessary. Equivalent but in fact inoperable provisions were made for England. No such orders had been made in either Scotland or Wales by the end of 1998, nor were any pending (Scottish Office 1998; Welsh Office 1999b). This provides clear confirmation that the worst fears regarding the impact of structural reform on service delivery have been confounded, confirming the fact that the transition has been well handled.

The position with respect to voluntary arrangements between local authorities is much less clear-cut. From the research interviews conducted, it is evident that for the first year or two after reorganisation the Scottish and Welsh authorities maintained existing collaborative arrangements more or less intact, a policy consistent with the need to achieve a seamless transition. However, it is also clear that some of these initial arrangements have been discontinued as the new councils have got into their stride. There seem to be two main reasons why voluntary joint arrangements are difficult to sustain. The first is human pride, the desire to be master in one's own domain. The second is the natural tendency for councils to set their own priorities and ways of working, a tendency which is entirely consistent with the concept of bringing local government 'closer to the people'. The differentiation of priorities and protocols is entirely legitimate and on certain criteria is to be welcomed but implies increasing difficulty in cooperating with other authorities. At the same time, agencies outside the local government system find that they must adjust their own procedures to mesh with the growing diversity of local government practices. These points have been explicitly identified as a result of inspections of three social services authorities in Wales:

> As each new authority develops in its own right, the common practice procedures and the joint arrangements supporting them are inevitably threatened. Hospital social work teams found themselves having to operate different sets of discharge procedures. The ACPC [Area Child Protection Committee] for 'pan-Gwent' (the area of the former Gwent plus the Rhymney Valley district) was about to be dismantled ... Cross authority training units faced an uncertain future. Social services and other public authorities were at different stages in coming to terms with the reality of this divergence. (Social Services Inspectorate for Wales 1997, para. 3.12)

A rather similar conclusion was reached by Davidson *et al.* (1997) in their study of child protection arrangements in Scotland. Inter-agency working was proving relatively effective for the three Islands councils, which had experienced no structural change, and also in the mainland unitary authorities based on former regions – Borders, Dumfries and Galloway, Fife, and Highland. Elsewhere, the disaggregation of the regions had created a situation in which cooperation between authorities was regarded as more problematical.

There appears to be no comprehensive study of voluntary joint arrangements in Wales comparable to the CoSLA (1998) study for Scotland. CoSLA identified 334 cooperative arrangements in 1996/7, the first year of the new councils. Of these, 302 definitely continued into the next year, 1997/8; 17 were known to have ceased; and 15 had come to an end. Only one new arrangement was started in 1997/8. The erosion of joint arrangements has been greater than is implied by these figures, since twelve of those that continued into the second year did so with a reduced number of participating authorities, and in an additional case plans were actively afoot for disbandment. These figures confirm the evidence from interviews and from social services in Wales, that transitional joint arrangements are being whittled away and are not being replaced by new ones.

Some examples reinforce the point. Prior to reorganisation, local authorities played a key role in funding the arts in Scotland (Vestri 1994) but since 1996 the finances of the major companies have been under particular stress. The arrangements which CoSLA had devised for all the councils to contribute, albeit in varying degree, for the maintenance of the national companies collapsed early in 1998 (*Municipal Journal*, 10 April 1998, p. 8), leaving the four primary cities to shoulder the burden of public support. These cities had provided 80 per cent of the local authority funding prior to reorganisation but found that the other twenty-eight authorities post-1996 were mostly unwilling to continue support. The host authorities were themselves under severe financial pressure and the net effect was a reduction in council funding somewhat greater than 50 per cent. CoSLA has been trying to find another formula for sharing the costs. On the positive side, it must be noted that virtually all the new authorities have taken steps to promote the arts within their own borders (Scottish Arts Council 1998). Serious difficulties have also been experienced by the Strathclyde Passenger Transport Authority. Because councils have not made available the planned financial support, annual capital expenditure has fallen from £25 million to just £5 million (*Local Government Chronicle*, 9 October 1998, p. 8).

Viewed in isolation, the fact that joint arrangements between local authorities in Scotland and Wales are proving hard to maintain and even harder to initiate may lead to one of two conclusions. It could be argued that as the councils settle down they can quite properly dispense with arrangements that may have been necessary in the transitional phase, so that we may be left with only a few voluntary cooperative ventures which are essentially technical in character, such as public analyst services and responsibility for weights and measures. This interpretation suggests that there are limited, or even non-existent, economies of scale over the greater part of local authority services, which would confirm the rhetoric of the New Right that even very small unitary authorities can be fully viable. The alternative interpretation is that the financial stringencies which have faced councils plus the political imperative of running the councils as autonomous units have combined to induce policy reponses that diverge from the rational needs of economical service provision, leading to long-term inefficiencies. Such an argument would conform with the case put forward by the counties in England and Wales, and the Scottish regions, that breaking them up would lead to significant diseconomies.

This second interpretation is consistent with the experience in London following the abolition of the Greater London Council and the Inner London Education Authority, exemplified by problems that have been identified with respect to residential facilities for young people in care (Chapter 2). That this second interpretation is probably correct is suggested by the fact that the 1998 CoSLA listing of joint arrangements in Scotland was compiled in order to encourage councils by example. CoSLA has taken the view that joint arrangements are a necessary feature of the present unitary structure in Scotland and that it is therefore important to maintain and to extend cooperative working. Given that CoSLA is the representative body for local government north of the Border, its concern suggests that in the absence of widespread cooperation the quality and efficiency of services will be impaired.

Much less information is available for England than for the other two countries, reflecting the limited nature of the structural reform that actually occurred. Therefore, to make further headway in deciding between the two conflicting conclusions that can be drawn from the Scottish and Welsh evidence about joint working it is necessary to turn to other evidence, and in particular to such information as may be available regarding the existence or non-existence of scale economies.

## Does scale matter?

There is no doubt that the Chief Inspector for Social Services in Wales has serious concerns about the ability of small authorities to provide adequate services in the long run:

At a strategic and a management level, the impact of a move from eight to twenty two (*sic*) authorities has become more apparent as time progresses. The change occurred at the same time as budgets came under particular pressure. Before reorganisation the larger authorities had some capacity to adjust budgets to meet specific requirements, for example the demand for specialised placements which can be unpredictable. SSDs [Social Services Departments], especially those in smaller unitary authorities, are finding this to be less possible. The need to forecast, plan and work effectively with others, particularly the health service, becomes even greater.

The requirement for SSDs to spearhead the overall planning of community care and children's services has placed a very great pressure on the unitary authorities. Technical expertise for planning is at a premium in Wales, and some small authorities have found it difficult to engage with others at the same time as maintaining operational services ...

... to maintain quality and effectiveness, organisations must be able to plan, monitor and review performance. Our work shows this to be an area of weakness where we all need to put more effort. (Social Services Inspectorate for Wales 1998, p. 2)

Rhondda, Cynon, Taff is the second largest authority in Wales, with a population of about 240,000. It has decided to cope with the problem of unpredictable calls upon resources for secure accommodation and for special educational needs by taking these items out of departmental budgets and treating them as a corporate responsibility. In effect, the severity of the management problem is eased through smoothing resource demands by amalgamating two independent sources of fluctuation but this strategy is less helpful for smaller councils.

Further light is thrown upon the implications of size by the possibility which arose in August 1997 that the boundary between Denbighshire and Wrexham might be reviewed. The Secretary of State announced that he was minded to direct the Local Government Boundary Commission for Wales to carry out a review to determine whether Llangollen should be transferred from Denbighshire to Wrexham. A considerable degree of local interest was aroused by this possibility. In the event, Ron Davies decided in February 1998 not to issue a direction, on the basis that local opinion did not support the boundary adjustment. Although the decision letter made no explicit mention of issues concerning the viability of the two authorities, the local view was quite clear, that the removal of Llangollen would call in question the continued existence of Denbighshire. Llangollen had a 1991 population of 3,900 (Hatton 1998), which compares with approximately 91,000 for Denbighshire and 123,000 for Wrexham in the late 1990s. The local press reported Eryl Williams, leader of Denbighshire council, to the effect that the loss of 3,900 people would compromise the viability of his authority, a view that was shared by Wrexham (Wrexham County Borough 1998) and by Martyn Jones, the MP for Clwyd South (*Evening Leader*, 17 March 1998).

The matter is now closed, with no change in the boundary. However, the episode illustrates two matters of general application. First, where local authorities are relatively small, it is difficult to contemplate boundary adjustments other than those which involve very few people indeed. Second, it would appear that a rural authority in Wales which has a population no greater than 91,000 must be regarded as vulnerable in terms of its ability to operate in a cost-effective manner in the long run.

Another aspect of size, which also links to the question of joint arrangements, is presented by the provision of secure accommodation for young people in Wales. In the year which ended in March 1997, fifty-five children were admitted to secure care, of whom eighteen, mostly from north Wales, were sent to England. Within Wales, there are only two units offering this facility – Hillside in Neath Port Talbot with eighteen places and the Children's Resource Centre in Rhondda, Cynon, Taff, equipped with just two places. The former, opened in November 1996, was started by the now disbanded West Glamorgan County Council in conjunction with the Welsh Office (Social Services Inspectorate for Wales 1998, p. 36). These facilities serve the whole of south Wales. The problem which is now emerging is that the Welsh councils are withdrawing from long-term contracts for the placement of children and are opting instead for spot purchases as and when they need to make a placement. This causes considerable funding and management problems for the 'host' authorities, creating conditions which could lead to a repeat of experience in London following the abolition of the Greater London Council. If the erosion and fragmentation of facilities is to be avoided, it is virtually certain that the Welsh Office will have to take a strong lead and commit funds, an outcome which would amount to the centralisation of control and power in Cardiff. Indeed, there has already been an explicit call for just such intervention in another aspect of child care, in the context of the difficult problems of child abuse in north Wales in the two former counties of Clwyd and Gwynedd. The author of a report on these matters questioned 'the capacity of the new authorities to undertake strategic planning and fulfil their mandatory obligations in respect of children's services plans without external assistance', calling on the Welsh Office to fund a special project to help local authorities up-grade their strategic planning capability (Jones 1996, para. 2.15). A similar message was conveyed to the author by the Finance Director of one of the smaller Welsh councils, who freely acknowledged that there has been a loss of scale economies; he fully expected that with the passage of time the small size of councils would lead to the centralisation of power in Cardiff.

Of course the evidence does not all point in one direction. As the Social Services Inspectorate for Wales (1997, para. 4.6) points out, the new authorities 'have gained the opportunity to have simpler, better integrated structures', though it is clear that the extent to which authorities have availed themselves of this opportunity has been patchy. Where options for better integration have been embraced, there have clearly been many positive developments but the operational managers have to cope with a wide range of policy issues in addition to day-to-day minutiae and pressures, with the result that 'only time will show how well these broader roles can be sustained' (Social Services Inspectorate for Wales 1997, para. 4.7).

The concerns which have been identified in the Welsh context regarding social services have close parallels in Scotland. In the absence of annual reports from the social work inspectorate reviewing Scotland as a whole, the most useful available assessment is contained in a report commissioned by the Scottish Office, which concluded that, with the creation of the new unitary authorities, merely to maintain services at the pre-reform level would require additional expenditure of about £21 million annually. In other words, structural reorganisation has increased costs and the savings which were envisaged as a consequence of reform can only be achieved by cuts in the quality and/or scope of services offered (Craig and Manthorpe 1998b, p. 198).

A survey of the twenty-nine mainland Scottish social work departments conducted in the spring of 1997 found that some respondents believed that reorganisation had led to improved service delivery and greater possibilities for integration but that: 'The weight of these comments, however, was not significant compared with the difficulties ... experienced by authorities in reconstructing relationships with other agencies, and with Health Boards in particular' (Craig and Manthorpe 1998a, p. 123). The most noteworthy issues raised by the respondents were the diseconomies associated with the small size of authorities and the proliferation of policy differences between councils.

Education is the other main service which has been affected by the disaggregation of councils. In both Scotland and Wales, the Inspectorate is concerned about the ability of the new authorities to maintain adequate support in specialist subjects, with the risk that the breadth of opportunities available to children will be reduced (HM Inspector of Schools 1999, p. 12; HM Chief Inspector of Schools in Wales 1998, p. 38). Experience in England with respect to music shows that these anxieties are well founded, though simultaneously showing just how difficult it is to isolate the effects of reorganisation from all the other factors. Early in the 1990s, Berkshire County Council hived off its support for music in the county's schools by setting up the Berkshire Young Musicians Trust (BYMT). Over a seven-year period, the contract with the Trust provided for a diminishing contribution from the county. The Trust enters into contracts with the parents of school children for the group teaching of instrumental and vocal skills by peripatetic specialists, and also individual tuition at four centres. The skills required are diverse – not just vocal, wind, string and brass, but individual instruments within those categories, such as 'cello and violin. At the time the new unitary authorities took over control in April 1998, they inherited the county contract with BYMT, amounting to an annual sum of about £1 million. When the contract expired in August 1998, Wokingham withdrew from the scheme but re-joined in September 1999, an episode which illustrates the fragility of joint arrangements for the provision of specialised services, in the provision of which there are clear economies of scale (Hazelgrove 1999).

The reason why Wokingham felt able to re-join BYMT may lie in an initiative taken by the Government in response to widespread problems in the provision of music for school children. These problems have arisen from the general pressure on council finances in combination with the transfer of most of the education budget to schools for them to manage. With devolved financial control and tight funding, many schools have felt that other needs must take priority over music, with the result that the viability of support facilities has been undermined. In response to this situation, the Government announced in December 1998 the provision of limited funds in England over three years for which authorities could bid. In the first year of the scheme, 1999–00, £41 million has been made available, to support existing services and to promote new initiatives, with explicit mention of cooperative ventures between councils. Having been successful in obtaining funds, Wokingham has felt able to re-join BYMT.

However, the complications of funding run wider than this. Grant Maintained schools reverted to local authority control as Foundation schools, with effect from April 1999, with consequential effects which can be illustrated by the case of Cambridgeshire, a county that supports music through the Cambridgeshire Instrumental Music Agency (CIMA). This Agency is part of the County Council, partially funded from education money which is retained by the county and partially by contracts with individual schools. These contracts reflect the subsidised costs of providing group tuition and ensemble work, except that GM schools have been paying the full cost of the service, since they otherwise make no contribution to the money equivalent to that contributed by the county. Peterborough became a unitary authority in April 1998, having previously been part of the county, and has entered into a three-year contract to buy into CIMA. The seven GM schools in Peterborough have been faced with reduced budgets on changing to Foundation status, as has been general for such schools throughout England and Wales. They therefore asked Peterborough to increase its contribution to CIMA so that they can buy CIMA's services at the subsidised price, in effect requesting that some of the money which the authority now retains be used for this particular purpose. This meant that Peterborough had to make an explicit decision. This situation adds to the uncertainties which are inherent in the separation of Peterborough from the county, removing about one-quarter of the population of the pre-reform council. The basic uncertainty is whether Peterborough's three-year contract will be renewed but all the uncertainties have implications not only for all the schools in Peterborough but also for all those in the rest of the county, since the uncertainties impinge on the range and quality of the resources which will be available for schools to call upon through CIMA (Lovell 1999).

Rather similar problems have affected the Department of Adult and Continuing Education (DACE) of the University of Glasgow. The Department used to operate throughout the former Strathclyde region as well as in Dumfries and Galloway; it developed courses which included ones for disadvantaged students and was able to cross-subsidise work in remote and sparsely peopled areas. With reorganisation, DACE was faced with negotiating contracts with a total of thirteen authorities, significantly increasing the complexity and cost of administration. In fact, some of the new authorities have felt unable or unwilling to make any financial contribution, while the others have reduced their collective funding, no doubt partly because of the general pressure on their resources. As a result, DACE has scaled down its activities outside the city of Glasgow, abandoning all activities in South Lanarkshire and East Ayrshire, despite the growth of income from fees and the receipt of support directly from the Universities Funding Council. In sum, the reorganisation of local government, in combination with other developments, has eroded the links between DACE and the local government sector and has had an adverse impact on the scope of its work (Davies *et al.* 1999).

Finally, as Craig and Manthorpe (1999) have shown, the fragmentation of local government poses serious problems for the voluntary sector. The multiplication of local authorities with which some voluntary bodies now have to deal imposes additional ongoing costs which are clearly a matter of concern for the organisations affected.

This account of the limited evidence regarding scale economies strongly suggests that the erosion of joint arrangements reported in the previous section is to be interpreted as evidence of the increase in costs associated with reorganisation into comparatively small units of local government, and not as evidence that the size of councils is unimportant.

## Service integration and management structures

Advocates of the unitary principle claimed that bringing all local government services together in the hands of a single authority would yield advantages from service integration, with housing and social services frequently cited as the prime example. The most visible manifestation of that integration would be the union of these two services into a single department or directorate. Consequently, it is of some interest to examine the extent to which the new unitary authorities have in fact adopted this form of integrated management structure.

The context for this enquiry is provided by a recent study of management structures in England and Wales (Whitford-Jackson 1998). Councils have been faced with general pressure in recent years to adopt 'flatter' management systems, with a smaller number of chief officers. Several factors have been instrumental in this, including structural reorganisation, financial pressures, the demands imposed on councils by the need to work with a multiplicity of other agencies, changing management theories, and so on. Whitford-Jackson defines a 'new' structure in terms of the number of directorates: for the English and Welsh authorities other than districts, a new structure is one which has five or fewer; in the case of districts, the criterion is three directorates or fewer. Table 8.7 provides a snapshot of the position in 1998, showing that the counties, districts and unitary councils in England have gone a good deal further in adopting these new structures than is the case for the boroughs of London and the Metropolitan authorities. Considering England on

**Table 8.7**   *Great Britain: management structures of local authorities, 1998*

|  | Percentage of authorities | |
| --- | --- | --- |
|  | *'New'* structures | *'Old'* structures |
| English authorities | | |
| Counties | 63.0 | 37.0 |
| Districts | 61.5 | 38.5 |
| Unitary authorities | 64.0 | 36.0 |
| London boroughs | 45.5 | 54.5 |
| Metropolitan councils | 47.0 | 53.0 |
| Scottish unitary authorities | 40.5 | 59.5 |
| Welsh unitary authorities | 32.0 | 68.0 |

*Source*: Whitford-Jackson (1998, pp.65 and 67).
*Note*: For definitions of 'new' and 'old' structures see text.

its own, this pattern could be interpreted as showing that the structural review, and reorganisation where this has occurred, served to stimulate councils to modernise. However, this conclusion would lead one to expect that the new councils in Scotland and Wales would have been equally innovative, but this clearly has not been the case.

The links between social services and housing are shown in Table 8.8. In the great majority of cases, the unitary authorities in England, Scotland and Wales have kept the services separate, in the manner which characterises the London boroughs and the Metropolitan councils. This is in fact a continuation of the position which existed at the time of the structural review, and suggests that the benefits of integrating the two services have not proved particularly notable. That this

**Table 8.8**   *Great Britain: separation or combination of housing and social services in single-tier authorities, 1997 (% of authorities)*

|  | *Services* separate | *Services* joined | *Ambiguous* |
| --- | --- | --- | --- |
| London boroughs | 72 | 19 | 9 |
| Metropolitan councils | 88 | 3 | 9 |
| Unitary authorities | | | |
| England[a] | 71 | 29 | |
| Wales | 86 | | 14 |
| Scotland | 87 | 10 | 3 |

*Source*: *Municipal Yearbook* 1997.
*Note*: [a] Those unitary authorities which became operational in 1995 and 1996.

should be so need occasion little surprise. A joint study by Cheshire County Council and Congleton Borough Council (1994, para. 19) found 'only about 15 per cent of clients' on the registers of their respective social services and housing departments had needs which required the *simultaneous* attention of both organisations.

Possibly of even greater interest is the following. The NHS and Community Care Act 1990 provided for the transfer of elderly long-stay patients from NHS hospitals to residential care or their own homes, responsibility being vested in the social services departments of local authorities. The Health Committee of the House of Commons examined the effects of this transfer, concluding:

> We consider that the problems of collaboration between health and social services will not be properly resolved until there is an integrated health and social care system, whether this is within the NHS, within local government or within some new, separate organisation. We acknowledge that such an integration would lead to an emphasis of the boundary between the health and social care body and other functions, for instance housing and education, but we believe it [the new body] is the only sensible long term solution to end the current confusion. (Health Committee 1998, para. 68)

This rather gloomy view of relations between health and social services is at variance with the evidence given to the LGCE (1995a, pp. 39–41) but nevertheless demonstrates that the simple rhetoric used during the structural review was divorced from the complexities of the real world.

Formal structures are one thing, how they work is quite another. Research interviews have shown general agreement that it is the attitudes which inform organisations, rather than the formal structures, that determine the level of cooperation and inter-agency collaboration. Structural reform is a very blunt instrument for achieving attitudinal developments, not least because so much depends on the experience and perceptions of those appointed to the senior posts. In any case, structural reform is a one-off event, whereas the evolution of working habits is an ongoing business. Thus the main benefit which the Chartered Institute of Housing could find as a result of the Scottish reforms was 'improved communications between departments', not just social services and housing, but generally (*Local Government Chronicle*, 30 May 1997, p. 2). Whether it really needed structural upheaval to achieve this is a moot point. More generally, unless a structural change is followed through with carefully considered changes in the training of officers, those in post and joining the service, the benefits actually realised may fall short of expectations. A recent historical example makes the point. The Local Authority Social Services Act 1970 embodied the widely accepted objective of bringing together the then separate social services to focus on family needs as a whole. Hitherto, staff in the separate services had specialist skills and experience, in children's problems, the elderly, and so on. Very quickly, they had to become generalists, or 'generic' workers, but limited provision was made for staff to have training or specialist back-up facilities upon which they could draw when needed. As a result, the benefits of the unified provision were less than had been intended and some adverse consequences linger to this day (Kahan 1999b).

## Decentralisation schemes

It will be recollected that the 1994 legislation laid a much stronger duty on the Scottish authorities than on those in Wales to consult with local communities – parish or community councils – and to establish decentralised systems of governance. This legal difference seems to be reflected in the extent to which decentralisation schemes have in fact been implemented.

By 1 April 1997, the Scottish authorities were obliged to have drawn up plans for decentralised administration within their respective jurisdictions. These schemes show wide variation in the way that councils have approached the task, reflecting, no doubt, the variety of geographical circumstances as well as political decisions (Elrick 1999). This variation is manifest in the internal political arrangements which councils are making, the managerial structures established and the physical infrastructure which is provided. Councils clearly regard decentralisation as an ongoing process which is still in its formative stages. Elrick's study provides no assessment of the success of the schemes nor the cost thereof. Nevertheless, there is a strong sense that the Scottish councils are taking serious steps to involve their communities.

Much less has been done in Wales. Indeed, the Welsh Local Government Association has felt sufficiently concerned that early in 1999 it was preparing a campaign to persuade all councils to adopt community plans (*Local Government Chronicle*, 26 February 1999, p. 2). In the view of the Association, which is the representative body for Welsh councils, authorities have not done enough to involve the various constituent communities in the governance of their areas, a view which is shared by the Welsh Council for Voluntary Organisations (*Municipal Journal*, 19 February 1999, p. 8).

The 1992 Act for England makes no provision for decentralisation schemes and the author is not aware of any study which shows the extent to which arrangements have been made in the new unitary authorities on the one hand, and more generally elsewhere. From the experience in Scotland and Wales, though, the following conclusion seems to be inescapable. In so far as decentralisation schemes are desirable, this reflects the fact that even quite small authorities are generally an amalgam of distinct communities, with the implication that the slogan of 'closer to the people' ignores the diversity which exists. Equally important, it is clear that structural reform on its own is not sufficient to ensure a proper system of decentralised administration. Conversely, if the goal is to involve the people in the governance of their area, it seems clear that some form of general initiative is necessary, possibly enshrined in legislation. If that is the case, then it is not self-evident that the two-tier structure had to be up-rooted to achieve an adequate degree of local involvement.

## Conclusion

The actual changeover to the new structures of local government has, without any doubt, been handled very well, and the public has been presented with a seamless transition. In this sense, the reforms have been an undoubted success. However, as we look to the future, there are important questions which arise from the post-reform experience, questions that will only be answered with the passage of time. These questions are intimately linked with key elements of the rhetoric used in favour of structural change, as discussed in Chapter 2.

The post-reform evidence suggests that the smaller unitary authorities in Scotland and Wales, and presumably also in England, do not enjoy the economies of scale available to councils with larger populations. An important reason for this lies in the fact that, despite the rhetoric about councils becoming enablers rather than providers, direct provision remains a very important part of local authority activities. Market alternatives to direct provision have proved to be less readily available than had been envisaged by the Government in the early 1990s. One means of coping with this situation is the use of joint arrangements between authorities but, as we have seen, it appears that these are being whittled away as the initial arrangements come to an end, rather than being multiplied and strengthened. One reason for this, signalled in the New Right thinking which justifies small councils, is the development of policies by individual authorities; the greater the diversity of policy packages, the harder it is to establish and maintain joint working. It is quite clear that policy differentiation is going on.

In the short period of their existence, there is little evidence to suggest that the new councils are able to deliver demonstrably better services than the two-tier authorities they replaced. While this may change in the future, the experience of unitary authorities in London and the Metropolitan areas of England since 1986 justifies some scepticism as to whether structural reorganisation is a very efficient means for achieving improved service delivery. At the same time, it is absolutely clear from Scotland and Wales that structural reorganisation on its own has not created authorities which are universally perceived to engage their constituent communities. Indeed, the provisions contained in the 1994 Act for Scotland, laying a duty on the new councils to draw up decentralisation schemes and methods for consulting the community councils, could well provide a model for England and Wales.

As for the efficiency savings which were expected to follow from reorganisation, the evidence points, if anything, to higher rather than lower costs for delivering the same quantity and quality of services. This is most clearly seen in the case of social work services in Scotland; just to maintain services at the pre-reform level annually requires some £21 million more than previously. Over-all in Scotland, the evidence is fully consistent with the conclusion reached by the Controller of Audit to the Accounts Commission, that CoSLA's assessment of the costs and benefits of change is more likely to be right than that of the Scottish Office; and CoSLA, it will be remembered, could see no evidence that there would be savings.

Indeed, it is probably the case that ongoing costs for a given level of activity will be permanently somewhat higher than hitherto.

In England, the representative body for local authority personnel officers has summed up the experience of reorganisation in the following terms:

> The cost benefit to emerge for the community in England appears doubtful ...
>
> One of the Government's aims was that reorganisation would bring about financial savings in the provision of local government services. Although it may be too early to say whether reorganisation will bring about savings in the longer term, there is no doubt that in the short term it has led to an increase in expenditure, and may do too in the longer term. (Society of Chief Personnel Officers 1998, pp. 7–8)

By the time that the English review had ended, neither the LGCE nor the Government was expecting that reorganisation would yield annual savings, a view which seems to be confirmed by the post-reform experience. In striking contrast, both the Scottish Office and the Welsh Office confidently asserted in the memoranda which accompanied the respective Bills for reorganisation that the cost of change 'will be offset by ongoing savings'; the Welsh Office offered no figure for these savings but the Scottish Office claimed that the annual benefit would be in the range of £22 million to £66 million. Yet the clear balance of the evidence since reform was implemented is that these savings have not materialised, and that in all probability costs have been increased by reorganisation.

Specialist services seem to be under increased pressure as a direct result of the fragmentation of the former county and regional services, though it is difficult to disentangle the impact of structural change from a whole host of other factors. The fact that specialist provision has been put under greater stress than previously has interesting implications for an important strand of public choice thinking. It will be recollected from Chapter 2 that from this body of thinking one may derive the proposition that bureaucracies tend to cater for the average person and that consequently allocational efficiency will be increased if councils are socially homogeneous, which implies that they should be relatively small. These ideas run counter to the observable fact that large authorities have been accustomed to providing a range of specialist facilities and services, catering for the special needs of minorities, whether these be children with special needs for residential care or pupils who wish to study a minority language or play a less popular instrument, or whatever. There is clear evidence that reorganisation has contributed to the difficulty of maintaining this diversity, which implies that the costs of provision must rise, or that the quality of the services will deteriorate. It may be that, in order to maintain some of these services, there will have to be greater involvement on the part of central government, as in the case of the recent initiative for music; in so far as this may be occasioned by reorganisation, it would run counter to the rhetoric of greater local accountability as a justification for the reforms.

Reorganisation in Scotland and Wales created conditions in which it became more rather than less likely that administrations in Cardiff and Edinburgh would have to become more closely involved in the work of councils, and similarly that central government in England would also become more intimately associated with policy decisions. This all happened at a time when devolved administration for Scotland and Wales was not on the political agenda, and therefore set the stage for some upward transfer of powers away from local government and away from local democratic control. To the extent that there may be a general tendency in this direction, it would be contrary to the arguments which were deployed in favour of structural change by the creation of councils based on 'natural' communities.

It is clearly too soon to make a final assessment of the effects of reorganisation. Nevertheless, the evidence does suggest that there are significant defects in the pattern of small unitary authorities created in Scotland and Wales, and to a lesser extent in England. How serious these defects may be will only become evident over time. To the extent that problems do become evident, it is essential that they should be analysed carefully, to identify the source or sources of the difficulties. The need for such care is contained in the following warning, based on an examination of social work services in Scotland:

> It is likely not only that some of the consequences of local government reorganisation will be laid, inappropriately, at the door of social work itself, but also that this tendency to 'blame the victim' may extend to local government altogether as its ability to respond effectively to local needs and issues is hampered by both inadequate funding and ill-founded structural arrangements. (Craig and Manthorpe 1998a, p. 125)

# 9

# Conclusion

There is nothing a Government hates more than to be well-informed; for it makes the process of arriving at decisions much more complicated and difficult. (John Maynard Keynes in Moggridge 1982, p. 409)

We are now in a position to take stock of the reorganisation of local government in the 1990s and to consider the conclusions to be drawn. For this purpose, it is convenient to identify four main subjects that warrant attention: the comparison of the reform's rhetoric and reality; the stability of the structures which are now in place; the role of independent commissions; and wider issues relating to national governance. These four topics will be taken in turn; they lead to the fifth section, which returns to the question posed in Chapter 2 – why did structural change occur in the 1990s? – and then to a final forward look to the possibility that there may be calls for further structural changes of a radical nature at some time in the future.

## Comparing rhetoric and reality

Chapter 2 set out the main strands of thought which contributed to the implementation of reform and provided the source for the rhetoric employed by the advocates of change, while subsequent chapters amplified some of these points. For ease of exposition, it is convenient to return to some of these ideas as a framework for discussion, so that we may compare the arguments which were advanced with the evidence that has been examined, though it is difficult to assign an order of priority in which these topics should be treated.

### Accountability

It was argued that the elimination of one tier of local government would improve the accountability of local authorities to their electorates, by making it absolutely clear to voters which council is responsible for their area. While it is manifest that there would be *some* clarification of accountability, it is also clear that the scale of this clarification is actually quite small, for three separate reasons. In the first place, early in the 1990s central government funded about 80 per cent of council expenditure, the total of which was capped; in addition, all councils operated in an environment of tight regulatory controls. Indeed, the level of regulation was such that in 1996 the House of Lords Select Committee under Lord Hunt issued a major report advocating considerable relaxation of control as a necessary part of rebuilding trust between central and local government. Subsequently, there has been some movement to redress the balance following the publication in 1998 of a White Paper issued by the DETR, but that movement has been much less than had been hoped for by many in the field of local government (Environment, Transport and Regional Affairs Committee 1999). Consequently, the situation remains that in comparison with the degree of central control exercised by the Government over local authorities generally, any increase in local accountability by the removal of one tier of councils was, and remains, small.

The second difficulty with the accountability argument is the existence of many bodies which impact on the governance of localities but which are not themselves locally acccountable. The list includes central government directly and also indirectly through the regional offices of Whitehall departments in England and the Scottish and Welsh Offices. However, the two latter bodies have now come under more direct democratic control as part of the devolution initiative of the Labour Government, a development which was not on the Conservatives' agenda at the time local government reorganisation was initiated. The new Regional Development Agencies, which became operational in England in 1999, remain outside of any local electoral accountability. In addition, there is a plethora of health trusts, Training and Enterprise Councils and other quangos which have no formal local accountability (Stoker 1997a), along with the major privatised utilities whose operations are potentially important for localities.

The third difficulty was abundantly clear during the LGCE's consultation process. Unitary protagonists claimed that one of the fundamental problems of the two-tier structure is the difficulty of reconciling the needs and aspirations of the districts with the priorities of the county, so that the abolition of one tier would eliminate major sources of friction and dispute. However, a unitary structure does not solve this problem, it merely transforms its manifestation. In a two-tier structure, the *vertical* conflicts of interest between the tiers are resolved by elected councils. With a unitary structure, many of these differences of interest become *horizontal* issues between neighbouring and/or nearby authorities; the smaller the unitary councils, the greater that horizontal transformation. These horizontal conflicts must be resolved in some way, even if that is by the absence of positive action, leaving the issues to fester. One form of horizontal resolution is through voluntary arrangements between councils; but as we have seen these cannot be relied upon. As a result, there is apt to be a diminution in the range of services provided, especially specialist services in the context of small councils; or the effective decisions are taken at a higher level of government, out of the reach of local accountability. Consequently, the rhetoric of bringing local government closer to the people by creating small unitary authorities almost certainly has the effect over time of removing important matters from local control, the precise opposite of what was supposedly intended.

## Communities

The Association of District Councils and the Government itself made considerable play with the concept of communities as the basis for the structure of local government, an idea encapsulated by the term 'natural communities' introduced by the Adam Smith Institute (1989a, 1989b). The very idea of community implies a sense of shared interests and concerns, a network of personal relationships and a shared sense of belonging. The LGCE quickly made the surprise-free discovery that this concept of the *affective* community finds its practical expression at the scale of the village, parish, small town or the neighbourhoods of big cities. This is a very local scale, much smaller than many districts or unitary authorities. At the same time, though, there is often a clear allegiance to a much larger area with historical connotations, such as the Ridings of Yorkshire or a county such as Hampshire. Consequently, the ADC's 'closer to the people' campaign, implying that the districts in all cases represented communities, was fundamentally flawed. Its case was strongest for distinct urban areas, including the Major Cities, and weakest in rural and semi-rural regions. Over much of shire England, Scotland and Wales, a community-based pattern of local authorities would have meant a pattern of councils considerably smaller than the districts which existed (and those which continue), and smaller than most of the new unitary authorities. The fact that the new councils in Scotland and Wales need to take explicit action to involve their community councils testifies to their need for devolved internal governance to cope with their heterogeneous nature; the Scottish councils appear to have gone further than their Welsh counterparts in this regard.

It was never realistic that the entire structure of local government units could be coterminous with natural communities. In general terms, the most that could be expected was that recognisable communities should not be split between two local jurisdictions. In addition, it was clearly desirable that any amalgamation of the very small communities into viable local authorities should avoid bringing together localities with greatly different circumstances – of income, housing, and so on – though the more socially homogeneous that a local authority is, the more likely it is that one political party will be dominant, which may not be good for the long-term health of democracy.

Thus, as is clearly apparent in the case of Scotland and Wales, the really important thing is the internal organisation of an authority. If matters are handled properly, all the communities will feel that their voice is heard, even if the decisions do not always go the way that they wish. The requirement placed on Scottish unitary authorities to draw up plans for consulting with and working with their community councils shows beyond reasonable doubt that structural reform on its own cannot fully achieve the ideal of community participation, and the provisions made in Scotland might well provide a model which could usefully be adopted elsewhere. Structural reform on its own was not a sufficient condition for achieving community participation and the Scottish provisions suggest that it was not even a necessary condition, since they could have been introduced in the two-tier context.

### Scale economies: the enabling authority

Although it is clear that the *ex ante* costing of change was seriously deficient in both the magnitude of transition costs and of the probable ongoing costs/savings, one feature is common to all the estimates. On a scale from individual districts to whole counties, the most cost-effective pattern of unitary authorities would have been the counties. The debate focused around the rate at which the benefits would diminish as one moved towards the district end of the scale, with the districts generally claiming that there would be positive, albeit modest, savings, whereas the counties held that costs would be increased. The latter position was endorsed by the LGCE. That *ex ante* evidence clearly confirmed the idea that there are economies of scale in local government, contradicting the advice from Government that scale was immaterial. The *ex post* evidence reviewed in Chapter 8, limited though it is, also points to the existence of scale economies. We may conclude with reasonable confidence that scale economies do remain significant, despite the rhetoric to the contrary.

As part of the scale economy argument, it was also represented that local authorities were rapidly becoming enablers rather than providers, with the extreme case held out that they would be little more than the focal point for a network of contracts with the independent sector. From this premiss flowed the argument that any economies of scale that there may be would be obtained by the contractors in the first instance and then passed back to councils through the downward pressure on prices occurring in the competitive service markets. In practice, though the balance between in-house and external provision has undoubtedly shifted in the enabling direction, the scale of that change has been a good deal less in practice than the Government had hoped, and a good deal less than required to underpin the scale economies argument. Local authorities remain what they have been for a long time – agents in a mixed economy of provision.

### Costs and savings

Early in the reorganisation process, the Government seemed to think that it would be possible to devise unitary structures which *simultaneously* were based on communities (i.e. small) and would deliver services more cheaply than hitherto. By 1993, the Welsh Office had recognised that a structure similar to the one actually enacted would probably be cost neutral. In the same year, the DoE relaxed its exhortation to the LGCE that structural change should yield financial savings, to allow that costs might actually be increased, though any such increase should be off-set by other benefits. The Commission itself pointed out that unitary authorities recommended from among the twenty-one councils it was asked in 1995 to review again would almost certainly increase the costs of administration, and not reduce them as, according to the earlier rhetoric, should be the case. This convergence to the recognition that reorganisation would probably raise costs was based on the *ex ante* cost estimates, which we have seen to have been optimistic in comparison with the actual situation post-reform. In particular, the key decision makers seriously under-estimated the one-off costs of reorganisation.

One of the key reasons for this assessment error was the refusal of the Government to look objectively at the then existing information, especially that from the abolition of the GLC and the Metropolitan counties. In addition, for whatever reasons, this earlier experience was not properly brought to the attention of the Local Government Commission, which understandably failed to track it down on account of the enormous pressure on the time of Commissioners and officers. Shaming though the admission is, as a Commissioner the author was unaware of much of the pre-1992 local government literature which is cited in this book and a good deal of that which appeared during the review, and the same was manifestly true of other Commissioners. In fact, the costing exercises commissioned by the Government in Scotland and Wales, and by the Commission in England, were based on accountancy principles and paid scant attention to historical experience. The most serious attempt to collate this prior knowledge of which the author is aware was that undertaken by CoSLA (1994). However, this study was ignored by the Scottish Office and was too late to have an impact in England – even supposing that it had been circulated to Commissioners, which was not the case.

In the light of the evidence assembled in this volume, there is no reason to suppose that reorganisation has served to reduce the costs of local government and there are many reasons for believing that expenses have actually been increased. That does not necessarily mean that reorganisation should not have occurred, at the very least in respect of the larger cities. It is quite clear that in many of the new unitary authorities there is enormous enthusiasm for the job in hand, and a considerable amount of good innovative work. However, structural reform is a one-off event, while service delivery and community leadership are continuing matters. Only time will tell how long the beneficial impetus will last. Even then, the question will remain unanswered as to whether that beneficial effect could not have been achieved in other ways.

*Summary on rhetoric and reality*

A pervading feature of the reorganisation process has been the divorce between the rhetoric employed in favour of unitary structures and the realities of the world. As a Commissioner, exposed to public meetings and many private ones as well, the author was himself acutely conscious of this disjuncture, and equally aware that members of the public, voluntary organisations, and so on, found it difficult to disentangle the real issues. If governments, both local and national, aspire to the confidence of the electorate, then it is essential that the public discourse be rooted in arguments which bear some relation to reality, otherwise the public will rightly become even more cynical than it currently is concerning politicians. And if, as has been claimed for one political party, they do 'trust the people' (Willetts 1997, p. 1), then that trust must be manifested in a discourse which gives the electorate the credit of being able to discern sound arguments from ones that are less plausible.

## How stable are the existing structures?

The conventional reaction to this question is that those areas of England which remain two tier will be reformed in the relatively near future, to bring them into line with the unitary structures which now exist elsewhere. While superficially attractive, that response ignores some crucially important facts (Davis 1997).

First among these facts is the clear evidence from the 1990s that it is a thoroughly non-trivial task to define a satisfactory set of boundaries in the tug-of-war between community identity and the effectiveness of authorities. In the light of our present knowledge, nobody could reasonably argue that a district-based unitary solution throughout the two-tier counties would be cost effective; nor could it be argued that the existing districts universally equate with communities. In any case, simply reorganising boundaries without at the same time considering the powers of local authorities and other important matters just will not do again. If that basic proposition is accepted, then there is an important corollary. If there were pressure for the general conversion of the remaining two-tier areas to a pattern of unitary authorities, it would be indefensible to apply the necessary wider investigation of the role and functioning of local government only to the two-tier areas of England. A proper review of the two-tier areas would have major implications for the rest of England and could not properly be done without these being fully considered. In the absence of a wider review of this nature, and a degree of consensus emerging therefrom, to embark on the conversion of the two-tier areas to unitary authorities would run the risk, the near certainty, of a politically damaging process which might well lead to rather limited benefits. It seems probable that the Government will wish to avoid these difficulties, implying that the present arrangements will remain in place for the foreseeable future, subject only to the possibility of very localised change.

There are other reasons why it would be premature to suppose that the main focus of instability lies in the two-tier areas. As Chapter 8 shows, there is no evidence that the two-tier structures are performing less effectively than unitary authorities elsewhere, in London, the Metropolitan areas and in shire England. Until and unless there is a demonstrable case that two-tier structures are less effective, it would be hard to sustain a rational case for their abolition. Meantime, there clearly is a large agenda of issues common to all local authorities on which action needs to be taken, and is in some respects being taken. On the evidence compiled in this book, there can be little doubt that these issues are considerably more important than the benefits which may flow from further structural change.

Apparently working in the contrary direction, however, are attitudes to two matters of contemporary concern. The Labour Government has been active in promoting the idea of elected mayors, first in London, as a means of increasing the effectiveness of local administration and also of increasing public interest in local elections. Protagonists of this innovation are apt to claim that it is not compatible with county councils, which should therefore be abolished. However, having elected mayors implies the complete reorganisation of the power relations in local government and the reassessment of the role of elected councillors, implications which so far have not been thought through. In other words, the concept of the elected mayor is a matter of political rhetoric at the present time and until and unless there is some actual experience of how the new system works it is impossible to be dogmatic about the kind of authority for which it might be suitable. For example, mayors have traditionally been associated with cities and urban areas, not with rural councils. At the present time, to argue that elected mayors imply the end of two-tier local government would be to argue for the imposition of structural change on the basis of political rhetoric, not on the basis of a carefully argued case.

An equally fallacious argument centres on the case for regional devolution in England. The simple proposition is made that, if there were to be elected regional bodies, it would be wasteful to have two principal tiers of elected authorities below them. This proposition begs the fundamental question: Would the elected bodies have powers transferred to them from Westminster and Whitehall, or would the transfer be upwards from the local government sector? If the former, there would be genuine devolution of power, which means the transfer of the upper tier from London to the provinces. This is not the same thing as creating yet another tier of government and therefore there is no automatic implication that structural change to local government must occur. If, on the other hand, the elected assemblies took powers from local government then there would be a centralisation of power at the regional centres; this would not be devolution but would certainly require serious consideration of the structure of local government which it would be appropriate to have, but such consideration might well need to go beyond the two-tier areas to the rest of England. At the time of writing, energies are focused on making the new (unelected) Regional Development Agencies function and it is unclear whether the Government will proceed with elected assemblies and, if so, what their powers would be. In so far as they would take control of the funds devolved to the Agencies, this would be part of a process of devolution, shifting the location of the upper tier rather than creating yet another layer of administration.

It may seem paradoxical but the main immediate sources of instability in the structure of local government probably lie in the areas controlled by unitary councils. The most obvious case is that of London. Barely fifteen years after the Greater London Council was abolished, London is to have an elected Authority and mayor, with a remit covering the whole of the conurbation. Although their powers will be limited by comparison with the former GLC and ILEA, and although many matters will remain in the hands of unelected bodies and/or central government, London is again to have two-tier local government. It seems unlikely that the initial distribution of powers between the councillors and mayor on the one hand, and between the Authority and the Government on the other, will remain constant over time, so it is probable that the new two-tier arrangements will evolve; the most likely direction of that evolution is to strengthen the London-wide powers of the new Authority, and this could have implications for the boroughs. If we assume that the new arrangements prove successful, the time may come when opinion coalesces around the idea that some equivalent institutional change is needed in the other conurbations, to cope with the thorny issues which run beyond the boundaries of a single council, such as transport matters and major planning issues. Although the time does not appear to be ripe for this at present, the re-creation of an upper tier in London may presage similar developments elsewhere. At the very least, the developments in London imply that there is life in the two-tier concept, such that an automatic dismissal of the concept is not appropriate.

Scotland and Wales must now be considered separately from England and also from each other, given the devolution of powers to the Scottish Parliament and the Welsh Assembly; in both cases, local government comes within their remit. For both countries, it is too early to know what the implications of this constitutional innovation will be. Yet, as we have seen in Chapter 8, in both countries there are sources of potential instability arising from the small average size of many councils. To ensure the maintenance of good services in the long run, some centralisation of decision making in Cardiff and Edinburgh is probable. To the extent that this does occur, it will represent the strengthening of the national tier and the diminution of the role of the elected local authorities.

While that is a likely scenario for the foreseeable future, two other possibilities must be considered. The first was signalled by the Scottish Conservatives in the 1999 elections for the new Parliament and amounts to the following. Given the structure of local government which now exists, what are the powers and duties it should have? In particular, should there be a reduction in their responsibilities because the structure contains authorities which may be too small to discharge all their existing functions adequately? The specific suggestions made by the Conservatives may or may not be appropriate; the fundamental point to recognise is that this particular political party is questioning whether powers should now be adjusted to structure. The second possibility to consider in the medium term is that the smaller authorities on the Scottish mainland and in Wales may find it difficult to maintain adequate service standards at costs which are comparable to those available in areas which are geographically similar but served by larger councils. If this were to become evident, there may be pressure for some reconfiguration of boundaries to create larger local authorities by amalgamation. Although one might visualise that similar pressures could arise in England, the majority of the new unitary authorities are larger than those created in Scotland and Wales and in the generality of cases are identifiably urban in character.

However, as already implied, there are powerful general reasons for supposing that there will not be any radical re-structuring for quite some time. If the evidence assembled in this book has any influence upon future policy, then the direction of that influence is not difficult to discern. The experience of the 1990s ought to have demonstrated that structural reform of local government should only be undertaken in the context of the powers, finance and internal organisation of councils, and in response to clearly identified problems for which structural change is a necessary, even if not a sufficient, condition. If that lesson has been learned, the existing structures throughout Great Britain are likely to be left substantially unchanged for a considerable time, since it is unlikely that any Government would wish to undertake such a review in the absence of pressing reasons for so doing.

A further reason for believing that stability is likely for some time arises from the need for new primary legislation. For both Scotland and Wales, the present structure of local government is enshrined in statute. The fact that in both countries the first elections for their new legislatures gave no one party outright control virtually ensures that no radical change will be contemplated for the first few years. A rather more complex situation exists in England. Under the 1992 Act, the Secretary of State could direct the Local Government Commission to undertake further structural reviews, but these could only be of the areas which currently are organised in two tiers. While it is conceivable that these powers might be used for a one-off review of a particular area, it is unlikely that there would be a direction to consider all the two-tier areas, since this would re-open all the battles which have just been fought, with a high probability of the same outcome irrespective of the wording of the guidance which the Secretary of State might issue, since that would be guidance only and of lesser standing than the Act. For any major structural review to be satisfactory, new legislation would be necessary, which in turn raises all the questions about the need for a structural review to include the other integral aspects of local government, a clear concept of the problems which structural change would be expected to solve and an equally clear idea regarding the range of structural options which ought to be considered.

In summary terms, a rational approach to changing the structure of local government would require a thorough review of the whole system. Until or unless there is a clear set of reasons for supposing that structural change is a necessary condition for achieving objectives which otherwise cannot readily be achieved, the prudent course of action will be to leave well alone.

## The utility of an independent commission

Feelings in both Scotland and Wales ran high, especially in Scotland, that the absence of an independent commission was a serious, even fatal, blemish on the process of reorganisation. In England, many participants and observers blamed the

LGCE for what they perceived to be a bungled review. On the face of it, therefore, the recent experience offers no guidance on the merits of having or not having an independent commission. However, by now the reader will be fully aware that this contrast does scant justice to the issues.

Some essentially irrelevant matters have been raised by Boyne *et al.* (1995) and McVicar *et al.* (1995). They point out that commissions are an imperfect way of proceeding, because individual commissioners bring their own prejudices to bear on the task in hand, commissions do not always operate on the basis of proper research, and they are subject to partisan pressures. These criticisms are manifestly correct, however well commissioners address their task, but they apply with equal force to any review process conducted by the Government itself. Therefore, these criticisms of the use of a commission are beside the point.

To make a reasoned case for having or not having a commission, two features of the recent experience must be emphasised. In his quinquennial review of the LGCE, Hazell points out that the Commission was given 'an impossible task', the difficulty of which was compounded by the attempts of ministers to manipulate the situation to achieve specific ends. This unhappy experience is often contrasted with the greater success of ministers in Scotland and Wales in getting their way without a commission, but: 'The allegations of gerrymander in Scotland were serious, and still linger. There was also a belief in Scotland and Wales that the consultation process which preceeded the reorganisation was something of a charade' (Hazell 1998, para. 4.4). To put matters bluntly, there were serious question marks over the integrity of the review process in all three countries.

To clarify the issues, it is useful to adapt the analysis which Wolf (1988) applied to the choice between market and government provision of goods and services. He points out that in the real world, as distinct from the world of the textbook, the choice lies between imperfect markets and imperfect governments, and not between one which is perfect and the other which is not. In our case, the choice to be made is between the imperfect instrument of a commission and the imperfections of a governmental process. With that in mind, two primary lessons may be drawn from the experience of the 1990s recounted in this book. For any future structural review, it is essential that sensible, clear and open procedures should be established at the outset, and then be maintained through the review. Second, those rules must then be operated honestly. If these two criteria are adopted, then it may make little difference whether the review is carried out by an independent commission or within the Government. However, the key proviso is contained in the word 'if'. It is an inherent feature of the exercise of power that there are temptations to use it in ways that are not entirely desirable. This is, in the author's opinion, a sufficient reason for believing that an independent commission is to be preferred to a procedure undertaken by the Government, a view with which Hazell concurs: 'I would advise that any future structural reorganisation of local government should involve the use of an independent commission' (Hazell 1998, para. 4.4).

Some may believe that a contrary argument is a sufficient reason for not having a commission namely, that in the absence thereof the review process is more streamlined, efficient and predictable. That view does not accord with the experience of one Chief Executive who experienced both the Welsh and the English review processes – from the vantage point of Powys and then Shropshire:

> There is an impression in England that the lack of a Commission in Wales made the process much more straightforward, less time consuming and more predictable. As someone with extensive experience of both, I can confirm that this was certainly not the case. The extensive time spent on the arguments, the disruption to normal business and the damper on new developments was just as evident in Wales as in England. (Barnish 1999)

Given that assessment of the two experiences, there can be little doubt that if or when major further reorganisation is contemplated then an independent commission should be used, as Hazell advises.

Assuming that this advice will be heeded, the next requirement is that any future reorganisation review should be conducted under legislation which is clear and purposeful, with ministerial guidance of the same quality. The Government must then school itself to respect the independence of the commission which is set up, and be willing to give it adequate time to do the job properly. The need for this admonition lies in the experience of the attempts to manipulate the Local Government Commission, an experience that is not unique (Cox 1991). Given the difficulties to which the phased review in England led, any commission that might be set up for a structural review should be charged to produce its recommendations in a single report. It is possible, of course, that the Government would not wish to accept the recommendations which the commission offers, or would wish to make significant modifications. This is what happened with the Wheatley Commission, its conclusions having been substantially modified in the drafting of the legislation which brought in the Scottish structure that was then swept away in 1996. Some commentators have suggested that this experience proves the futility of having an independent commission in the first place and is a sufficient reason for believing that there is no need to have one. That must surely be a mistaken view for the reason already given, that the use of a commission should ensure that the relevant considerations are examined in a report which is in the public domain, so that if the Government of the day should choose to follow a different course it would be clear to everyone what was going on, making for a more transparent process.

The need for such transparency is underlined by the experience of the 1990s reviews. Whatever the defects of the Local Government Commission may have been, it did serve as a forum for eliciting information and opinions, and making these public, which was not true in Scotland and in Wales. As a result, there was a powerful check on the propensity to use Parliament as a form of elective dictatorship.

## National governance

The present book is about an episode in the history of local government. However, it is apparent that the local government arena is a mirror in which we see central government, whose image has been sharpened because England is itself a mirror for Scotland and Wales, and vice versa. The image which has become visible has lineaments which, in important respects, do not inspire confidence.

The focal period of the present study is one in which the Conservatives held office, with the result that an examination of the failings of the Government is to a substantial degree the examination of a single political party. However, though primary responsibility must lie with the party which had a majority in Parliament, that does not exonerate the Opposition parties. The Opposition had embraced the unitary concept, though generally without bothering to specify the relevant criteria, and there was no sustained critique by the other parties of the way in which the Government handled the reviews. In fact, there was considerable cooperation by the Opposition parties. Therefore, the following discussion is about a governmental machine, which happened to be controlled by a particular party, and is intended to focus on issues which rise above party politics.

### Parliament

Attention has already been drawn to serious defects of parliamentary scrutiny as they related to the Local Government Act 1992 (see also Chisholm 1995). Although the central provision of the Act is neutral as between a recommendation for change or no change, important parts of the Act are written on the assumption that the outcome would be an all-unitary structure. Those who drafted the legislation and the parliamentarians did not visualise the range of possible outcomes, including the creation of free-standing unitary authorities within a two-tier county. As a result, some severe constraints are placed on any future structural review under the Act in an area which is fully unitary, these constraints being so severe that in practice the Act could not be used. In the hybrid counties, the constraint is less stringent but nevertheless serious, in that the free-standing unitary authorities would be exempt. In addition, the provisions which enabled the Secretary of State to intervene to ensure that proper arrangements were in place for the delivery of services, by requiring the setting up of joint operations, had little impact because they only applied in areas, such as the former Avon County Council, where the two-tier structure had been entirely replaced. (This particular defect has been overtaken by more recent legislation giving the Government general powers to intervene.) As enacted in 1992, the legislation for structural reform in England was a careless piece of work.

The Environment Committee of the House of Commons went on record with some opinions which betrayed a failure to understand the 1992 Act. It stated that if the LGCE came up with the 'wrong' recommendations, ministers would be fully justified if they imposed their own solutions (Environment Committee 1994, p.

xi). In taking that view, the Committee failed to recognise that the Act gives ministers no power to substitute a wholly different structure from that recommended by the Commission. Thus the MPs sitting on this Committee were willing to encourage ministers to ignore the express provisions of the Act they had passed, blurring the distinction between the legislature on the one hand and the executive on the other, and making a nonsense of the legislation passed by Parliament.

The third failure of Parliament was noted in Chapter 6, the failure taking the form of the perfunctory and inadequate way in which the Scottish and Welsh Bills were discussed during the committee stage. If the rhetoric of parliamentary sovereignty is to be accepted, then the quality of the parliamentary scrutiny process needs to be improved. Confirmation of this need is provided by the determination of those responsible for setting up the new Scottish Parliament to conduct business in a manner that improves upon the procedures in Westminster, a determination which had support from all the Scottish political parties; only time will tell whether that resolve will be maintained.

## Costing legislation

When the Government lays a Bill before the Westminster Parliament, it is customary for there to be an explanatory and financial memorandum, giving summary details of the financial implications of the proposed legislation. This procedure was followed in the case of the Scottish and Welsh Bills, which proposed a specific structure; there were no financial details given when the Bill for England was published, since the outcome of the review to be undertaken was uncertain. Chapters 7 and 8 together show that the one-off costs of reorganisation were seriously under-estimated for both Scotland and Wales, and that there was similarly misplaced optimism concerning the savings expected on an ongoing basis. These errors of estimation were not an isolated event, the Layfield Committee having complained about the inadequate costing of legislation in its 1976 report.

The entirely general point is the following. If a legislature is given seriously inaccurate information at the time a Bill is being considered, then the assessment of that Bill is bound to be affected and hence, possibly, the conclusions to which MPs come as a result of their deliberations. Of course, one has to recognise that *ex ante* estimates are likely to be proved wrong in some degree in the light of experience, but the scale of the misjudgement in the case of local government reform in both Scotland and Wales must call into question the utility of the information which was supplied to Parliament. In principle, therefore, serious thought should be given to the mechanisms which are in place, so that in the future legislation is considered with the benefit of more accurate costings, or a greater awareness of the errors which are attendant upon forward estimates. This must be a fundamental feature of a good legislative process.

From the enquiries which have been made, it seems quite clear that the Westminster Parliament itself does not have the resources to scrutinise the costing data adequately and that there is no other body which has the responsibility for providing the necessary check. The most obvious body to undertake this work would be the National Audit Office, but it has no role prior to the enactment of legislation and does not systematically monitor the *ex post* situation for comparison with the *ex ante* evidence supplied to Parliament (National Audit Office 1998). Therefore, there is a strong case for establishing in Britain something equivalent to the Congressional Budget Office in the United States, charged to scrutinise the financial implications of legislation and to keep track of the subsequent experience. For this purpose, it might well be appropriate to expand the remit of the National Audit Office. The establishment of such a mechanism would impose a valuable discipline on the manner in which the legislature and the executive inter-act, the kind of discipline which the Government very properly prescribes for other sectors of the economy and society.

## The role of evidence

One of the features of local government reorganisation in the 1990s was the unwillingness of the Government to recognise and to act upon the evidence which existed prior to the initiation of the reviews, and also the material which became available as the reviews progressed. The Local Government Commission was criticised from many quarters, implicitly including the Government, for the fact that it followed the requirement of the Act to consult 'persons who may be interested in the review' of an area and reported the findings of its consultation, that in general the proposed unitary structures were not very popular. This characteristic of the Government's stance during the reviews in Great Britain is consistent with the view of Cabinet government painted by Foster (1999) and Foster and Plowden (1996) and with the wider critique of government by several authors, three of whom published their studies in 1995 (Hutton, Jenkins and Marr). With respect to the role of information in the formulation of policy, a particularly savage comment has recently been made from experience in the education field within the civil service: 'You might also expect good policy to be research- or evidence-based. Too often in the past you would have been disappointed. One of my distinguished predecessors lamented that the former Education Department was a knowledge-free zone' (Bichard 1999, p. 11). That these concerns are widely shared is shown by the two-day seminar held in St Andrews in September 1998 on 'Evidence-based policy and practice', the papers from which have been published in a special issue of *Public Money and Management* (vol. 19.1, January 1999). From these papers, it is clear that there are serious problems in bringing evidence and research to bear on the practical problems of policy making. Nobody is likely to suggest that these problems could ever be fully solved. However, the general situation leaves much to be desired, and the local government review provided clear testimony to the need for major improvements.

## Why structural reform in the 1990s?

This question was posed as the title of Chapter 2 and a partial answer was given on the basis of the historical material which had been assembled at that juncture. The subsequent discussion has thrown further light on the matter.

We have seen that much of the rhetoric deployed in support of unitary local government as the norm throughout Great Britain had but limited congruence with the available evidence. There was reliance upon structural reorganisation as the means for achieving the stated aims of improved efficiency and greater community identity, ignoring the possibility that other initiatives might be more suitable for achieving these ends. Consequently, one is entitled to wonder whether the arguments which the Government deployed reflected the real reasons for embarking on, and then persevering with, reorganisation. At the time the structural review for England was announced in December 1990, the view was widespread that it was designed to provide cover for the highly embarrassing policy reversal involved in scrapping the Poll Tax. We have clear evidence that in Scotland an important reason for reforming local government lay in considerations of party advantage, Strathclyde Regional Council having never been controlled by the Conservatives and being a large enough authority to have real clout with the Scottish Office. In both Scotland and Wales, there were serious concerns that the proposed unitary authorities amounted to a gerrymander, at least in part. The fact that the Conservatives did not win control of a single unitary authority when the first elections were held does not disprove the charge of gerrymandering, as one senior former minister asserted in an interview. In England, also, at a time when Conservative electoral fortunes in local government were at a low ebb, there were clear short-term political advantages to be had if the LGCE recommended relatively small unitary authorities, since it was clear that this would serve to separate areas with differing political affiliations.

These thoughts lead us to an alternative view of these recent events, for which the summary of the Thatcher legacy provided by the political commentator Hugo Young provides the key: that while the Government preached the doctrine of power to the people, it acted to increase central control at the expense of local discretion:

> As a result, one of the unconsidered outcomes of the Thatcher years was nothing less than a major constitutional change, unargued for and not presented to the electorate in such terms, but amounting to the decimation of local control over public services which local politicians had traditionally delivered ... The imperfections of local democratic control had been replaced by the fiction of parliamentary accountability. (Young 1991, pp. 613–14)

The Government's expressed desire for small unitary authorities is consistent with that interpretation, since small authorities implied the illusion of greater local control whereas the reality would be the transfer of the real decision making upwards, to Cardiff, Edinburgh and London. Edwina Currie, Conservative MP for South

Derbyshire until 1997, not only confirms this interpretation but goes even further. In her view, the structural reform was part of a deliberate programme to emasculate local government (Currie 1999).

It will not be until Cabinet and other documents become available under the thirty-year rule that historians will be able authoritatively to confirm, reject or modify this assessment of what it was that really drove the reorganisation forward in the manner that was actually adopted. On the evidence currently available, though, it does seem that the Government embarked on the wholesale reorganisation for essentially the wrong reasons. Stoker (1993, p. 4) opined that the review of local government in Great Britain could be characterised in the following terms: 'Solutions appear to be chasing problems', words almost identical to those used on several occasions by John Banham, Chairman of the Local Government Commission. If, by 'problem', one understands those problems which were identified in the rhetoric, both men were right. However, if the real issue was that identified by Young and Currie, then both were wrong.

## Looking to the future – or SPIF

A major theme which has run throughout this book is the folly of reorganising the Structure of local government without the simultaneous consideration of the Powers which councils should exercise, the Internal arrangements for devolved governance and the means by which authorities should be Financed – in other words, **SPIF**. Above everything else, this must surely be the lesson to learn from the experience detailed in the preceding pages. This is not a novel conclusion: Chapter 2 noted that this point had been made in the post-war period by local government commissions; it was reiterated by Stewart in 1989 (p. 237). However, the events chronicled in this study allow one to assert this conclusion with particular vehemence. At some time in the future, however distant that future may be, thought will once again be given to the structure of local government. When it is, the over-riding need to consider structure in the round with powers, internal organisation and finance must be recognised. If it is not, the ghost of Keynes will continue to haunt us.

# Epilogue

If it be true that good wine needs no bush,
'Tis true that a good play needs no epilogue;
Yet to good wine they do use good bushes,
And good plays prove the better by the help of good epilogues.
(William Shakespeare, *As You Like It,* Epilogue)

The reader might well ask why, given the account of the English review provided in Chapter 3, I chose to serve the full three-year appointment on the Commission. As my wife and a few close friends will testify, there were occasions when I was on the point of resigning. The trouble with so doing, however, is that it can only be done once and that the scope for shaping events is then reduced to minimal or non-existent proportions.

At the time of starting in July 1992, I was not at all clear in my own mind what the best structure of local government would look like and, given the constraints of the particular exercise, what kinds of recommendation the Commission should make. As a result, I travelled to visit two friends in different quarters of England, to talk over the issues in general terms. Once engaged in the task, and faced with the accumulating evidence, I very quickly concluded that the larger cities had a strong *prima facie* case to become unitary authorities and that the balance of advantage would be for that to happen. However, it was less clear how far down the urban hierarchy this process should go. Outside the bigger urban areas, I believed that a general district-based solution of unitary authorities could not be justified. They would in general be too small to provide services effectively and efficiently and would result in more costly administration, while at the same time the claim that they equated with communities was palpably difficult to sustain. In any case, a district-based structure would imply the potential – near certainty – for conflicts between councils which would almost certainly need some mechanism for resolution, and any such resolution in the context of the policies on offer by the Government could only mean a further centralisation of control to Westminster and Whitehall. From that point, the conclusion was quite straightforward. If there were to be structural change, it would be much better for the authorities to be large than small – the large cities and otherwise whole counties or perhaps one-half or one-third. But that would entail major changes in the way that authorities were organised internally, a matter over which the Commission had no jurisdiction.

In any case, as the first tranche reviews proceeded, it quickly became clear that rural unitary authorities on such a large scale would not be well received by district politicians, the Government or the public. Consequently, the best course of action in the majority of cases would be, I felt, the retention of the two-tier structure, modified in some places by the creation of cities as unitary councils. Though I did my best to retain an open mind, it was not easy to hide these predilections. The ADC and the districts, I am quite sure, detected that I was not in favour of a general district-based solution.

The reader may be tempted to assert that this predisposition means that I could not approach the task of writing this book in an objective manner, a charge that was made by an individual in the early days of preparation in an attempt to dissuade me from continuing with the enterprise. I would be the first to acknowledge that it is impossible for anyone to be completely impartial. However, my invitation to those who doubt the evidence which has been assembled, and the conclusions based thereon, is the following. Indicate where the evidence is mistaken or wrongly interpreted, produce for me the evidence which I have overlooked, and, if you are persuasive, I am prepared to revise my opinions.

Meantime, it is for the reader to decide whether I was right to think that a pattern of small unitary authorities in England would have been a mistake, and that in the absence of large ones the best general solution was to continue with the existing two-tier structure, modified to accommodate unitary status for large cities. The real answer will only come as the durability of the Scottish and Welsh structures is tested over time, along with the structures in England.

Michael Chisholm
Cambridge

# Appendix 1

# Initial directions to the
# Local Government Commission
# for England for the review timetable

**Table A.1** *Counties allocated to tranches*

| First tranche | Second tranche | Third tranche | Fourth tranche | Fifth tranche |
|---|---|---|---|---|
| Isle of Wight | Leicestershire | Bedfordshire | Dorset | Cornwall |
| Derbyshire | Nottinghamshire | Berkshire | Essex | Hertfordshire |
| Cleveland | Cumbria | Oxfordshire | Hereford and Worcestershire | Northumberland |
| Co. Durham | Lancashire | Buckinghamshire | Norfolk | Shropshire |
| Avon | Staffordshire | Cheshire | Suffolk | Surrey |
| Gloucestershire | Cambridgeshire | East Sussex | Wiltshire | Warwickshire |
| Somerset | Devon | West Sussex | | |
| Humberside | Hampshire | Kent | | |
| Lincolnshire | | Northamptonshire | | |
| North Yorkshire | | | | |

**Table A.2** *Timetable for first tranche counties*

| Counties | Start of review | Publication of draft recommendations | Completion of final report |
|---|---|---|---|
| Isle of Wight | 3 Aug. 1992 | 21 Dec. 1992 | 25 April 1993 |
| Derbyshire | 7 Sept. 1992 | 22 March 1993 | 19 Sept. 1993 |
| Cleveland, Co. Durham | 14 Sept. 1992 | 26 April 1993 | 21 Nov. 1993 |
| Avon, Gloucestershire, Somerset | 28 Sept. 1992 | 14 June 1993 | 23 Jan. 1994 |
| Humberside, Lincolnshire, North Yorkshire | 28 Sept. 1992 | 14 June 1993 | 23 Jan. 1994 |

*Source*: (DoE 1992d).
*Note*: Intermediate dates have been omitted.

# Appendix 2

# Supplementary credit approvals and capitalisation directions

## England

Local authorities in England wishing to finance capital expenditure by borrowing have to obtain permission from the DETR for the purpose. In the ordinary course of events, these permissions are known as Basic Credit Approvals. Capital costs for reorganisation included items such as the purchase of IT equipment and premises, and the borrowing for these purposes needed permission in the form of Supplementary Credit Approvals. Data are published for the SCAs granted.

Unfortunately, that is not the end of the matter. As a general rule, councils are not permitted to borrow in order to finance revenue expenditure. However, local authorities have been faced with revenue expenditure for staffing and redundancy in particular but have been able to finance these costs by borrowing, subject to obtaining an SCA for the purpose. Therefore, the SCA data contain both capital and revenue components.

The revenue element of an SCA must be authorised in a second way, by means of a capitalisation direction. However, if a local authority has the resources which make it unnecessary to increase its indebtedness by borrowing, it does not need an SCA but does need to obtain a capitalisation direction to use some of its BCA and/or unused capital receipts. Such expenditure is therefore outwith the sums covered by the SCAs.

Consequently, the SCA data do not show the full extent of expenditure which the Government has acknowledged as being occasioned by reorganisation and one needs to have data for both the SCAs and for capitalisation directions. Furthermore, one needs to know how much of the SCA authorisations relate to capital and how much to revenue expenditure. The capital part of the SCAs does not need a capitalisation direction but the revenue part does. Consequently, to obtain the true picture, one needs to subtract the sum of the revenue SCAs from the aggregate of the capitalisation directions in order to know how much of the latter did not need an SCA and should therefore be added to the SCA figures to obtain the over-all amount authorised (Sumby 1999).

It is at this point that the difficulties begin. Although data are available for the SCAs granted, the published information does not distinguish between the capital and revenue components; and there are no published data for capitalisation directions. For this reason, it was necessary to ask the DETR for information. The response obtained to this enquiry reads as follows:

The total amount of SCAs issued for reorganisation costs up to the end of 97/98 scheme is £307.981m and the total amount of capitalisation directions issued for this period is £268.607m. The figures given are up to the end of 97/98 scheme, as SCAs and capitalisation directions are not issued until September following the end of the financial year to which they relate.

We do not keep separate records of SCAs issued for capital and revenue expenditure. However, the total amount of capitalisation directions near reflects revenue expenditure for reorganisation costs. But you should bear in mind that it also includes amounts for debt free authorities requiring capitalisation directions. (DETR 1999)

The clear implication is that most of the capitalisation directions were granted in respect of revenue expenditure which would also have required the grant of SCAs. If the total sum of capitalisation directions had been granted in respect of expenditure which also required an SCA, then only £39.374 (£307.981 – £268.607) million of the SCA expenditure would have been for capital purposes, which seems to be a very small proportion. In any case, the further implication is that the SCA data provide a reasonably accurate assessment of the total allowed costs, subject to the element of the capitalisation directions which related to those authorities which received no SCA and funded the transition costs in other ways that required only a capitalisation direction. So the next question to consider is the value of these 'missing' SCA allowances.

In the summer of 1998, the author conducted an exercise with the published SCA data to ascertain the probable value of the 'missing' entries (see Appendix 3). At that time, there were outturn SCA data for 1994/5 to 1996/7, plus mid-year review data for 1997/8 and initial allocations for 1998/9. On conservative assumptions, the total value of the 'missing' SCAs was £23.2 million, or 5.6 per cent of the £417.2 million which at that time had been approved.

It seems reasonable to suggest that this conservatively estimated figure of 5.6 per cent is representative of the over-all position. Further, it is reasonable to suggest that the capitalisation directions relating to authorities which did not request an SCA have covered such a sum. Therefore, we may up-rate the aggregate of £478.2 million of SCAs granted (as shown in Table 7.1) by 5.6 per cent to obtain a figure of £505 million. This aggregate must, however, be regarded as the *minimum* increase to be applied to the published SCA data.

In contrast to the DETR, the Welsh Office was able to supply figures which distinguish the revenue and capital elements of the aggregate SCAs granted, as shown in Table 7.3. Of the total of £85.1 million of SCAs, £38.4 million was for revenue purposes, or only 45.1 per cent; this is a much lower proportion than is implied by the DETR for England. If we now assume that the Welsh ratio actually applied in England, we may perform the following calculations from the data supplied by the DETR which are noted above. The Department records that £307.981 million of SCAs was granted in the time period specified. If we take 45.1 per cent of that sum, we have £138.9 million applied to revenue purposes. Subtract this sum from £268.6 million capitalisation directions to obtain a residue of £129.7 million, this last sum representing capitalisation directions for which no SCA was required. Hence we add £129.7 million to the aggregate of £308 million of SCAs to obtain £437.7 million as the estimated cost of reorganisation recognised by the DETR. This means that the SCA data have been increased by 42 per cent.

This increment of 42 per cent may now be applied to the aggregate value of SCAs reported in Table 7.1 for England, £478.2 million, to give a figure of £679.0 million, this last figure being regarded as setting a probable *maximum* limit to the costs acknowledged by the Government.

## Wales

Table 7.3 shows that the value of SCAs allowed amounted to £88.101 million, a figure which almost certainly under-states the actual costs, even allowing for the special grants which amounted to £19.5 million. One way of estimating this under-statement is to assume that the rules which applied in England for SCAs and capitalisation directions also applied in Wales, to give an estimate of Welsh costs based on English criteria. In England, the capitalisation directions amounted to 87.2 per cent of the SCAs. If that ratio applied in Wales, capitalisation directions would have amounted to £76.8 million, from which we may subtract the sum of £40.7 million revenue SCAs; the difference of £36.1 million is to be added to the value of SCAs granted, to give a total of £124.2 million. However, in England there were no special grants to help defray costs as there were in Wales. Thus the sum of £124.2 million estimated above is to be compared with the figure of £107.6 million shown in Table 7.3 as the sum of the SCAs allowed and the special grants (publicity and so on excluded), a difference of £16.6 million, which amounts to 15.4 per cent of the officially acknowledged costs for local authorities.

The estimation process described above explicitly assumes that the criteria used in England also applied in Wales. The fact that very few capitalisation directions have been issued in Wales (Welsh Office 1998) does not invalidate the procedure.

*Note: The estimates presented above should not be used without reference to other evidence discussed in the text, for which see Chapter 7.*

# Appendix 3

# Estimation of 'missing' data for supplementary credit approvals: England

The data for SCA allocations show that some authorities received no SCA allocation and in several of the cases that no bid was made by the authority concerned. The purpose of this Appendix is to estimate the 'missing' figures. The reason for doing this is not so much to obtain figures for the individual authorities as to gain an over-all estimate of the significance of the 'missing' numbers. The exercise was undertaken in the summer of 1998.

The estimates have been made entirely on the evidence which is internal to the table of allocations published by the DETR. Where there is no SCA for an eligible authority, A, in just one year, but there is a figure for the preceding year, then for that preceding year the ratio of A's SCA to the SCA for an appropriate comparator, B, may be obtained. This ratio may then be applied to the SCA for B for the relevant year to obtain the 'missing' figure for A. An example is the former county of Cleveland. No SCA allocation was made for Redcar and Cleveland Council in 1998/9 but allocations were made to the other three authorities. Therefore, it has been assumed that the share Redcar and Cleveland had of the total SCAs in the preceding year, 1997/8, also applied in 1998/9, and hence its imputed SCA for that year could be estimated from the amounts allowed to the three other authorities in the former county area. In some cases, rather more heroic assumptions have been made. In the case of the Isle of Wight, the two 'missing' years have been estimated from the aggregate amounts of SCA for the authorities in the former county areas of Avon, Cleveland and Humberside, taking account of the 'missing' number for Redcar and Cleveland already mentioned. These counties were comparable to the Isle of Wight in being all-change areas, with the change taking place a year later than the Isle of Wight. The aggregate for these authorities shows that the third and fourth year SCAs were about half the amounts for the first and second. Therefore, the mean for the first two years was compared with the mean for the second pair of years. This ratio was then applied to the mean SCA for the Isle of Wight as recorded for its first two years of eligibility to obtain the 'missing' values for the two later years.

An extension of these procedures was used for some counties which have zero entries in the published data in 1996/7 and 1997/8. To estimate these 'missing' values, data were aggregated for each year separately for all the county areas where SCAs were made available to both the county and the one or two districts/unitary authorities. These aggregates give a ratio between the county and the district/unitary authority SCAs. It was then assumed that this average ratio would apply in the cases of the 'missing' data, so that the county figure could be estimated from the SCA for the district/unitary authority or authorities.

The county estimates shown for 1998/9 have been obtained on the assumption that the county figure would be 20 per cent of the figure for the relevant district/unitary authority or authorities. This ratio is slightly lower than the ratio observed in earlier years.

There are so many zero entries for the North Yorkshire county area that no estimates for 'missing' entries have been made.

The results of these estimation procedures are shown in Table A.3. Individual figures will have a substantial margin of error. The aggregate of the 'missing' entries is £23.2 million, which is 5.6 per cent of the over-all total of SCAs allocated at the time the analysis was done, £417.2 million. Given that no estimate is offered for entries in North Yorkshire, the aggregate figure of £23.2 million probably represents an under- rather than an over-estimate of the position.

**Table A.3** *Estimates of 'missing' SCA data for English authorities (£ 000)*

| Local authority and year of reorganisation | 1995/6 | 1996/7 | 1997/8 | 1998/9 |
|---|---|---|---|---|
| **1995 and 1996** | | | | |
| Redcar and Cleveland Council | | | | 1,439 |
| Isle of Wight Council | | 818 | 818 | |
| Ryedale D. C. | * | * | * | * |
| Selby D. C. | | | * | * |
| North Yorkshire C. C. | | | * | * |
| **1997** | | | | |
| Bedfordshire C. C. | | | | 395 |
| Buckinghamshire C. C. | | 1,362 | 843 | 450 |
| Derbyshire C. C. | | | | 320 |
| Dorset C. C. | | 2,905 | 1,658 | 320 |
| Durham C. C. | | 2,057 | | 199 |
| East Sussex C. C. | | | | 241 |
| Hampshire C. C. | | | | 776 |
| Leicestershire C. C. | | | | 782 |
| Leicester City Council | | | | 2,846 |
| Staffordshire C. C. | | | | 270 |
| Wiltshire C. C. | | | | 180 |
| **1998** | | | | |
| Bracknell Forest B. C. | | | | 1,413 |
| Newbury D. C. | | | | 1,615 |
| Royal Borough of Maidenhead and Windsor | | | | 1,481 |
| Total | | 7,142 | 3,319 | 12,727 |

*Source*: DETR Local Government Reorganisation Costs Scheme, via the Internet
*Note*: * For these authorities it was not possible to estimate the 'missing' data.

# References

Accounts Commission (1997), *The Commissioning Maze. Commissioning Community Care Services*, Edinburgh, Accounts Commission.

Accounts Commission (1998), *Performance Information for Scottish Councils 1996/97*, Edinburgh, Accounts Commission.

Adam Smith Institute (1989a), *Wiser Counsels*, London, Adam Smith Institute.

Adam Smith Institute (1989b), *Shedding a Tier*, London, Adam Smith Institute.

Alexander, A. (1991), 'Managing fragmentation – democracy, accountability and the future of local government', *Local Government Studies*, 17, 63–76.

Alexander, A. (1992), 'Constitutional stalemate and institutional reform: reforming Scottish local government', *Scottish Affairs*, 1, 55–65.

Alexander, A. and K. Orr (1994), 'The reform of Scottish local government', *Public Money and Management*, 14:1, 33–8.

Arrow, K. J. (1951), *Social Choice and Individual Values*, New York, Wiley.

Ascher, K. (1987), *The Politics of Privatisation. Contracting Out Public Services*, Basingstoke, Macmillan.

Assembly of Welsh Counties (1991), 'Review of structures, finance and functions of local government in Wales', submission to the Secretary of State for Wales, 25 February, Cardiff, AWC.

Assembly of Welsh Counties (1992a), 'The structure of local government in Wales. Costing the options – a financial model', Cardiff, AWC.

Assembly of Welsh Counties (1992b), 'Supplementary response to the Secretary of State', Cardiff, AWC.

Association of County Councils (1990), *Strengths of the Counties*, London, ACC.

Association of County Councils (1991a), 'Review of local government. Proposals of the Association of County Councils', London, ACC.

Association of County Councils (1991b), 'The structure of local government in England. ACC response to the government consultation paper', London, ACC.

Association of County Councils (1992), 'Unitary authorities: the costs and savings. Draft report', August, London, ACC.

Association of County Councils (1994), *Improving the Two-Tier Structure*, London, ACC.

Association of District Councils (1987), *Closer to the People*, London, ADC.

Association of District Councils (1990), *Closer to the People*, London, ADC.

Association of District Councils (1991a), 'Heseltine review', internal typescript for a committee meeting in early September, London, ADC.

Association of District Councils (1991b), 'Structure of local government in England – ADC views', London, ADC.

Association of District Councils (1994), *Can Two Tier Local Government be Significantly Improved?*, London, ADC.

Audit Commission (1988), *The Competitive Council*, London, HMSO.

Audit Commission (1998a), *Local Authority Performance Indicators. Council Services in Wales*, London, Audit Commission.

Audit Commission (1998b), *Local Authority Performance Indicators 1996/97*, 2 vols, London, Audit Commission.

Audit Commission (1999), *Local Authority Performance Indicators 1997/98. Education Services*, London, Audit Commission.

Banham, J. (1994), *The Anatomy of Change. Blueprint for a New Era*, London, Weidenfeld & Nicolson.

Barnish, A. J. (1999), Private communication, 10 February.

Bennett, R. J. (1990), 'Decentralization, intergovernmental relations and markets: towards a post-welfare agenda?', pp. 1–26 in R. J. Bennett (ed.), *Decentralization, Local Government and Markets. Towards a Post-Welfare Agenda*, Oxford, Clarendon Press.

Bichard, M. (1999), *Modernizing the Policy Process*, London, Public Management and Policy Association.

Black, S. (ed.) (1995), *Wheatley to ... What? On the Re-organisation of Scottish Local Government.* vol. 2; *The Impact of Re-organisation on Particular Services*, Edinburgh, Unit for the Study of Government in Scotland, University of Edinburgh.

Black, S. (1996), 'The impact of the re-organisation of Scottish local government', pp. 5–53 in S. Black (ed), *Wheatley to ... What? On the reorganisation of Scottish Local Government. Vol. 5. An Overview Assessment of the Re-organisation*, Edinburgh, Unit for the Study of Government in Scotland, University of Edinburgh.

Boddy, M. and C. Fudge (eds) (1984), *Local Socialism? Labour Councils and New Left Alternatives*, Basingstoke, Macmillan.

Boyne, G. (1992), 'The reform of local government structure in Wales: a critique of the case for unitary authorities', *Public Policy and Management*, 12:4, 49–52.

Boyne, G. (1995), 'Population size and economies of scale in local government', *Policy and Politics*, 23, 213–22.

Boyne, G. (1996), 'Competition and local government: a public choice perspective', *Urban Studies*, 33, 703–21.

Boyne, G. (1997), 'Comparing the performance of local authorities: an evaluation of the Audit Commission indicators', *Local Government Studies*, 23, 17–43.

Boyne, G., G. Jordan and M. McVicar (1995), *Local Government Reform: A Review of the Process in Scotland and Wales*, London, LGC Communications.

Boyne, G. and J. Law (1993), 'Bidding for unitary status: an evaluation of the contest in Wales', *Local Government Studies*, 19, 537–57.

Brooke, I. G. (1993), 'Transitional costs of restructuring local government in England', Kirkby-in-Ashfield, Ashfield District Council.

Brooke, R. (1989), *Managing the Enabling Authority*, London, Longman.

Burns, D., R. Hambleton and P. Hoggett (1994), *The Politics of Decentralisation. Revitalising Local Democracy*, Basingstoke, Macmillan.

Butler, D., A. Adonis and T. Travers (1994), *Failure in British Government. The Politics of the Poll Tax*, Oxford, Oxford University Press.

Butler, D. and I. McLean (1996), 'The redrawing of parliamentary boundaries in Britain', pp. 1–38 in I. McLean and D. Butler (eds), *Fixing the Boundaries: Defining and Redefining Single-Member Districts*, Aldershot, Dartmouth.

Calpin, D. (1997), 'Finding new roots back to power', *Municipal Journal*, 3 October, 12–13.

Charlesworth, J. and J. Clarke (1995), 'Managing mixed economies of care', *Environment and Planning A*, 27, 1419–35.

Chartered Institute of Public Finance and Accountancy (1993), 'Critique of the Touche Ross report', Edinburgh, CIPFA. Contained in CoSLA (1994).

Cheshire County Council and Congleton Borough Council (1994), 'Cheshire: keep the best - improve the rest. Making two-tier local government even more effective', Chester, Cheshire County Council.

Chisholm, M. (1975), 'The reformation of local government in England', pp. 305–18 in R. Peel, M. Chisholm and P. Haggett (eds), *Processes in Physical and Human Geography*, London, Heinemann.

Chisholm, M. (1995), 'Some lessons from the review of local government in England', *Regional Studies*, 29, 563–9.

Chisholm, M. (1997), 'Independence under stress', *Public Administration*, 75, 97–107.

Chisholm, M., R. Hale and D. Thomas (eds) (1997), *A Fresh Start for Local Government*, London, CIPFA.

Clarke, Y. (1997), Correspondence and telephone conversation, June, Institute of Public Finance.

Cochrane, A. (1993), *Whatever Happened to Local Government?*, Buckingham, Open University Press.

Cole, M. and G. Boyne (1996), 'Evaluating the structure of local government: the importance of tiers', *Public Policy and Administration*, 11:1, 63–73.

Controller of Audit to the Accounts Commission (1998), *Overview Report on the 1995/96 Audits of the Former Local Authorities*, S.R. 98/5, Edinburgh, Accounts Commission.

Convention of Scottish Local Authorities (1992), 'A response to the Secretary of State for Scotland's consultation paper on the future of local government in Scotland', Edinburgh, CoSLA.

Convention of Scottish Local Authorities (1993), 'The cost of restructuring local government in Scotland. a critical analysis by CoSLA of the Touche Ross report', Edinburgh, CoSLA. Contained in CoSLA 1994.

Convention of Scottish Local Authorities (1994), *Local Government Reorganisation in Scotland: A Critical Evaluation of Costs*, Edinburgh, CoSLA.

Convention of Scottish Local Authorities (1998), *Voluntary Joint Working Arrangements by Councils*, Edinburgh, CoSLA.

Convention of Scottish Local Authorities; Chartered Institute of Public Finance and Accountancy (1996), *Survey on the Costs of Local Government Reorganisation*, Edinburgh, CoSLA.

Council of Welsh Districts (1990), *Closer to the People of Wales*, Cardiff, CWD.

Council of Welsh Districts (1992), 'Models for the costing of options for local government reform', Cardiff, CWD.

Council of Welsh Districts (1993), 'The transitional costs of local government reform. A comparison of CWD and AWC costings', Cardiff, CWD.

Cox, B. (1991), *Cox on Cox. An English Curriculum for the 1990s*, London, Hodder

& Stoughton.

Craig, G. (1999), Private communication, 27 May.

Craig, G. and J. Manthorpe (1996), *Wiped off the Map? Local Government Reorganisation and Community Care*, Kingston-upon-Hull, School of Policy Studies, University of Lincolnshire and Humberside.

Craig, G. and J. Manthorpe (1998a), 'Blaming the victim?: local government reform and Scottish social work', *Scottish Affairs*, 24, 109–27.

Craig, G. and J. Manthorpe (1998b), 'Small is beautiful? Local government reorganisation and the work of the social services departments', *Policy and Politics*, 26, 189–207.

Craig, G. and J. Manthorpe (1999), 'Unequal partners? Local government reorganisation and the voluntary sector', *Social Policy and Administration*, 33, 55–72.

Crewe, I. (1994), 'Electoral behaviour', pp. 99–121 in D. Kavanagh and A. Seldon (eds), *The Major Effect*, London, Macmillan.

Crick, M. (1997), *Michael Heseltine. A Biography*, Harmondsworth, Penguin Books.

Currie, E. (1999), Private communication, 4 March.

Davidson, K., J. Fairley and A. Stopford (1997), 'Local government restructuring and the management of the child protection system', *Scottish Affairs*, 20, 74–94.

Davies, G., J. G. MacDonald and M. Slowey (1999), Private communication, 1 June.

Davis, H. (1997), 'Reviewing the review', *Local Government Studies*, 23, 5–17.

Dearlove, J. (1979), *The Reorganisation of British Local Government. Old Orthodoxies and a Political Perspective*, Cambridge, Cambridge University Press.

Delafons, J. (1994), 'Thoughts of chairman Banham', *Town and Country Planning*, 63, 343.

Department of the Environment (1979), *Organic Change in Local Government*, Cmnd 7457, London, HMSO.

Department of the Environment (1991a), *A New Tax for Local Government: A Consultation Paper*, London, Department of the Environment. Published jointly with the Scottish Office and the Welsh Office.

Department of the Environment (1991b), *The Structure of Local Government in England: A Consultation Paper*, London, Department of the Environment.

Department of the Environment (1991c), *The Internal Management of Local Authorities in England: A Consultation Paper*, London, Department of the Environment.

Department of the Environment (1992a), *The Functions of Local Authorities in England*, London, HMSO.

Department of the Environment (1992b), *Policy Guidance to the Local Government Commission for England*, London, Department of the Environment.

Department of the Environment (1992c), *Procedure Guidance to the Local Government Commission for England*, London, Department of the Environment.

Department of the Environment (1992d), 'News release', 20 July, London, Department of the Environment.

Department of the Environment (1993), *Policy Guidance to the Local Government Commission for England*, London, Department of the Environment.

Department of the Environment (1994), Letter to the Chief Executive of the Local Government Commission for England, 18 August.

Department of the Environment (1995), *Policy and Procedure Guidance to the Local Government Commission for England*, London, Department of the Environment.

Department of the Environment, Transport and the Regions (1998), *Modern Local Government. In Touch with the People*, Cm 4014, London, Stationery Office.

Department of the Environment, Transport and the Regions (1999), Private communication, 18 February.

Department of the Environment, Transport and the Regions; Scottish Office; Welsh Office (1998), *Housing Construction Statistics 1987–1997. Great Britain*, London, Stationery Office.

Department of Health (1996), *Social Services: Maintaining Standards in a Changing World. An Introduction for Elected Members and Chief Officers of Local Authorities*, London, Department of Health.

Department of Health (1997), *Better Value for Money in Social Services. A Review of Performance Trends in Social Services in England*, London, Department of Health.

Department of Health (1999), 'Local authority circular, LAC (99)9', London, Department of Health.

Department of Health; Welsh Office (1997), *Social Services. Achievement and Challenge*, Cm 3588, London, Stationery Office.

Dowding, K. (1996), 'Public choice and local governance', pp. 50–66 in D. King and G. Stoker (eds), *Rethinking Local Democracy*, Basingstoke, Macmillan.

Dowding, K., P. John and S. Biggs (1994), 'Tiebout: a survey of the empirical literature', *Urban Studies*, 31, 767–97.

Elrick, D. (1999), *Decentralisation: Analysis of the Scottish Local Authority Decentralisation Schemes*, Edinburgh, Scottish Community Education Council.

Environment Committee of the House of Commons (1994), *Third Report: DOE Estimates 1994–95 and Annual Report 1994*, Session 1993–94, London, HMSO.

Environment, Transport and Regional Affairs Committee of the House of Commons (1999), *Local Government Finance. Vol. 1. Report and Proceedings of the Committee*, HC 78–1, London, Stationery Office.

Ernst & Young (1993a), 'Local government review – financial appraisal of options', London, Ernst & Young.

Ernst & Young (1993b), 'Local government review – advice on the preparation and submission of the financial appraisal options', London, Ernst & Young.

Filkin, G. and C. Moor (1997), 'Reflections on the local government review', *Public Administration*, 75, 129–40.

Flowerdew, R., B. Francis and S. Lucas (1994), 'The standard spending assessment as a measure of spending needs in nonmetropolitan districts', *Environment and Planning C*, 12, 1–13.

Forrester, A., S. Lansley and R. Pauley (1985), *Beyond our Ken. A Guide to the Battle for London*, London, Fourth Estate.

Foster, C. D. (1999), *The End of Cabinet Government?*, London, Public Management and Policy Association.

Foster, C. D. and F. J. Plowden (1996), *The State Under Stress. Can the Hollow State be Good Government?*, Buckingham, Open University Press.

Gall, A. (1999), Private communication, 26 May.

Game, C. (1997), 'Unprecedented in local government terms – the Local Government Commission's public consultation exercise', *Public Administration*, 75, 67–96.

Goodwin, M. and J. Painter (1996), 'Local governance, the crises of Fordism and the changing geographies of regulation', *Transactions*, Institute of British Geographers, 21, 635–48.

Gray, C. (1994), *Government Beyond the Centre: Sub-national Politics in Britain*, Basingstoke, Macmillan.

Griffiths, P. (1994), 'Cross border tendering – the key issue for Wales', *Local Authority Law*, March, 7–8.

Griffiths, P. (1996), 'Legislating for Wales – Local Government (Wales) Act 1994', *Journal of Legislative Studies*, 2, 63–78.

Gummer, J. (1999), Private communication, 18 February.

Hambleton, R. and L. Mills (1993), 'Local government reform in Wales', *Local Government Policy Making*, 19:4, 45–53.

Hatton, S. (1998), Private communication, 17 November.

Hayton, K. (1993), 'Two into one won't go – an analysis of the proposals for the reform of Scottish local government', *Local Government Policy Making*, 19:4, 7–18.

Hazelgrove, B. (1999), Private communication, 26 May.

Hazell, R. (1998), *Quinquennial Review of the Local Government Commission*, London, Constitution Unit, University College London.

Health Committee of the House of Commons (1998), *The Relationship between Health and Social Services*. Vol. 1. *Report and Proceedings of the Committee*, Session 1998–9, 74–1, London, Stationery Office.

Hebbert, M. and T. Travers (eds) (1988), *The London Government Handbook*, London, Cassell.

HM Chief Inspector of Schools in Wales (1998), *The Annual Report of Her Majesty's Chief Inspector of Schools in Wales 1996–97*, London, Stationery Office.

HM Inspector of Schools (1999), *Standards and Quality in Scottish Schools 1995 to 1998*, Edinburgh, Scottish Office.

Hodgson, N. (1998), Private communication, 16 October.

Hutton, W. (1995), *The State We're In*, London, Jonathan Cape.

Jenkins, S. (1995), *Accountable to None. The Tory Nationalization of Britain*, London, Hamish Hamilton.

John, P. (1997), 'The policy implications of Tiebout effects', *Local Government Studies*, 23, 67–79.

Johnston, R. J., C. J. Pattie and D. J. Rossiter (1997), 'The organic or the arithmetic: independent commissions and the redrawing of the UK's administrative maps', *Regional Studies*, 31, 337–49.

Jones, A. (1996), *Report of the Examination Team on Child Care Procedures and Practice in North Wales*, London, HMSO.

Jones, B. (1986), *The Future Role and Organisation of Local Government. The Welsh Experience*, Birmingham, Institute of Local Government Studies.

Jones, G. (1993), *Local Government. The Management Agenda*, Hemel Hempstead, ICSA Publishing.

Kahan, B. (1999a), Private communication, 21 March.

Kahan, B. (1999b), Private communication, 1 May.

Keeble, D. (1987), 'Industrial change in the United Kingdom', pp. 1–20 in W. F. Lever (ed.) *Industrial Change in the United Kingdom*, Harlow, Longman.

Keeble, D. (1990), 'Small firms, new firms and uneven regional development in the United Kingdom', *Area*, 22, 234–45.

Keith-Lucas, B. and P. G. Richards (1978), *A History of Local Government in the Twentieth Century*, London, Allen & Unwin.

Kellner, P. (1997), 'The nationalization of local government', pp. 11–21 in M. Chisholm, R. Hale and D. Thomas (eds), *A Fresh Start for Local Government*, London, CIPFA.

Kerley, R. and K. Orr (1993), 'Joint arrangements in Scotland', *Local Government Studies*,

19, 309–18.

King, D. N. (1984), *Fiscal Tiers: The Economics of Multi-level Government*, London, Allen & Unwin.

King, D. S. (1987), *The New Right Politics, Markets and Citizenship*, Basingstoke, Macmillan.

King, D. S. (1989), 'The new right, the new left and local government', pp. 185–211 in J. Stewart and G. Stoker (eds), *The Future of Local Government*, Basingstoke, Macmillan.

Lang, I. (1994), 'Local government reform: change for the better', *Scottish Affairs*, 6, 14–24.

Latham, R. (1993), Letter to Tina Day of the Association of County Councils, 15 April.

Lawson, N. (1993), *The View from No. 11. Memoirs of a Tory Radical*, London, Corgi Books (first published by Bantam Press in 1992).

Layfield, F. (1976), *Local Government Finance. Report of the Committee of Enquiry*, Cmnd 6453, London, HMSO.

Leach, R. (1994), 'Restructuring local government', *Local Government Studies*, 20, 345–60.

Leach, S. (1992a), 'The disintegration of an initiative', pp. 1-10 in S. Leach *et al.*, *The Heseltine Review of Local Government. A New Vision or Opportunities Missed?*, Birmingham, Institute of Local Government Studies.

Leach, S. (1992b), 'The abolition of the Metropolitan County Councils; implications for the reorganisation of local government in the shire counties', pp. 24–43 in S. Leach *et al.*, *The Heseltine Review of Local Government. A New Vision or Opportunities Missed?*, Birmingham, Institute of Local Government Studies.

Leach, S. (1994), 'The local government review: from policy drift to policy fiasco', *Regional Studies*, 28, 537–43.

Leach, S. (1995), 'The strange case of the local government review', pp. 49–68 in J. Stewart and S. Leach (eds), *Local Government in the 1990s*, Basingstoke, Macmillan.

Leach, S. (1997), 'The local government review: a "policy process" perspective', *Local Government Studies*, 23, 18–38.

Leach, S. and G. Stoker (1997), 'Understanding the local government review: a retrospective analysis', *Public Administration*, 75, 1–20.

Leach, S., H. Davis, C. Game and C. Skelcher (1991), *After Abolition: The Operation of the Post-1986 Metropolitan Government System in England*, Birmingham, Institute of Local Government Studies.

Leach, S., M. Clarke, A. Campbell, H. Davis and S. Rogers (1996), *Minimising Fragmentation. Managing Services, Leading Communities*, Luton, Local Government Management Board.

Lilley, P. (1999), 'Rab Butler memorial lecture', 20 April, London, Adam Smith Institute.

Lipietz, A. (1987), *Mirages and Miracles. The Crises of Global Fordism*, London, Verso.

Lloyd, M. G. (1996), 'Disruption costs and local government reorganisation: managing problems, policies and priorities', *Scottish Affairs*, 14, 8–21.

Local Government Association for Wales (1997), Private communication, 21 March.

Local Government Commission for England (1993), *Renewing Local Government in the English Shires. A Progress Report*, London, HMSO.

Local Government Commission for England (1994), *The Future Local Government of Derbyshire. Draft Recommendations*, London, HMSO.

Local Government Commission for England (1995a), 'Renewing Local Government in the English Shires. A report on the 1992–1995 structural review', London, HMSO.

Local Government Commission for England (1995b), *Final Recommendations on the Future Local Government of Derbyshire. Second Review*, London, HMSO.

Local Government Commission for England (1995c), *Final Recommendations on the Future Local Government of Basildon and Thurrock, etc.*, London, HMSO.

Local Government Commission for England (1995d), *The 1995 Review of 21 Districts in England. Overview Report*, London, HMSO.

Local Government Commission for England (1995e), 'Local government review. Procedural advice for respondents', London, Local Government Commission for England.

Local Government Commission for England (1997), 'Financial appraisal of structural reviews', London, Local Government Commission for England.

Local Government Commission for England (1998), Private communication, 6 November.

Local Government Management Board (1998), *LGMB Service Delivery and Competition Data Base*, London, Local Government Management Board.

Lord Hunt of Tanworth (1996), *Rebuilding Trust*, Report of the Select Committee on Relations between Central and Local Government, HL Paper 97, London, HMSO.

Lord Hunt of Wirral (1999), Private communication, 25 March.

Lord Lang of Monkton (1999), Private communication, 17 February.

Lord Redcliffe-Maud (1969), *Royal Commission on Local Government in England 1966–1969. Report*, Cmnd 4040, 3 vols, London, HMSO.

Lord Redcliffe-Maud and B. Wood (1974), *English Local Government Reformed*, London, Oxford University Press.

Lovell, W. (1999), Private communication, 1 June.

Lynn, P. (1992), *Public Perceptions of Local Government: Its Finance and Services*, London, HMSO.

Major Cities (1991), 'Proud of the past. Hungry for the future. The Major Cities' case for the return of unitary powers', submission to the Secretary of State for the Environment and the Secretary of State for Wales, in conjunction with the Association of District Councils. Typescript, pages not numbered.

Marr, A. (1995), *Ruling Britannia. The Failure and Future of British Democracy*, London, Michael Joseph.

Mason, C. M. (1987), 'The small firm sector', pp. 125–48 in W. F. Lever (ed.), *Industrial Change in the United Kingdom*, Harlow, Longman.

McCrone, D., A. Brown and L. Paterson (1992), *The Structure of Local Government in Scotland. An Analysis of Submissions to the Scottish Office Consultation Paper*, Edinburgh, Unit for the Study of Government in Scotland, Edinburgh University.

McCrone, D., M. McPherson, A. Brown and L. Paterson (1993a), *The Structure of Local Government in Scotland. An Analysis of Non-Local Authority Submissions to the Scottish Office Consultation Paper 'Shaping the New Councils', October 1992*, Edinburgh, CoSLA.

McCrone, D., L. Paterson and A. Brown (1993b), 'Reforming local government in Scotland', *Local Government Studies*, 19, 9–15.

McQuaid, R.W. (1993), 'Costing local government reform', *Local Government Studies*, 19, 477–86.

McVicar, M., G. Jordan and G. Boyne (1994), 'Ships in the night: Scottish political parties and local government reform', *Scottish Affairs*, 9, 80–96.

McVicar, M., G. Boyne and G. Jordan (1995), 'Recurring issues in Scottish local government reform', *Public Policy and Administration*, 10:3, 1–14.

Midwinter, A. (1992), 'The review of local government in Scotland – a critical perspective', *Local Government Studies*, 18, 44–54.

Midwinter, A. (1993a), 'Shaping Scotland's new local authorities: arguments, options, issues', *Local Government Studies*, 19, 351–67.

Midwinter, A. (1993b), 'Local government reform: taking stock of the Conservative approach', *Scottish Affairs*, 5, 58–71.

Midwinter, A. (1995), *Local Government in Scotland. Reform or Decline?*, Basingstoke, Macmillan.

Midwinter, A. (1998), 'The fiscal crisis in Scottish local government', *Local Governance*, 24:1, 157–65.

Midwinter, A. and N. McGarvey (1994), 'The restructuring of Scotland's education authorities: does size matter?', *Scottish Educational Review*, 26, 110–17.

Midwinter, A. and N. McGarvey (1995), 'Organising the new Scottish local authorities – some problems with the new management agenda', *Local Government and Policy*, 22:1, 3–15.

Midwinter, A. and M. McVicar (1993), 'Population size and functional efficiency in public library authorities: the statistical evidence', *Journal of Librarianship and Information Science*, 25, 187–96.

Mobbs, T. (1997), 'LGR: a bizarre can of worms', *Local Government Studies*, 23, 107–12.

Moggridge, D. (ed.) (1982), *The Collected Writings of John Maynard Keynes*, vol. xxi, London, Macmillan.

National Audit Office (1998), Private communication, 27 November.

Newman, P. and A. Thornley (1997), 'Fragmentation and centralisation in the government of London: influencing the urban policy and planning agenda', *Urban Studies*, 34, 967–88.

Nicholson, G. (1996), 'Place and local identity', pp. 110–23 in S. Kraemer and J. Roberts (eds), *The Politics of Attachment. Towards a Secure Society*, London, Free Association Books.

Oates, W. E. (1972), *Fiscal Federalism*, New York, Harcourt Brace.

Office for Standards in Education (1998), *The Annual Report of Her Majesty's Chief Inspector of Schools. Standards and Quality in Education 1996/97*, London, Stationery Office.

Painter, C., K. Isaac-Henry and J. Rouse (1997), 'Local authorities and non-elected agencies: strategic responses and organizational networks', *Public Administration*, 75, 225–45.

Painter, J. (1991), 'Regulation theory and local government', *Local Government Studies*, 17, 23–44.

Peters, B. G. (1998), 'Managing horizontal government: the politics of co-ordination', *Public Administration*, 76, 295–311.

Piore, M. J. and C. F. Sabel (1984), *The Second Industrial Divide. Possibilities for Prosperity*, New York, Basic Books.

Popper, K. R. (1959), *The Logic of Scientific Enquiry*, London, Hutchinson.

Redwood, J. (1999), Private communication, 2 February.

Richards, P. G. (1973), *The Reformed Local Government System*, London, Allen & Unwin.

Ridley, N. (1988), *The Local Right: Enabling not Providing*, London, Centre for Policy Studies.

Rigg, D. P. (1993), Letter with annex written to county treasurers, 14 October.

Rita Hale & Associates (1998), 'Briefing paper on SSAs for the coalfields', London, Rita Hale & Associates.

Rita Hale & Associates with IPF Ltd (1996), *Fair Shares for Rural Areas?*, London, Rural Development Commission.

Scottish Arts Council (1998), Private communication, 22 December.

Scottish Office (1991), *The Structure of Local Government in Scotland: The Case for Change. Principles of the New System. A Consultation Paper*, Edinburgh, Scottish Office.

Scottish Office (1992a), *The Structure of Local Government in Scotland: Shaping the New Councils. A Consultation Paper*, Edinburgh, HMSO.

Scottish Office (1992b), *The Structure of Local Government in Scotland: The Case for Change. Summary of Responses*, Edinburgh, Scottish Office.

Scottish Office (1993), *The Structure of Local Government. Shaping the Future – the New Councils*, Cm 2267, Edinburgh, HMSO.

Scottish Office (1998), Private communication, 14 December.

Scottish Office (1999), Private communication, 14 June.

Secretary of State for the Environment, Secretary of State for Scotland and Secretary of State for Wales (1986), *Paying for Local Government*, Cmnd 9714, London, HMSO.

Secretary of State for Scotland (1993), *Scotland in the Union: A Partnership for Good*, Edinburgh, HMSO.

Smith, B. C. (1985), *Decentralization. The Territorial Dimension of the State*, London, Allen & Unwin.

Smith, S. and S. Watson (1988), 'Consequences of the abolition of the Inner London Education Authority', *Fiscal Studies*, 9:3, 67–85.

Social Services Inspectorate (1996), *Local Government Reorganisation. Managing the Transition for Personal Social Services*, Gateshead, Social Services Inspectorate.

Social Services Inspectorate (1997), *Better Management, Better Care. The Sixth Annual Report of the Chief Inspector Social Services Inspectorate 1996/97*, London, Stationery Office.

Social Services Inspectorate for Wales (1997), *Management Arrangements in the Personal Social Services. Overview Report of Inspections in Blaenau Gwent, Monmouthshire and Wrexham Local Authorities*, Cardiff, Social Services Inspectorate for Wales.

Social Services Inspectorate for Wales (1998), *Social Services in Wales 1996–98*, Cardiff, Social Services Inspectorate for Wales.

Society of Chief Personnel Officers (1998), *LGR in the 1990's. Strategic Pointers for Future Change*, Meopham, Society of Chief Personnel Officers.

Stewart, J. (1989), 'A future for authorities as community government', pp. 236–54 in J. Stewart and G. Stoker (eds), *The Future of Local Government*, Basingstoke, Macmillan.

Stewart, M., L. Gaster and G. Smart (1997), *The Local Government Commission. Oversized Cloak or Emperor's Clothes?*, York, Joseph Rowntree Foundation.

Stodart, A. (1981), *Committee of Enquiry into Local Government in Scotland. Report*, Cmnd 8115, Edinburgh, HMSO.

Stoker, G. (1989), 'Creating a local government for a post-Fordist society: the Thatcherite project?', pp. 141–70 in J. Stewart and G. Stoker (eds), *The Future of Local Government*, Basingstoke, Macmillan.

Stoker, G. (1991), *The Politics of Local Government*, Basingstoke, Macmillan (2nd edition).

Stoker, G. (1993), 'Introduction: local government reorganisation as a garbage can process', *Local Government Policy Making*, 19:4, 3–5.

Stoker, G. (1997a), 'New forms of local governance', pp. 79–91 in M. Chisholm, R. Hale and D. Thomas (eds), *A Fresh Start for Local Government*, London, CIPFA.

Stoker, G. (1997b), 'Hearing but not listening: the local government review process in West Sussex', *Public Administration*, 75, 35–48.

Storey, D. J. (1994), *Understanding the Small Business Sector*, London, Routledge.

Sumby, A. (1994), 'Validity of the Ernst and Young model for England', Nottingham, Nottinghamshire County Council.

Sumby, A. (1999), Private communication, 13 January.

Sutherland, S. (1999), *With Respect to Old Age. A Report by the Royal Commission on Long Term Care*, Cm 4192–1, London, Stationery Office.

Terry, F. (1999), 'Editorial', *Public Money and Management*, 19:2, 3.

Thatcher, M. (1993), *The Downing Street Years*, London, Harper-Collins.

The Times (1992), *The Times Guide to the House of Commons, May 1992*, London, Times Books.

Thomas, A. (1994), 'The myth of consensus: the local government review in Wales', pp. 47–60 in G. Day and D. Thomas (eds), *Contemporary Wales. An Annual Review of Economic and Social Research*, Cardiff, University of Wales Press.

Tidball, M. and J. Robinson (1999), 'Care for the future', *Local Government Chronicle*, 19, February, 16–17.

Tiebout, C. (1956), 'A pure theory of local expenditures', *Journal of Political Economy*, 64, 416–24.

Touche Ross (1993), 'Report to the Welsh Office on transitional costs of local government reorganisation', London, Touche Ross.

Travers, T., S. Biggs and G. Jones (1995), *Joint Working Between Local Authorities. Experience from the Metropolitan Areas*, London, LGC Publications.

Travers, T., G. Jones and J. Burnham (1993), *The Impact of Population Size on Local Authority Costs and Effectiveness*, York, Joseph Rowntree Foundation.

Travers, T., G. Jones, M. Hebbert and J. Burnham (1991), *The Government of London*, York, Joseph Rowntree Foundation.

Tutt, N. (1999), Private communication, 29 March.

Vestri, P. (1994), 'From structural pivot to walk on part? The arts and local government reorganisation', *Scottish Affairs*, 7, 32–42.

Waldegrave, W. (1993), *The Reality of Reform and Accountability in Today's Public Service*, London, CIPFA.

Walsh, K. (1989), 'Competition and services in local government', pp. 30–54 in J. Stewart and G. Stoker (eds), *The Future of Local Government*, Basingstoke, Macmillan.

Walsh, K., N. Deakin, P. Smith, P. Spurgeon and N. Thomas (1997), *Contracting for Change. Contracts in Health, Social Care, and Other Local Government Services*, Oxford, Oxford University Press.

Welsh Office (1991), *The Structure of Local Government in Wales*, Cardiff, Welsh Office.

Welsh Office (1993), *Local Government in Wales. A Charter for the Future*, Cm 2155, London, HMSO.

Welsh Office (1998), Private communication, 27 August.

Welsh Office (1999a), Private communication, 30 June.

Welsh Office (1999b), Private communication, 18 January.

Wendt, R. (1997), 'The last word? Reflections on the local government review', London, Association of County Councils.

West, T. (1993), 'Forgotten costings?', *Public Finance and Accountancy*, July, 10–11.

Wheatley, G. A. (1969), *Royal Commission on Local Government in Scotland 1966–1969*.

*Report*, Cmnd 4150, Edinburgh, HMSO.

Whitehead, A. (1994), 'Redistributing the remains: a commentary on the 1993-4 local government review', *Local Government Policy Making*, 21:1, 3–19.

Whitford-Jackson, P. (1998), *New Management Structures in Local Government. A Personal View*, Hemel Hempstead, PCSA Publishing.

Widdicombe, D. (1986), *The Conduct of Local Authority Business. Report of the Committee of Enquiry into the Conduct of Local Authority Business*, Cmnd 9797, London, HMSO.

Willetts, D. (1997), *Why Vote Conservative?*, London, Penguin Books.

Wilson, D. and C. Game (1994), *Local Government in the United Kingdom*, Basingstoke, Macmillan.

Wilson, D. J. (1996), 'The Local Government Commission: examining the consultative process', *Public Administration*, 74, 199–219.

Wistow, G., M. Knapp, B. Hardy and C. Allen (1994), *Social Care in a Mixed Economy*, Buckingham, Open University Press.

Wolf, M. (1988), *Markets or Governments. Choosing Between Imperfect Alternatives*, Cambridge (Mass.), MIT Press.

Wood, B. (1976), *The Process of Local Government Reform, 1966–1974*, London, Allen & Unwin.

Wrexham County Borough (1998), 'Press statement', 24 February, Wrexham, Wrexham County Borough.

Young, H. (1991), *One of Us. A Biography of Margaret Thatcher*, final edition, London, Macmillan.

Young, H. (1998), *This Blessed Plot. Britain and Europe from Churchill to Blair*, London, Macmillan.

Young, K. (1994), 'Local government', pp. 83–98 in D. Kavanagh and A. Seldon (eds), *The Major Effect*, London, Macmillan.

Young, K., B. Gosschalk and W. Hatter (1996), *In Search of Community Identity*, York, Joseph Rowntree Foundation.

# Index

Numbers in bold identify the main page references